Another Brick in the Wall

THIS IS A CARLTON BOOK

This edition published in the USA by
Carlton Books Limited 1999
20 Mortimer Street
London
W1N 7RD

Reprinted in 2002

ISBN 1-85868-849-3

Executive Editor: Lorraine Dickey
Editor: Duncan Noble, Ian Cranna
Art Direction: Vicky Harvey
Designer: Andy Jones
Picture Research: Charlotte Bush
Production: Sarah Schuman

Printed in Dubai

Another Brick in the Wall

THE STORIES BEHIND EVERY PINK FLOYD SONG

Najlepsze Życzenia
z okazji urodzin
Składają : Aneta i Adam
11-12-2002

CLIFF JONES

CARLTON

Contents

Preface

With the possible exception of Syd Barrett, whose talent was tragically eclipsed by terminal psychedelia before it had the chance to develop, Roger Waters is the lyrical mastermind behind Pink Floyd. There are Floyd-o-philes out there who will baulk at this, as Waters hasn't been a member of the band for nearly ten years, and his latter lyrical efforts bordered on the mundane, but it was Waters alone who shaped the powerful lyrical concepts that underpin all of the Floyd's classic albums. Not to diminish Gilmour, Wright and Mason's obvious talents (if we are talking about the music itself then Gilmour is the uncontested figurehead), but the lyrical focus was always Roger Waters's exploration of his own troubled psyche.

With Syd Barrett still languishing in a hopeless schizophrenic limbo, Waters was naturally my first point of enquiry during the research for this book. He is well known for his reclusive persona, and I was not hopeful of an interview. I sent cuttings and polite letters outlining the scope and angle of the book. After long consideration the verdict came down from on high. It was brief and unequivocal. "Roger Waters does not want such a book to be written."

It was only as I got further into researching this book, exploring just what lies behind the Pink Floyd enigma, that I began to understand some of the reasons why Waters might feel so strongly that a book seeking to explain the thinking behind his words and the Floyd's music might not be welcome. The Pink Floyd enigma has to be treated with care.

Everyone perceives music in different ways; this is no longer metaphysical debate but science fact. Different races, classes and ages perceive music differently - it's a matter of brain chemistry and physiology as much as of our social conditioning. This is especially true of the work of Pink Floyd.

For much of the Floyd's music there is no definitive meaning - just a feeling, an emotion, that has evolved through the band's improvisations and the relentless studio craft of the four musicians involved. Pink Floyd's music is aural impressionism. Unlike the songs of, say, The Beatles, there simply isn't one direct and unequivocal meaning. Heck, in many cases there aren't even songs, as such. But that is all part of their appeal.

Pink Floyd are a cult of unpersonality, a band who, after the departure of Syd, were bereft of a personal focal point and so let the icons and imagery of their albums do the job for them. This created one of the great marketing strategies of all time - the anti-image image. This is a band who are not only aware of their own cultish appeal, but who exploit it at every possible turn, seeding their albums with secret messages, puzzles and visual cues that lead some to assume there is some higher power at work behind it all. Think about the powerful icons the band have created - huge visual monoliths that dominate their covers: pigs, power stations, walls and prisms. These are amongst the most recognised and evocative images on earth, reinforcing the Pink Floyd global brand image, yet their creators could walk through any shopping mall in any country unrecognised. Roger Waters has quipped that the band's image is so strong that the band could conceivably still be playing in 200 years time - the mantle simply passed down through the generations to other anonymous-looking musicians. "Pink Floyd are anything you want us to be," remarked Gilmour during the recent Division Bell world tour. "I hesitate to define meanings to songs because someone will read something I've written and it might be completely different to the spin they put on it. 'Whatever works for you,' is my motto." The fear that Gilmour, Waters and the rest have is that if one starts making things too specific the enigma is destroyed, the magic evaporates and the compelling mystique that the brand has built up over thirty years will be lost forever. It's a fear with which one can sympathise.

On the other hand, of course, Waters has often complained that his lyrics are constantly being misunderstood. Indeed, in one particular case, the lyrics to the hit 'Money', in which Waters paints an ironic picture of money and its deleterious effects, were interpreted by some as a capitalist rallying call, an enforcement of the American Dream of wealth and power. You can't win either way.

This book does not attempt to explain the absolute truth behind every track. In most cases, there is no absolute meaning. Even the writers admit that many of the lyrics are a result of chance phrases stuck together in a Burroughs cut and paste fashion. They might assume a meaning later on, but at the time of writing the words are there to echo the vague emotions inherent in the music. This tradition goes right back to the origins of the band in the late 60s, when Syd Barrett first began abandoning literal meaning in favour of impressionistic writing.

While there may often be no specific event or person to whom a lyric relates, there are, however, central themes and ideas that underlie many of the lyrics which I hope you will come to see as crucial to an understanding of the band and their music. I have not performed psychoanalysis on Barrett, Waters and the rest of Pink Floyd. Everything contained within these pages is based around facts and the comments of those who were there when the music was made.

Nor is this book a critique. I know that not all of Pink Floyd's music is great. Some of it is not even good. But my role is not to play critic. One man's meat, and all that. You will, however, notice that some entries are longer than others. This does reflect my own bias as to the tracks' relative importance in the Floyd canon.

My approach here has been to supplement existing interview texts and articles on the band, using my own interviews with those who were in the studio or present when the tracks were cut.

Then of course there's Syd. Despite being absent for nearly a quarter of a century, Syd Barrett's spectre still hovers over the Floyd, casting long shadows. For some of his songs there is no definitive answer to the question of what exactly they are about. Though his condition provided the Floyd with many of the themes for their classic albums including *Dark Side Of The Moon*, *Wish You Were Here* and *The Wall*, I did not want to intrude on his semi-peaceful existence. Since his mother died in 1991, he has remained a reclusive character in his Cambridge semi-detached house, rarely venturing outside unless it's to empty his dustbins or go shopping. He listens to jazz and classical albums, drinks beer and watches TV - including *Top Of The Pops* - though what he makes of the music now is anyone's guess. He does not play the guitar or write music, and finds any talk of the past profoundly upsetting - often sending him into month-long depressions. Coupled with his severe diabetic condition, the chances that he would be in any way receptive to enquiries about his past were minimal. Whatever his present condition, the man remains a legend, whose music is still a crucial influence on British popular music of the 90s - a fact often forgotten by newspapers and magazines worldwide, who every so often decide to hunt him down like a fox to ground. In this book there is very little reference made to the tragic and disturbing incidents surrounding his illness - except where it is directly relevant to the music. Those aspects of his sad but brilliant life have been tactfully and comprehensively covered in Mike Watkinson and Pete Anderson's account of Syd's life, *Crazy Diamond*, also in the late Nicholas Schaffner's excellent account of Pink Floyd, *Saucerful of Secrets*. In the absence of Syd, I drew on the recollections of those who knew him in the halcyon days before stardom consumed him, when he was writing great music and was happy doing it. In particular I am indebted to Nigel Gordon, Peter Jenner and Andrew King for their perceptive and very frank comments on the man and his songs.

Alongside each entry you'll find illustrations of the band at work in the studio or playing live, or a picture that directly relates to the idea that triggered the lyrics or to the music itself. There are 200 of these, many of which have never been seen before. There are precious few shots of the band at work in the studio - they hated any intrusion on their workmanlike sessions. The book prints many of those available, and special thanks go to Ron Geesin for access not only to his notes and score for *Atom Heart Mother*, putting the album and the band in context, but to his photo library as well.

The definitive book on the band will not be written until all five members contribute their recollections for posterity. In Syd's case this will probably never happen, and with Roger Waters still not on speaking terms with his ex-bandmates, this kind of rounded and comprehensive portrait will probably never be written.

Ultimately, however, my aim here was to side-step all the internecine wranglings that obscured the music for so long, and take things back to basics. I didn't come to destroy the Pink Floyd enigma or erode their mystique, simply to give the band's many fans the world over an insight into the musicians, their methods and inspiration. I hope Roger Waters can see my point: understanding the muse behind the art doesn't diminish that art one little bit.

Turn up the stereo and let Pink Floyd Rock it to the Right Side Of The Mooooon!

Cliff Jones, Clapham Junction, May 1996.

Introduction

Captive in a giant electric fish tank of light, Pink Floyd are working their way through a devastating set culled from thirty years' worth of albums. They're laying the foundations for 'One of These Days', the sound steadily building from a delicate synthesized whisper to a full blown hurricane of sound, the light show perfectly synchronized. Without warning we're delivered into a spooky limbo, with only the strobe lights to guide us. There are thousands of people, their faces frozen into grimaces by the pure white light. A family of Floyd fans - mum, dad and two younger facsimiles - dressed identically in their *Division Bell* T-shirts, have their fingers in their ears and a look of unbridled terror on their faces. Two amusing long haired relics from 1971 have ceased their curious uncoordinated gyrations and are standing bolt upright like statues, the look of stoned simpletons replaced by one of amazement and wonder. As the bass assaults the audience at a terrifying volume, the strobe goes on and on, bludgeoning repeatedly until we're beaten down, cowering, trembling in its wake. Dave Gilmour, a lone figure bathed in a chrysanthemum of violet light, sits behind his lap steel, sending great swathes of slide guitar scything from the PA. It's the sound of a 747 taking off, an ultra heavy four to the floor rock'n'roll terror trip that would leave even the most abrasive of the current alternative rock acts quaking in their leather biker boots. Pink Floyd are still as uncompromising and deliciously perverse as they were when they burst onto the scene in late 1966.

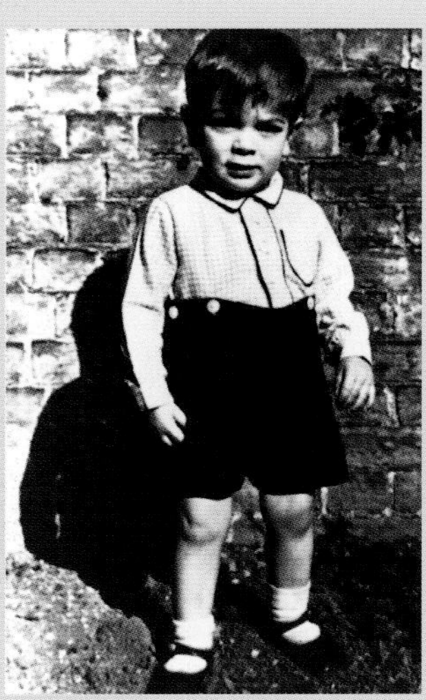

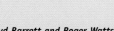

Syd Barrett as a four-year old.

Syd Barrett and Roger Watts rehearse in the basement of Mike Leonard's London home, 1966.

Pink Floyd are the biggest rock act on the planet. Their recent world tour was the highest grossing in history, playing to an estimated five million people in 55 cities, and their back catalogue, remastered for CD, is selling faster than ever. The Floyd's idiosyncratic music sounds as fresh and relevant to people today as when first released. In short, Pink Floyd are that rarest of breeds - an utterly timeless rock act.

Those who have witnessed their latest live performances will attest that the Floyd now are more relevant, powerful, accomplished and downright inspiring than at any time since their heyday between 1966 and 1976. As they rattle through a stupendously loud 'greatest hits' set, taking in everything from 'Astronomy Domine' through to *The Division Bell*, you begin to realise that they are still invoking the *avant-garde* sensibilities that brought them onto the scene in a flurry of frenetic, unstructured chaos, back in late 1966. This, and the band's incredible capacity to salvage their past and reinvent themselves for each new age, appear to be the only constant factors in their thirty year career. They abandoned traditional influences and pioneered a spontaneous approach to making music, everything from curious psychedelic pop songs like 'Arnold Layne' and 'See Emily Play' (arguably the finest British pop song of the late 60s) to vast impressionistic soundscapes like 'Echoes' from the *Meddle* album. In addition, they drew on the emerging multimedia culture - lights, film, theatre and animation - to create icons and huge conceptual structures that are known across the world - visual metaphors that communicate beyond language. Look behind the spectacular images, the inflatable pigs, power stations, pyramids and styrofoam bricks, however, and you discover a story in the best rock'n'roll tradition: glory, insanity, tragedy, humour, excess and internecine wrangling in equal measure.

There have been four distinct phases to the Floyd's career - each with a character all its own: the early days of free-form freakouts and Syd's psychedelic pop, the innovative phase which saw Waters's conceptual and lyrical ability in equilibrium with Gilmour's musical evolution (reaching its zenith in the early

Syd Barrett, Bob Klose, Chris Dennis and Roger Watts playing as The Pink Floyd in Autumn 1964.

70s), the period of Waters's conceptual dominance and the Gilmour-led post-Waters band. The music has changed dramatically - Barrett-era Floyd and the latest incarnation may appear to have little in common but the name. However, there are strong thematic and conceptual links running throughout. What unites all four phases is a humanism, a universal examination of love, loss, good, evil, madness, sanity, boredom, sadness. Syd Barrett's early Floyd songs expressed this in a more elliptical fashion than those of Roger Waters, but this strong sentiment was one which Waters and, latterly, Gilmour have taken as their muse.

Thirty years on, 22 albums and well over two hundred tracks later, and the Floyd are still the undisputed custodians of the rock 'n 'roll chemistry set, manoeuvring themselves onto the cutting edge of technology, striving to take the experience one step beyond. There was no precedent for the Floyd sound in 1966, and there's very little for what they do now. Consistently evolving like a chaotic pattern of fractals, the band are moving forward in a way that no one could have predicted - indeed the latest reports have Dave Gilmour working with a poetry collective to create a new conceptual framework for the next album. With stadiums tentatively booked for the end of 1997, and rumblings of a multimedia spectacular on the way, we can only wait with baited breath.

The Floyd enigma remains curiously intact - their influence on the current map of contemporary music is vast and irrefutable - even if many acts would prefer to deny any connection at all. From hard-core techno to indie guitar music, from Oasis (Noel Gallagher is Floyd fan) to Blur and U2, the Floyd's influence is profound. Yet few know anything about the curious band who shun the spotlight and the idiosyncratic way they made their music. *Echoes* is your track by track guide to the people and the music of this most enigmatic of acts. Enjoy.

POSTSCRIPT:

At the time of writing, Syd Barrett lies resting in a private ward at Addenbrookes hospital in Cambridge. He is now almost totally blind, the result of a severe diabetic condition.

This book is respectfully dedicated to Syd Barrett and all those who burn brightly but are eclipsed by the moon. Shine on.

The Joshua Tree Inn, CA, June 1996.

LEMON
HART
RUM
Have a Coke

Tonite Let's All Make Love In London

1965

Late in 1965, 20-year-old student Peter Whitehead moved into the Cambridge house of family friends, the Mitchells. Syd Barrett, then a student at Cambridge Technical College, doing an art foundation course, was seeing the Mitchells' daughter Juliet, who'd persuaded her parents to let Syd and his friends practise their music in the basement. "It sounded awful to me," recalls Whitehead," . . . like listening to Schoenberg."

A year later, Whitehead moved to London to become a film maker, sharing a flat with Anthony Stern, another old friend from Cambridge. Stern and Whitehead became members of a loose group of Cambrigians - which also included members of Syd's new band, now re-named The Pink Floyd - who hung out together at various London pubs, in the common room at Hornsey College of Art and at the gigs and happenings the band had started to play, including a Sunday afternoon residency at The Marquee Club.

For Whitehead, the main draw wasn't the cacophonous music of The Pink Floyd but Syd Barrett's latest girlfriend, Jenny Spires. Unknown to Syd, Peter and Jenny had a "tempestuous fling", after which, in an attempt to appease a guilty conscience, Spires persuaded a sceptical (and jealous) Whitehead to help fund a studio session for the band, with a view to including their music in the film he was making about the new style aristocracy of 'Swinging London'.

Inspired by Allan Ginsberg's poem of the same name, the feature-length film *Tonite Let's All Make Love In London* sought to capture the essence of 'Swinging London', circa 1967. Mildly amusing, full of Minis, micro skirts and union jack lunacy, laced with cameo appearances from David Hockney, Mick Jagger and a bizarre military-clad Lee Marvin, the film is nevertheless a fascinating period time capsule.

On 11 January, 1967, guitarist Syd Barrett, bass player Roger Waters, organist Richard Wright and drummer Nick Mason entered Sound Techniques studio in Chelsea with engineer John Woods and producer Joe Boyd (who, together with managers Peter Jenner and Andrew King, was also putting up money for the recordings). In two short sessions on successive days, The Pink Floyd cut four songs, the long freewheeling instrumentals 'Interstellar Overdrive' and 'Nick's Boogie' followed by two of Barrett's eccentric pop tunes, 'Arnold Layne' and 'Let's Roll Another One' (later to become 'Candy And A Currant Bun').

The Pink Floyd, March 1967.

Interstellar Overdrive

(BARRETT, WATERS, WRIGHT, MASON)

INTERSTELLAR OVERDRIVE

(INSTRUMENTAL)
BARRETT *guitars and effects*
WATERS *Rickenbacker bass*
WRIGHT *Farfisa organ*
MASON *drums*

RECORDED:
11 January, 1967 at Sound Techniques, Chelsea, London
PRODUCED BY *JOE BOYD*
UK release on the soundtrack album (Various Artists)
'TONITE LET'S ALL MAKE LOVE IN LONDON', *early 1968*
(edited version, parts I, II & III)
re-released as
'TONITE LET'S ALL MAKE LOVE IN LONDON . . . PLUS, *1990'*
(full version plus hitherto unknown track, 'Nick's Boogie')

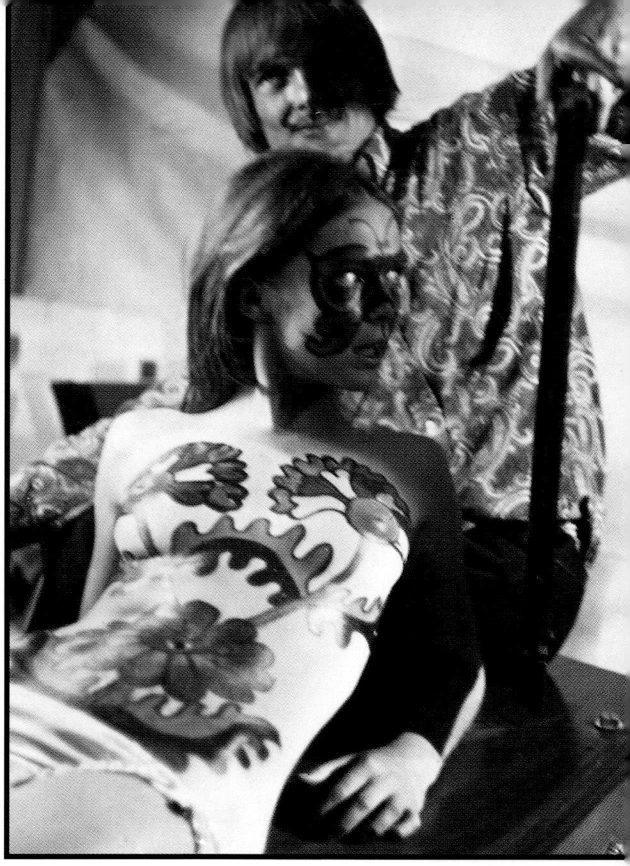

A scene from* Tonite. *Alan Aldridge and a youthful Vanessa Redgrave.

At 16 minutes and 46 seconds, this is the track which defined The Pink Floyd's early music. It is also the closest they ever came to capturing the frenetic sound of their early live performances on tape. During their residencies at The Marquee and later the UFO club, 'Interstellar Overdrive' became the cornerstone of the set, and a curious anthem for the emerging underground scene. Often played for over half an hour, and always sonically disorientating, it was, in retrospect at least, an aural evocation of the dislocation and confusion of the LSD experience, and it paved the way towards the abandonment of conventional musical structures that began in earnest in mid-1966. "It was mostly dope around then," says Miles, one of the key figures in the UK underground scene and one of the journalists who worked on the newspaper *International Times (IT)*. "The Floyd's music could be quite disturbing if you were on LSD. To most people LSD was a sacrament, something you did with the serious goal of enlightenment in mind, not simply for kicks. To most people in that very small scene it was just something radically different and new. The word psychedelic came later, once the media caught on."

If The Beatles unlocked the door with *Revolver*, The Pink Floyd (the definite article would be dropped in 1968) led the underground community through to the other side. 'Interstellar Overdrive' established the Floyd's enduring reputation as innovators, steering rock away from its obsession with American blues roots and into an entirely new territory - psychedelia - through liberal use of sound effects, feedback and wild improvisation.

There was no real precedent for the Floyd's sound. Although contemporaries, such as The Move and Soft Machine, were also experimenting with free-form rock, the Floyd's set was unequivocally modernist. When they began performing 'Interstellar Overdrive' in April 1966, The Beatles' psychedelic B-side 'Rain' had yet to be released, and *Revolver* was still four months away. A meandering LSD-inspired instrumental of indeterminate length required a considerable leap of faith for a pop audience weaned on blues or Merseybeat.

Syd Barrett, just turned 19, took his first LSD trip in the back garden of his longtime friend, Dave Gale, in Cambridge, late in 1965. LSD had not yet been criminalized and, thanks to Cambridge LSD evangelist Nigel Gordon, supplies of the drug in liquid form were being ferried to the Cambridge set straight from the ESP Disk LSD scene in New York and ex-Millbrook Leary acolyte Michael Hollingshead.

Syd and his friends - including Storm Thorgerson, who'd go on to design many Floyd album covers - would spend weekends smoking dope and experimenting with LSD. According to Thorgerson, Syd was "always experimenting, a very open sort of mind, empirical to an almost dangerous degree. But whether he was any more enlightened as a result is anyone's guess."

On his second trip, Syd became deeply anxious as the drug took hold, and underwent the sensation of a terrifying rush into the depths of space, before being left in limbo between the planets of Jupiter and Venus, represented in reality by an orange and a plum that he had in his pockets (see 'Astronomy Domine'). The structure of 'Interstellar Overdrive' perfectly parallels that trip: initial dislocation and fear at the onset of the drug, submission to the rush, the period of exploration and suspension and, eventually, the slow descent into contemplation.

The Pink Floyd's love of free jazz and LSD-inspired pop was much less contrived than that of other would-be psychedelic acts of the time. "They would take musical innovation out further than it had ever been before," recalls journalist Miles, "dancing along crumbling precipices, saved sometimes only by the confidence beamed at them from the audience sitting at their feet."

Despite its apparent chaotic nature, the recorded version of 'Interstellar Overdrive' is, in fact, tightly structured, the result of months of nightly live performances. The opening riff, a descending major triad in E flat, dates back to March 1966. Peter Jenner had just been given, by Miles, a copy of the debut album by West Coast psychedelic folk band Love. Jenner was so impressed with what he heard that, when he next met Syd, he attempted to explain how the songs sounded. "I was trying to tell him about one song I couldn't remember the title of, so I just hummed the main riff. Syd picked up his guitar and followed what I was humming, chord-wise. I've got a terrible sense of pitch. He played back a riff on his guitar, said, 'It goes like this?' And of course it was quite different, because my humming was so bad! The chord pattern he worked out he went on to use as his main riff for 'Interstellar Overdrive'."

The song Jenner was attempting to hum was Love's version of the Burt Bacharach and Hal David song 'My Little Red Book'. Others, most notably Roger Waters, also detected a hint of Ron Grainer's theme tune to the long running BBC sitcom *Steptoe And Son*.

At first, the band took to playing the riff at a galloping double-picked clip. It was Waters's suggestion that they cut the gallop to a trot, and reduce the double time to a single barred chromatic descent. From December 1966, the basic structure of 'Interstellar Overdrive' was fixed in this form, though it was still as wildly unpredictable, in terms of the free form music that grew from those basic structural foundations.

Another influence on this and on many other Barrett free form excursions was hearing Handel's *Messiah* performed at the Albert Hall, while he was tripping on LSD. Living in Earlham Street, Soho, Barrett had become fascinated by classical and free jazz records, which, he said, inspired his painting (Coltrane's *Om* album was repeatedly played on the Barrett stereo). 'Interstellar Overdrive' can almost be seen as Syd's attempt to recreate the impact and complex beauty of *Messiah*, using feedback and guitars. Peter Wynn Wilson, who shared a flat with Barrett, confirms the impact that evening had: "Quite the most extraordinary thing I'd ever encountered."

No other song in the Floyd's early canon better illustrates the dualism at the heart of the group: on the one hand, Barrett the undisciplined art student, who'd constantly profess that there were "no rules" and, on the other, Waters the architecture student, the cautious structuralist. Waters put parameters around Syd's free jazz ethic. "Given the chance, Syd would have jammed the same chord sequence all night," recalls Andrew King. "Roger gave the track a form, and dynamic boundaries within which Syd could run free." Waters retained the song's *avant-garde* intent but made it more accessible.

The group's light show, overseen by Pip Carter, proved to be another major factor in the evolution of the Floyd's music. The band originally felt that the lights, projections and oil slides should achieve symbiosis with the music, offering a direct stimulus to what was being played live.

Before the January session, there'd been an earlier attempt to put 'Interstellar Overdrive' on tape; in November 1966, at Thompson Private Recorders, a basic 2-track demo studio in Hemel Hempstead[1], where the basic structure was set. The band was totally unaware of how to record in a professional studio. Nevertheless, the sound achieved at Sound Techniques was a fair representation of the way the piece would have sounded to the audience of UFO. They found the recording process fascinating, yet intimidating. Their approach was simply to plug in and play as they would on stage, while John Woods attempted to wrestle the enormous sound onto tape. They cut just one take.

The rhythm is established, and leads into the first section of extemporization, in which Syd runs a plastic ruler over the guitar strings to create a textural wash of cascading clicks and notes, emerging from his Binson Echorec tape delay system[2]. As studios were beginning to be used as a creative tool, and musicians were experimenting with amplification, echo and feedback, Syd gave the guitar an entirely new sound. Heavy on the delays, it was the aural equivalent of an expressionist painting; spontaneous, colourful, primal. "It was all very much part of Syd's approach not to separate things into categories," recalls Andrew King. "He saw art and music as complementary ideas and he was always trying to get his music to sound like his art and visa versa."

Syd had seen the Binson Echorec in use at a an earlier session at Sound Techniques, in May 1966, when he'd been invited to watch experimental electronic free form artists AMM (who later worked with the pioneering electronic composer Cornelius Cardew, a huge influence on such musicians as John Cale) recording their debut album with Joe Boyd. The guitarist with AMM was Keith Rowe, who favoured an unsentimental approach to the instrument, making use of effects, treatments and various household implements. One of his favourite effects was achieved by taking a plastic ruler and running it up and down his guitar strings for an unusual grating sound (Syd also used this trick on the middle section of 'Arnold Layne'). Seeing AMM (the Floyd later played with AMM at The Happening Club) liberated Syd from thinking of the guitar as a conventional instrument. While he was still deeply attracted to the sound of Bo Diddley, Syd began to use his guitar as much an effects generator as a device for playing chords and solos.

'Interstellar Overdrive', though wilfully uncommercial, provided the wild aesthetic for much of the next ten years of Pink Floyd's career.

1. Apart from a shorter take of 'Interstellar Overdrive' the group recorded two further Barrett compositions, 'Stoned Alone' and 'Lucy Leave', and a Bo Diddley track.

2. The Binson Echorec was based on circuitry originally designed by the GPO as a telephone switching device, until it was patented for use as a tape delay system for studios. A rotating drum with tape heads on it was run past a loop of tape producing variously timed delays and repeats. You could then feed these signals back on themselves resulting in a saturated crescendo that built to a horrific epiphany before dying away again. "Syd would play his echo box as if it were an instrument," recalls Andrew King.

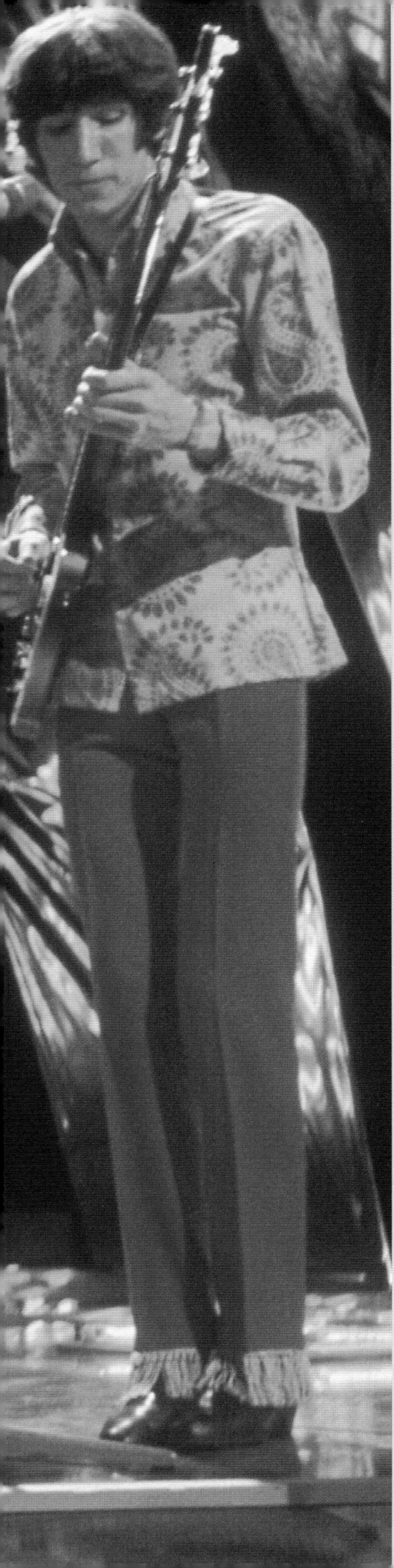

The Early Singles 1967

The Pink Floyd's attitude to the music industry was one of studied disdain. Which was just what the London underground set expected. Being good middle class boys, watched over by solidly middle class managers and originating from a very ordered middle class background, Pink Floyd saw the machinations of the music business as grubby, and somewhat beneath them. However, when pressed, the Floyd made no attempt to hide their desire for stardom's trappings. They wanted money, cars, girls and lavish lifestyles and were shrewd enough to realise that they had to make certain compromises with their music or else remain a marginal act, of interest only to a trendy clique.

This compromise, coupled with the enormous pressure to write chart hits, would ultimately lead to problems of a most profound nature, for Syd Barrett in particular. But during these early days of innocence, Syd would passionately proclaim that the band were pop stars first and musicians second. In the 60s pop stardom was no disgrace. Syd's bizarre, inspired pop singles unconsciously shunned the US blues roots of artists like Bo Diddley and Muddy Waters - the very musicians who had first attracted him to rock music. Instead, Syd's music brought forth a white, middle class, art school agenda, creating an arch, literate style that would be passed down through David Bowie, Marc Bolan and Bryan Ferry, on to modern artists like Blur and Pulp. The Floyd's short run of singles was clearly tongue in cheek - psychedelic pop songs partly intended to 'Trojan Horse' the Floyd's underground free form excursions into the charts, while tipping the nod to the enlightened members of the underground set. In this sense the singles are, in places anyway, as extreme as any of their sonic experiments. Radio-friendly production and the logic and brevity of the singles format were fine, for

'The Pink Floyd made three appearances on* Top of the Pops*, each more peculiar than the last. The first was for 'Arnold Layne' in April 1967. The last was for the single 'See Emily Play' in June of the same year and Syd's mental state had deteriorated. Syd changed into scruffy painters rags he had brought with him in a carrier bag. It was he claimed a protest at being forced to appear on the show. Argueing that because his idol John Lennon no longer had to appear on the program but could use a promo film, he shouldn't have to appear in person either.

these purposes, but didn't appeal to the band when they played live, and they quickly shunned their hits in concert.

'Arnold Layne' and 'See Emily Play' were performed only under duress from managers Jenner and King, who faced flack from disgruntled promoters who'd booked a chart act and got sets of ear-splitting free-form psychedelia for their trouble. In London, the Floyd's *avant-garde* aesthetic was taken more for granted, but an improvisation called 'Reaction In G' was commonly performed as a protest at having to play the hits ('See Emily Play' in particular), whenever the Floyd performed outside the capital.

Nearly all of the songs that became singles, and most of the tracks that made up the Floyd's first album *The Piper At The Gates Of Dawn*, were brought to fruition over the short six month period between the time the band made the transition into a semi-pro college band and then became full professionals in January 1967. Once stardom and the pressures of constant touring, the relentless round of interviews and the scrutiny of the adoring fans became a very real intrusion into his life, Syd Barrett withdrew and stopped writing. The incredible speed at which the Floyd rollercoaster took off overwhelmed Barrett, whose mind was still having difficulty dealing with the profound experience of his many LSD trips. 'See Emily Play' was, to many of those who knew him, the last point at which the Barrett genius was intact.

Arnold Layne

(BARRETT)

ARNOLD LAYNE

BARRETT *double tracked vocal, lead guitar*
WATERS *Rickenbacker bass, backing vocal*
WRIGHT *Farfisa organ, backing vocals*
MASON *drums, backing vocals*

RECORDED *27 February, 1967 Sound Techniques Studios Chelsea, London*
PRODUCED BY *JOE BOYD*
UK RELEASE *11 March, 1967*

Syd Barrett's influences were diverse. "Anything that fell within his orbit would end up recycled into something else," says Peter Jenner. "He'd see something or read something, and go 'That's nice, I'll use that'. It would get written down, or tucked away in his folder of lyrics, and then magically reappear in a song a week later. He didn't have definite influences, like poetry, but he read, and I know he came across poetry and children's books, pictures, art books, anything really." One particular influence on Barrett was a book of French symbolist poetry that included Baudelaire. Indeed, as Andrew King points out, "Many of his songs actually had the slightly dislocated metre of poetry in translation." Arnold Layne's comic verse, reminiscent of Hilaire Belloc's *Cautionary Tales* - another Barrett childhood favourite - has more parochial roots.

After the death of her husband in World War Two, Roger Waters's schoolteacher mother began taking in female college lodgers to help pay the bills. Washing, particularly knickers, bras and 'smalls' belonging to these girls kept vanishing from her line, always in the dead of night. The Cambridge Knicker Snatcher became the cause of much local gossip, and Roger would keep Syd abreast of events as more laundry disappeared from the Waters garden. Amused, Syd turned the story into a song whose apparently benign simplicity belies the fact that it took him three weeks to perfect. During frequent train journeys between London and Cambridge, Syd would work on the couplets, rolling images and ideas together into some deceptively simple poetry. While to the casual listener it is a fairly straightforward song telling a story, to the LSD set its imagery and delivery were obviously influenced by LSD. Syd invents a name for the thief, gives him a hobby - transvestism - and builds the song into a tale of how he steals washing by moonlight, only to end up 'doing time' for his crime. Arnold Layne is a classic English pervert.

'Arnold Layne' became a long, rambling song in The Pink Floyd's live set, with a full 'freakout' section where the free form instinct would once again take over. But when mutterings of a potential record deal were made, and singles were discussed, 'Arnold Layne' seemed like the most suitable candidate for condensation into a three minute hit. Even a song that presents a *risqué* subject in such a humorous and moral light was too much for Radio London, who refused to play the record because it was "too smutty". Syd's response was, "Arnold just happens to dig dressing in women's clothing. A lot of people do, so let's face up to reality." Rick Wright believes the record was banned simply because the establishment, who had only just come to terms with The Beatles as the future of popular music, were outraged by the loud formless music of the Floyd and the reports that had appeared in *The News Of The World* about LSD sex orgies. "I think the record was banned . . . because they're against us as a group, and against what we stand for."

Despite only peaking at number 21 in the charts, 'Arnold Layne's impact on the British pop landscape was profound. Pete Brown, lyric writer with Cream, maintains it marked a decisive turning point in 60s pop, shifting rock away from its predominantly American R&B influence. 'There'd never been anything quite like it. Previous to that, I was completely into blues. Things like 'White Room' wouldn't have happened without Syd." Certainly one of the first pop songs to be delivered in a resolutely English accent and address the perennial British preoccupation with cross-dressing, it wasn't entirely without precedent. The Kinks' 'Dedicated Follower Of Fashion', of May 1966, had featured a defiantly dandified delivery and the line, "he pulls his nylon panties right up tight". Syd's vision of Arnold, however, was more sinister; the sound the Floyd achieved decidedly darker. Therefore, while it connected with pop's new sense of lyrical daring, it also sought to make the pop experience slightly unpleasant. 'Arnold Layne', like its protagonist, teeters on the brink of a perverse insanity. More importantly, Syd's was the first truly middle class pop voice. Just as psychedelia itself was a middle class phenomenon, so Syd's delivery and subject matter echoed a resolutely English obsession with eccentricity and minor perversion.

Though containing only a few seconds of the kind of instrumental mayhem that had made them infamous, Miles notes that 'Arnold Layne' nevertheless became "a pop anthem for the underground movement". In this sense, along with 'Interstellar Overdrive' and 'See Emily Play', it is among the most important recordings the Barrett-fronted Pink Floyd made.

Candy: *dope smoking and casual sex.*

Candy And A Currant Bun

(BARRETT)

An early Barrett song, recorded after 'Arnold Layne' at the first Sound Techniques session, then re-recorded during the subsequent Joe Boyd sessions, the original version of this track was performed live as early as September 1966 under its original title 'Let's Roll Another One'. In that form at least, it was a fairly unequivocal adolescent ode to pot-smoking, hash-eating and casual sex, and grew from one of Barrett's earliest compositions, written in mid-1965, called 'Stoned Alone'. The lyrics to this were straightforward and unequivocal: "Sitting here alone I get stoned". Like many Barrett songs of the era, it had less to do with excursions on LSD and more to do with Syd's simple observations of his own life and bohemian surroundings.

Played to the UFO crowd the original lyrics to the song were par for the course. Once the band were considering radio play and commercial suitability, its drawbacks were immediately obvious. "It had lines in it like, 'Tastes right if you eat it right' and 'Let's roll another one'," recalls Roger Waters. "The BBC didn't like that at all - nor did a lot of other people - so the lyrics and title had to be changed." Syd, as anxious as the rest of the band to have another hit, decided the song should undergo a drastic rewrite. The result is that candy, currant buns and ice cream become bizarre cuisinal metaphors for dope and sex. This became the B-side of The Pink Floyd's first single, 'Arnold Layne', and is one of Syd's great fractured masterpieces.

CANDY AND A CURRANT BUN

BARRETT *lead vocals, rhythm and lead guitar*
WATERS *Rickenbacker bass, backing vocals*
WRIGHT *Farfisa organ, backing vocals and arrangement*
MASON *drums*

RECORDED *27 February, 1967, Sound Techniques Studios, Chelsea, London*
PRODUCED BY *JOE BOYD*
UK RELEASE *11 March, 1967*

See Emily Play

(BARRETT)

The Pink Floyd's second single was a reworked version of the song 'Games For May', which was written for and performed at the *Free Games For May* happening at the Queen Elizabeth Hall on 12 May 1967. This concert was for many members of the underground community the first moment of collective consciousness. The Floyd, through Blackhill's connections with Hoppy Hopkins, founder of *IT* and leading light among the underground community, were asked to write the 'theme' song to celebrate the event. "Syd was incredibly productive for that brief time," recalls Andrew King. "You'd ask him to write something and he'd have a finished song a few days later. I don't even think it was a conscious thing. He kept lyrical and musical ideas in his little scrapbook of lyrics and poems and would piece it all together in his head."

The Pink Floyd's performance at *Games For May* was split into two sections, a number of individual performances followed by a full Floyd set that remains in the minds of those who witnessed it as one of their most innovative and spectacular performances. "[The first half began with] pre-recorded tapes; Roger and Rick got some together, but no-one else did really, because Syd was in the middle of writing 'See Emily Play'. The band

SEE EMILY PLAY

BARRETT *lead vocal, rhythm and lead guitars*
WATERS *Rickenbacker bass, backing vocals*
WRIGHT *Farfisa organ, backing vocals*
MASON *drums, backing vocals*

RECORDED *18-23 May, 1967, Sound Techniques Studios, Chelsea, London*
PRODUCER *NORMAN SMITH*
UK RELEASE *16 June, 1967*

Free Games for May. Queen Elizabeth Hall, 12 May, 1967.

Right: The view down George Street in Richmond, Surrey, scene of the Barrett shopping expedition which resulted in the song 'Apples And Oranges'.

played with full timpani, amplifiers, various gongs and percussion, it was like an *avant-garde* arts lab," recalls Andrew King.

The *Games For May* show passed into legend, but Jenner and King felt certain that Emily had 'hit ' written all over it, and suggested Syd rewrite it for the charts. Needing a new lyrical theme to fill the now redundant chorus line of "Free games for May", Syd, as he had done with all his songs, looked around him for inspiration. The underground community was a close knit clique in 1967. You could be assured of seeing the same faces at each happening or event. One of those faces belonged to The Honourable Emily Kennett, a 16 year-old raver that the UFO crowd had nicknamed 'the psychedelic schoolgirl'. The psychedelic underground attracted wealthy middle class kids, and Emily Kennett and her crowd, regulars at the UFO, Middle Earth and Marquee, were seen by many of the underground hard core as indulged charlatans. Many of the lines in the song are critical, and refer to Syd's feelings that people like Ms. Kennett misunderstood the scene. It contained some of Syd's most caustic observations on the emerging culture, not least of which is the line "Emily tries but misunderstands". Syd remained guarded about the Emily Kennett connection, for fear that it might embarrass her parents or cause a scandal. He told journalists that Emily was a girl he'd seen dancing and singing in a vision while he was sleeping in a wood after a gig that spring.

'See Emily Play' was recorded mid-way through the sessions for the album *The Piper At The Gates Of Dawn*. However, producer Norman Smith wanted to ensure that the song had the same clear, high-quality sound as their debut single. The band vociferously insisted to Smith that the sound they needed could only be obtained at Sound Techniques. They wanted the Joe Boyd sound. After several abortive attempts to record the song at Abbey Road (18-22 May), Norman and the band ended up traipsing down to Chelsea to record at Sound Techniques.

The music was a combination of a melody and guitar line that Syd had been toying with since late 1965, grafted onto a surging instrumental section that came from live performances and spelt the beginning of a lengthy freakout section. Through this, Syd laid down some of his most delicate slide work, using a Zippo lighter on his guitar strings to give a thin, wiry sound, as a development of the plastic ruler technique borrowed from Keith Rowe of AMM (see 'Interstellar Overdrive'). For all his conservatism, Norman Smith perfectly succeeded in making the track accessible and commercial. "The sanity of Norman helped ensure that the Floyd made hits," confirms Peter Jenner. "Which was vital. If the Floyd hadn't had a hit they would never have got through the difficult times that they went into."

Emily was indeed a big hit, and earned the Floyd praise from the likes of Paul McCartney, Eric Burdon and the numerous sceptics who now had to grudgingly admit that the Floyd were a real force to be reckoned with. However, this sudden new success took an immediate toll on Syd. "'Emily' was the last time Syd was focused and together, in my view," says Jenner. "The speed of it all was overwhelming. Suddenly, from just being Syd, he was a pop star and unwilling spokesman for a social movement. Combine that with the extraordinary information overload of LSD, world travel and the pop industry and you're in for problems. He was a terribly nice lad but it did his brain in." During these sessions, Dave Gilmour, on leave from his tour with Jokers Wild, popped into the studio to see his old friend Syd recording. Syd failed to even recognise him. It was a sad but telling moment that warned all concerned of the troubles to come.

Apples And Oranges

(BARRETT)

Syd Barrett's decline into schizophrenic exile came so swiftly that before his friends could do anything about it it was too late. By the time the band came to record their third single, the signs of his looming catatonia were becoming increasingly apparent. After rejecting 'Scream Thy Last Scream', a strange, disturbing, chirping chipmunk falsetto, recorded, along with 'Vegetable Man' and 'Jugband Blues', at De Lane Lea Studios in one madcap session, the band went back into Abbey Road to record, for the third single, the humorous vignette 'Apples And Oranges'.

Barrett was a shopoholic. He enjoyed nothing more than trailing from store to store looking for new clothes, trinkets and records. Now living with his new girlfriend, model Lyndsey Korner, at another LSD madhouse in Richmond, Surrey, he would spend much of his time, when the band were not recording or touring, wandering the streets or walking the banks of the River Thames. While out and about in the town centre, Syd was attracted to a young woman, out doing her shopping, and decided to follow her. The song's lyrics are a simple description of that shopping trip, finally ending up at the duck pond on the nearby Barnes Common, where the woman spent some time feeding the ducks. Unfortunately, this lyrical masterpiece is ruined by the ham-fisted production. The band's instruments were not even tuned properly. The Floyd didn't want it released, but they were persuaded by EMI that it was the most chart friendly of all the recent songs. "It was another example of our *naïveté* and inexperience," admits Nick Mason, "There wasn't anything else lying around."

Unlike the previous two singles, this one failed to chart. It was Syd's first taste of failure. "I couldn't care less," said Barrett to one journalist. "All we can do is make records which we like. If the kids don't, then they won't buy it." This flippancy masked a deep fear and unhappiness that his own talents were fading.

APPLES AND ORANGES

RECORDED *11 August, 1967, Abbey Road Studios, London*
PRODUCED BY *NORMAN SMITH*
UK RELEASE *18 November, 1967*

Paintbox

(WRIGHT)

By November 1967, Barrett was a shadow of his former self, and had stopped writing altogether. With EMI still making demands on the band for singles, the rest of the band were prompted to take up the slack.

'Paintbox' was Rick Wright's first sole writing credit, and displays his early disaffection with the world of pop stardom. This is the first of many ironic commentaries on fame, and the sycophants who follow pop groups. Wright, in particular, believed that the petty concerns of the pop music machine were intruding on the band's desire to extend the boundaries of *avant-garde* rock,

PAINTBOX

RECORDED *2 November 1967 Abbey Road Studios, London*
PRODUCED BY *NORMAN SMITH*
UK RELEASE *as B-side of 'Apples And Oranges', 18 November, 1967*

Rick Wright, May 1967.

forcing them to abandon their uncompromising approach. The lyric was written after a trip to Newcastle, when a disillusioned Wright threatened to walk out after the band were pelted and booed during 'Interstellar Overdrive'.

Released while the band were playing a disastrous package tour with Jimi Hendrix, it predictably bombed, and, coupled with Syd's inability to play and ever more withdrawn behaviour (the band had taken to passing him notes on pieces of paper because he wouldn't talk), the Floyd were on the brink of giving up.

It Would Be So Nice

(WRIGHT)

IT WOULD BE SO NICE

WRIGHT *lead vocals, piano*
GILMOUR *lead and rhythm guitar*
WATERS *Rickenbacker bass*
MASON *drums*
RECORDED *28-29 March, 1968*
PRODUCED BY *NORMAN SMITH*
UK RELEASE *12 April, 1968*

Pink Floyd's fourth single is the first released track to feature David Gilmour on guitar, and was recorded during the sessions for *A Saucerful Of Secrets*. Released only six days after the press announcement that Syd had left the band, it was a defiant memo from all concerned that The Pink Floyd were still a viable concern (relations with Barrett had taken an irreconcilable turn for the worse during February 1968: the errant guitarist had taken to turning up at gigs and scowling at his replacement, Gilmour, believing his old schoolfriend to be an interloper).

Determined to make a go of it, Wright attempted to fuse the sound of both The Beatles and The Beach Boys into one overwhelming pop package. Indeed The Beatles' 'Good Morning' from *Sergeant Pepper*, where Beatle-weary Lennon manages to turn the fact that he has nothing to say into an observation on his state of mind, is a strong lyrical influence. Wright's attempts to do the same are not so successful - the lyrics describe someone's dull and ordinary day. "Fucking awful, that record, wasn't it?" says Nick Mason. "At that period we had no direction. None at all. We were being hustled about to make hit singles so we did what we had to."

Despite this valiant attempt to prove themselves, those watching the group's career undoubtedly lost hope. 'It Would Be So Nice' is certainly one of the least distinguished songs Pink Floyd ever recorded. Except for the final few seconds during the fade-out it is, at best, described as mundane.

In one of the most curious lyric changes of all time, the BBC asked that a line that mentioned the *Evening Standard* newspaper be changed to the non-existent *Daily Standard*, because otherwise it might be misconstrued as advertising. "In fact what you do is exactly what was done - you make as much press out of it as possible," comments Mason. "You ring up the *Evening Standard* and say, 'Did you know that the BBC won't play our record because it mentions your paper?'." The Floyd needn't have bothered; no one played the record anyway.

Julia Dream

(WATERS)

JULIA DREAM

GILMOUR *lead vocals, lead and rhythm guitar*
WATERS *Rickenbacker bass, lead vocals on chorus*
WRIGHT *lead vocals, piano*
MASON *drums*
RECORDED *13 February, 1968, Abbey Road, Studio 3*
PRODUCED BY *NORMAN SMITH*
UK RELEASE *As B-side of 'It Would Be So Nice' 12 April, 1968*

In late December of 1967, Dave Gilmour was asked to join The Pink Floyd to supplement the line-up and cover for Syd's erratic playing at live shows, following a gig in Brighton when the guitarist went missing on the day of the show. Gilmour received a telephone call from old Cambridge friend Nigel Gordon, asking if he'd deputize for the errant Barrett. Though not a fan of Syd's music or the Floyd sound, Gilmour seemed to fit in and at the beginning of the new year, he began rehearsing with the band and learning the numbers. The band attempted to struggle on briefly as a five piece, but no one really believed the situation was acceptable.

'Julia Dream' was the first track to be recorded without Syd's involvement, and is the first Pink Floyd song to feature the voice of Dave Gilmour.

'Julia Dream' is underrated; an early pastoral classic, of the kind that would feature frequently in the Floyd canon for the next three years. Waters did not believe

Post-Barrett Floyd. Dave Gilmour (front).

POINT ME AT THE SKY

GILMOUR *lead vocals (verses 1,2,4 and chorus), lead and rhythm guitar*
WATERS *Rickenbacker bass, lead vocals (verses 3,5,6,except chorus)*
WRIGHT *lead vocals, piano*
MASON *drums*

RECORDED *November 1968*
Abbey Road Studio 3
PRODUCED BY *NORMAN SMITH*
UK RELEASE *17 December, 1968*

himself to be a capable lyric-writer at this early stage, and initially had trouble finding his own voice. Early on in his writing career he looked to the poets for inspiration, subtly adapting them to fit his own ideas. 'Julia Dream' drew on the poems of Rupert Brooke, who effectively evoked in his poems the spirit of the land around Cambridge. While Syd's memories of his childhood were, on the surface at least, bright and innocent, Waters's imagery was darker, questioning, dealing with nightmares, the fear of darkness, absence, loneliness and death itself - constant themes in his writing. Rick Wright plays some of his finest flute mellotron over the song, which is laden with the kind of spacey sound effects that would become the band's trademark in future years.

Point Me At The Sky

(WATERS, GILMOUR)

Rudderless, and desperately trying out new styles, this track, more than any other from the period, shows the emergence of the kind of grand musical and lyrical style that would come to dominate the band's output for the next decade. More prosaic, but ultimately more immediately accessible than Syd's idiosyncratic poetry, this was a deliberately constructed song, whose origins and execution hint at the progressive rock epics to come.

A song of escape, Pink Floyd's fifth and last single until 1979's 'Another Brick In The Wall Part 2', 'Point Me At The Sky' tells of an imaginary character's attempts to fly free of the endless cycle of failure and unenlightened behaviour that shapes man's dismal destiny. Although written in a deliberate parody of the whimsical children's verse of Edward Lear, the song metaphorically comments on such weightier issues such as the shortage of natural resources in the future, and how such a shortage may force a more strict and equal method of sharing them out. Waters was a fervent and idealistic young socialist, who as a student was quite fiery in his denunciation of the capitalist hierarchy. While the hippies were busy engaging in a revolution of the head, Waters was looking for a revolution of the means of production and distribution of wealth. This is another trait he inherited from his mother, who proved to be a vociferous campaigner for equality and human rights at a time when such beliefs were considered radical and not altogether desirable. Through the various meetings and campaigns that Mary Waters ran from her home in Cambridge, Roger was exposed to the great inequalities in less developed countries, and the way that natural resources are squandered by capitalism. Waters touches on all of these subjects in this song, which, though humorous in its delivery, is deadly serious in its message.

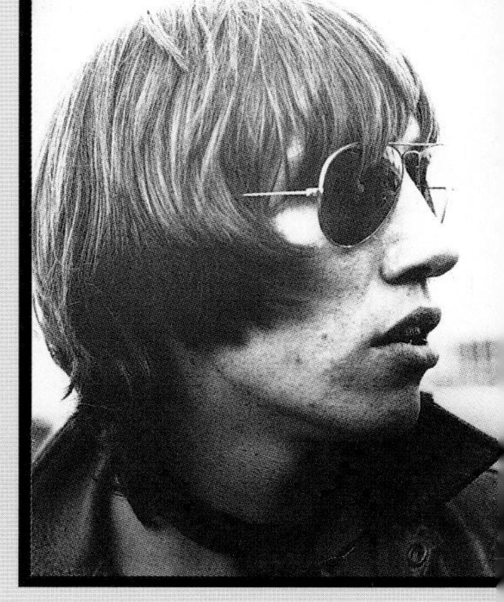

Roger Waters, fronting the Floyd by default.

The Piper At The Gates of Dawn

1967

Pink Floyd's first album was very much Syd Barrett's baby, much of its atmosphere down to his unique fusion of psychedelia, pop sensibility and child-like innocence. Syd took the record's title from chapter seven of Kenneth Grahame's children's novel *The Wind In The Willows*, in which Rat and Mole encounter the great god Pan. Pan, half man, half goat, was the god of flocks, woods and fields, wandering the mountains and grottoes of Arcadia amusing himself with nymphs and playing his pipes. Rat and Mole encounter him as a golden, dream-like vision, after Rat takes Mole to "the place of my song dream . . . . the Holy place". Portrayed in the book as a friendly but powerful naturalistic force, Pan comes to the animals' aid in the search for a lost otter cub.

This simple way in which Grahame conveyed profound spiritual concepts to his young readers intrigued Syd, who took it as the basis of his approach during the making of this album. Whether via LSD or not, Syd would often tell friends of how he'd met Pan and had been instilled with the natural spirit of the forest. "He thought Pan had given him insight and understanding into the way nature works," recalls Andrew King. "It formed itself into his own holistic view of the world." Seen in this context, *Piper* is not merely a pastoral album of whimsical English psychedelia, but a suite of songs that reflects a deep concern for mysticism, nature and man's place within the universe - unwittingly, a Gnostic concept album.

RECORDED *16 March, 15 April, 4 May-16 July, 1967, Abbey Road Studio 3, London*
PRODUCED AND MIXED BY *NORMAN SMITH*
UK RELEASE *5 August, 1967*
CHART PLACING
Number 6 in the UK
REAR COVER DESIGN
SYD BARRETT

Pink Floyd, dandy darlings of the 'psychedelic underground'.

The Beatles, a huge influence on Syd Barrett, next door finishing **Sergeant Pepper** *while the Floyd were recording their debut album.*

Most of the songs that made up the album were written in a brief golden period when Syd was happy and had the time to dedicate himself to writing, often spending entire days strumming and setting lyrics from his scrapbook to his simple chords. "Those were the halcyon days," recalls Peter Wynn Wilson, Syd's flatmate at Earlham Street. "He'd sit around with copious amounts of hash and grass and write these incredible songs. There's no doubt they were crafted very carefully and deliberately." Some part of Syd's subconscious may even have sensed that this album would be his last coherent moment. He threw himself into it with the passion of one seeking to express everything he could in the short time left. Recording began almost immediately after signing to EMI in March 1967, and continued during an intense touring schedule through June and early July. Though Syd was still lucid and maintained a strong artistic control, he was becoming increasingly withdrawn and difficult to communicate with.

Norman Smith, the EMI staff producer assigned to work with the Floyd, found Syd especially tiresome. Sceptical of the band's musical ability and inclined to dismiss Barrett's songs as infantile, the sessions were not an altogether happy affair for Smith. He'd been chief engineer for The Beatles up to and including *Rubber Soul*, had seen the Floyd live and was anxious to get to grips with a new band who might benefit from the production skills he'd picked up from George Martin. Initially his role was that of a sensitive pilot, enabling the Floyd to record what they heard in their heads. "He was a safe pair of hands," says Andrew King. "He wasn't terribly inspired. He'd give them suggestions and Syd would say something back and he'd try to interpret it as best he could. But, actually, I think Syd was a complete mystery to him."

"When I look back, I wonder how we ever managed to get anything done," says Smith. "It was sheer hell. There are no pleasant memories. I always left with a headache. Syd was undisciplined and would simply never sing the same thing twice. Trying to talk to him was like talking to a brick wall, because the face was so expressionless. His lyrics were child-like and he was a child in many ways; up one minute, down the next."

Faced with the unreceptive Smith, Syd found another line of communication into the studio control room, engineer Peter Bown. An eccentric Abbey Road 'lifer' in his early 40s, Bown struck up an unlikely friendship with Barrett, resulting in some of the more unusual sounds on the album. "Bown was as loopy as they come," remembers King. "He'd sit at the mixing desk painting plastic skin on his fingers because he was worried they'd wear out through overuse."

"With Syd you just never knew what was going to occur," says Bown, who retired in 1991. "We all knew he was taking drugs fairly heavily but, nevertheless, Syd was very creative. The fact that he didn't understand the recording process terribly well meant that he was less rigid about what could and couldn't be done. No one really understood Pink Floyd, particularly Norman. Pink Floyd were different and they were meant to be different." Smith's input did help the band create an accessible album that is mercifully free of the psychedelic platitudes that plague much of the music of the era. As bootlegs of the rough mixes performed by Syd attest, if Barrett had had his way the album would be full of aimless phase-shifting and heavy reverb.

The Beatles were another key influence on the sound. On 21 March, Pink Floyd were taken by Peter Bown to meet The Beatles - then putting the finishing touches to *Sergeant Pepper* in Studio 2. Bown had worked on many Beatles sessions and was friendly with Paul McCartney. "It was during the mix of 'Lovely Rita' and there was a bad atmosphere in Studio 2 that day. But the Floyd all stood there like dummies, riveted to the floor while McCartney said hello.

"Syd was very impressed, because McCartney said he liked what he had heard of the band and thought they were doing something unique and creative."

It has always been supposed that it was Lennon and Barrett who got together and recorded the rambling 'What's The New Mary Jane', but there is no solid evidence that such a session ever occurred.

On the day that McCartney met the Floyd, Lennon was enjoying his fabled unscheduled LSD trip during the making of *Sergeant Pepper* after getting his supply of pills and tabs confused.

"I'm sure the Beatles were copying what we were doing, just as we were copying what we were hearing down the corridor!" says Peter Jenner, of the bands' proximity during that epochal summer.

"Paul was patting them on the back, saying they were great and were going to do fine," adds writer Miles. "He wasn't being patronising; it was almost like The Beatles passing on the mantle. McCartney had always been convinced that there would be a new synthesis of electronic music and studio techniques in rock 'n' roll."

There were mixes of *Piper* made in both mono and stereo. The band – and Syd in particular – participated in the mono version, but the stereo version, the one currently available on CD, was hastily done without their supervision and is somewhat inferior. Syd certainly had nothing to do with the heavy handed panning effects used in the stereo mix of 'Interstellar Overdrive'.

For all the problems involved in its inception, the album was well received, though some of the hardened UFO crowd felt it was a betrayal of the Floyd's free-form intent.

For those who really bothered to listen, the album had a curious and delicate beauty, infused with Syd's dark spirit, that few, not even the band, really understood. "I love listening to it just to listen to Syd's songs," says Rick Wright reflectively, "It's sad in a way because it reminds me of what might have been. Syd could have easily been one of the finest songwriters around today."

Astronomy Domine

(BARRETT)

ASTRONOMY DOMINE

BARRETT *guitars, lead vocals*
WATERS *bass guitar, vocals*
WRIGHT *Farfisa organ, piano, double tracked lead vocals*
MASON *drums*
PETER JENNER *spoken intro*

RECORDED *15 April, 1967, Abbey Road Studio 3*
PRODUCED BY *NORMAN SMITH*

Syd Barrett's Cambridge friends, Ian 'Imo' Moore, Dave Gale, Storm Thorgerson and Nigel Gordon, had arrived back in Great Britain, where they began experimenting with a sample of

The Floyd light show, UFO club.

pure liquid LSD-25. Gordon had married, and moved to London to become a film maker. He had made connection with dealers who were importing LSD direct from the West Coast scene via Englishman Michael Hollingshead (the man who turned Timothy Leary on).

Moore and Gordon were anxious to initiate Syd into the ways of the new wonder drug. Moore set up a psychedelic garden party, at Dave Gale's parents' home while they were away on vacation. Sugar cubes were laced with huge doses of liquid LSD. By the time Syd arrived everyone was already tripping, having absorbed the drug through their skin during preparations. Syd took his sugar cube with little idea of what to expect, and spent the next twelve hours, according to Storm Thorgerson, "lost in space". Syd seized an orange and a plum from the household fruit bowl and carried them everywhere during his trip. In his altered state, the fruits came to represent the planets Jupiter and Venus. Syd imagined himself suspended in a place between the two planets for hours, until someone ate his plum (Venus) and his universe collapsed.

"We were all seeking higher elevation, and wanted everyone to experience this incredible drug," says Gordon. "Syd was very self-obsessed and uptight in many ways so we thought it was a good idea. In retrospect I don't think he was equipped to deal with the experience, because he was unstable to begin with. He simply didn't have it up top. Syd was a very simple person."

Like 'Interstellar Overdrive' this track evokes, albeit in more detail, the spirit of that first epic LSD excursion. Syd felt he had encountered the grandeur and majesty of the universe. He owned a small *Times Astronomical Atlas* that he often carried with him. Full of facts about the planets, including speculation from noted astronomers on the likely surface conditions on the planets in the solar system, this provided many of the song's lyrics. Syd mixed this information with pop references to astronaut 'Dan Dare, Pilot Of The Future', a regular strip in popular British boys comic *The Eagle*.

At the very beginning of the song, buried at the back of the mix before the Morse code blips come in, Peter Jenner can be heard speaking through a megaphone, naming astrological star signs and astronomical facts from Syd's atlas. The final version was the best take of the song - three were attempted - and despite the fact that the band had played it live for almost five months by this time, engineer Peter Bown recalls how each take was often a matter of chance. "You had to be quick with the Floyd. Syd was quite moody and would pace around, then suddenly want to do things, and he wouldn't wait. Nothing was ever played the same way twice." The band used two of the four available tracks to record the music, and on the remaining two they overdubbed vocals, backing vocals and Syd's soaring echo-laden guitar. Live, the track took over from 'Interstellar Overdrive' as the set's psychedelic highlight, Syd often performing some of his most inspired lead guitar work. "It was a curious number, because the group seemed to periodically change gear, using the feedback echo as the clutch," observes Miles.

Lucifer Sam

(BARRETT)

LUCIFER SAM

BARRETT *guitars, lead vocals*
WATERS *bass guitar, vocals*
WRIGHT *Farfisa organ, piano*
MASON *drums*

RECORDED *May 1967, Abbey Road Studio 3*
PRODUCED BY *NORMAN SMITH*

By March 1967, Syd Barrett was a star, and had moved from Earlham Street, Soho, into a flat at 101, Cromwell Road, in the Earls Court area of London. It was a place that Nigel Gordon, one of the inhabitants, describes now as "the most iniquitous den in all of London." Surrounded by proselytising LSD converts and a constant supply of drugs, Syd travelled further into inner space. His flatmates were so fervent that they would often lace Syd's morning Nescafé with liquid LSD. "Put it this way, you never drank anything round there unless you got it yourself from the tap," says Andrew King. This constant diet of LSD resulted in accelerated creativity, but also prompted the onset of Syd's slide from reality. "The poor lad didn't know whether he was awake or dreaming. He never had the chance to re-establish reality."

'Lucifer Sam' is a lyrical snapshot of Syd's fragmented life. Originally titled 'Percy The Rat Catcher', there were plans to expand the song into a half hour film, scheduled

Syd, 19, before his LSD excesses.

for production in June 1967. Lucifer Sam, the Siamese cat, was the rat-catching sidekick of Percy. Syd took this idea from his notebook, and mixed scraps taken from the *I Ching*, fragments of counterculture cod-psychology and a reference to his girlfriend of the time, Jenny Spires (who appears as Jennifer Gentle in the song).

The line, "That cat's something I can't explain", which ends each verse, refers, according to Nigel Gordon, to the comings and goings of the Cromwell Road flat's cat Elfie. One of the song's more oblique lyrics, "You're the left side/He's the right side", is a reference to the preoccupation then current in psychology with the functional differences between the two hemispheres of the brain. People who were logical and pragmatic were said to be dominated by the right side, whereas the artistic and intuitive primarily used the left.

The music was based around the riff to Bo Diddley/Billy Boy Arnold's 'I Ain't Got You' to which Syd added some of his tautest and most accomplished rhythm and lead guitar. Using his trusty Binson Echorec, Syd created some inspired elastic 'slapback' echo returns which have baffled guitarists for years. Waters doubles the stepped descending chromatic riff on the bass, while Mason keeps a steady 2/4 beat pounding away relentlessly.

Children's writer Hilaire Belloc.

Matilda Mother

(BARRETT)

'Matilda Mother' is a beautiful evocation of being read a bedtime story by mother. Most of the imagery derives from Hilaire Belloc's popular children's verse, *Cautionary Tales*. When the song was originally played live, Syd would sing verses lifted straight from the book. These versions opened with the stanza, "There was a boy whose name was Jim, his friends were very good to him/They gave him cakes and tea and jam and slices of delicious ham/Oh mother tell me more".

When it came time to record the track, Andrew King approached the Belloc estate, but was refused permission to use the poem, so Syd wrote his own version. Like John Lennon, childhood would become a refuge for Syd when the rude intrusions of the real world became unbearable. "It was the place where things were simple," says Jenner. "I think it all became disturbed when Syd's father died when he was twelve. That was the last time Syd probably felt really happy and so he was always looking back to childhood." The dream of being a pop star had turned sour as the endless touring, indifferent audiences outside London and the compromises he was being asked to make to score hits took their toll. When Syd finally left London and the world of rock in 1970 it was to his mother's home in Cambridge that he returned to live, until her death in 1991.

The instrumental jam in the middle of this track, which would extend for fifteen minutes or more on stage, was literally cut short by Norman Smith, who took a razor blade to it at a randomly chosen point. There was time, however, for a great B minor organ solo by Rick Wright.

MATILDA MOTHER

BARRETT *guitars, lead vocals (verses 2, 4, and 5)*
WATERS *bass guitar, backing vocals*
WRIGHT *Farfisa organ, piano, lead vocal (verses 1-4)*
MASON *drums*
RECORDED *29 June, 1967, Abbey Road Studio 3*
PRODUCED BY *NORMAN SMITH*

Flaming

(BARRETT)

Yet another song that Syd had written before The Pink Floyd came together, and another evocation of childhood. Inspired by one of the Cambridge set's LSD trips in the autumn of 1965, when the group went on a psychedelic picnic on the banks of the river Cam, Syd mixes this memory with those of childhood games of hide and seek, played with his sister Rosemary. As a child, Syd had always had a strong affinity with nature, and using LSD he had explored the exquisite form of his natural environment. "In the same way that poets would use nature as a reference point, Yeats or Joyce for example, who Syd was particularly fond of, so the songs used had nature, flowers, light as their focus," says Andrew King. "It was the same with his paintings. Syd was trying to paint colours with his songs because it was all the same thing to him."

One of the most profound sensations produced by LSD is 'flaming', a visual experience involving ordinary things

FLAMING

BARRETT *electric and 12 string acoustic guitars, lead vocals*
WATERS *Rickenbacker bass guitar, backing vocals*
WRIGHT *Farfisa organ, piano, lead vocal (verses 1-4)*
MASON *drums, finger cymbals, percussion.*
RECORDED *June 1967, Abbey Road Studio 3.*
PRODUCED BY *NORMAN SMITH*

cigarettes or fingers appearing to emit light and sparks, like the traces of hand-held fireworks in the dark. This appeared as a visual reference in many of his post-LSD paintings, and also in songs like 'Flaming'. Syd may also have taken it from free jazz surrealist group AMM's first and only album (he was invited to witness the sessions for this, at the behest of Joe Boyd) - the track that took up the whole of side one was a surreal *tour de force* entitled 'Later During A Flaming Riviera Sunset'.

The production on 'Flaming' is Norman Smith's crowning moment. Syd wanted the instrumental section to evoke the sensation of being born away on a celestial breeze, looking down and being able to see the minute details of the earth with absolute clarity. Smith's response was to set up a very delicate echo, feeding it back on itself to give the effect of a billowing wind, while Nick Mason provided a chattering percussion sound. It perfectly mirrored the dream-like state Syd was recalling in the song.

'Toc H': Flanders, World War One.

Pow R. Toc H.

(BARRETT, WATERS, WRIGHT, MASON)

POW R. TOC H.

(INSTRUMENTAL)
BARRETT *guitars, vocalisations*
WATERS *bass guitar, vocalisations*
WRIGHT *Farfisa organ, piano*
MASON *drums*
RECORDED *15 April, 1967, Abbey Road Studio 3*
PRODUCED BY *NORMAN SMITH*

Although credited to the whole band, this was based on Roger Waters's bass line, and was a conscious attempt to produce a sequel to 'Interstellar Overdrive' (the band were anxious to ensure that their debut album had enough of the underground Floyd style to appease their fans). Though lacklustre by comparison, it dates from early in 1967, when the band was at the height of its improvisational powers.

"Someone would walk up to the mike, usually Roger, and go, 'Ba-boom-chi-chi, Ba-boom-chi-chi', and everyone would just start improvising around that, playing drones, or whatever came to them at the time," recalls Nick Mason. "It's hard to explain the kind of freedom and absolute insanity that surrounded us at that time." Despite the skilled use of sound effects to create a collage reminiscent of some primeval jungle, the spirit of the Floyd's best free-form excursions is somehow absent.

The bizarre title, for so long the subject of speculation, is meaningless, a nonsense phrase made up by Roger because it sounded good phonetically when shouted into the mike at gigs. 'Toc H' was signaller's code for the Talbot House army signaller's club, a serviceman's billet, behind the Allied lines in Flanders during World War One, where rank was ignored, and officers and privates alike were on first name terms as equals. It later became a charity, the name applied to "An interdenominational Christian fellowship of men and women which attempted to promote an understanding life through involvement in the community". Looking for an accompanying phrase that was similarly arcane, Waters hit upon the 'power' pun, 'Pow R', for no other reason than it sounded right, and was a syllabic match.

Take Up Thy Stethoscope And Walk

(WATERS)

TAKE UP THY STETHOSCOPE AND WALK

BARRETT *guitars, lead vocals*
WATERS *bass guitar, second lead vocal*
WRIGHT *Farfisa organ*
MASON *drums*
RECORDED *June 1967, Abbey Road Studio 3*
PRODUCED BY *NORMAN SMITH*

The first Roger Waters composition to be recorded once again displays the Floyd's talent for jamming. The band rocks out in the middle section, with some overdriven Rick Wright organ, and splatter drumming from Mason, but, like 'Pow R. Toc H.', it's another formulaic attempt to recreate their on-stage sound. "A very bad song," admits Waters. Live, the song was a completely different beast, everything radiating around the improvised middle section, where all four entered into a frenzied tempest of feedback and noise that left audiences disorientated. Not surprisingly, it was Norman Smith's idea to excise this middle section. His edit is clearly audible in the stereo mix.

Interstellar Overdrive

(BARRETT, WATERS, WRIGHT, MASON)

Having already recorded this track twice, once at Thompson Private Recorders and again with Joe Boyd at Sound Techniques, the Floyd decided it was the perfect way to ease themselves into the unfamiliar process of recording at Abbey Road with an unknown producer. More importantly, the band wanted to use 'Interstellar Overdrive' as a statement of intent to whomever EMI had assigned to produce the session.

Recording began late on the night of 16 March, 1967, when the band convened with their equipment in Studio 3. Engineer Peter Bown was the first member of EMI staff to encounter the group. "I got a call at home saying, 'Peter, I want you back here at the studio at ten. You will be doing a new group, and it's called 'Underground Music'. You may find them very difficult to get on with. They don't communicate much.' So I get back to the studio and the Floyd were rehearsing 'Interstellar Overdrive'. I opened the door and I nearly shit myself. By Christ, it was loud! I thought, 'How the fuck are we going to get this on tape?' I had certainly never heard anything quite like it, and I don't think I ever did again. It was very exciting."

Norman Smith was tipped off that "one of the boys in the group, and some of the people around them, seem a bit strange". Smith listened to them play through the track, then called them into the control room to discuss his approach. The band told him that the previous two versions of the track they'd cut had failed to capture the intensity and impact of the live performance. Smith and Bown's solution was to try and capture the live sound using expensive stereo microphones, and have the band record the track onto two tracks of the four available on the Studer/EMI four track machine - the same type of machine used by The Beatles - then overdub a second set of bass, keyboard and guitar parts on the remaining two tracks, effectively double-tracking the entire performance. Syd was the main obstacle to the smooth execution of this plan, as Smith remembers: "I think Syd used music . . . [as] a statement being made at a given time, which meant that if you came back five minutes later to do another take, you probably wouldn't get the same performance. You probably wouldn't even get the same tune."

"Syd's guitar was always a problem because he would not keep still and was always fiddling with his sound," agrees Bown. "He used to go and kick his echo box every now and then, just because he liked the sound it made. We wrecked four very expensive microphones that night. They got louder and louder until everything was overloading and the mikes just gave up the ghost."

While not as extreme as Joe Boyd's Sound Techniques version, it does sound more powerful. When it came to the mono mix , Smith achieved a near perfect blend of the two performances. For the stereo mix the two takes were simply separated into the left and right channels.

INTERSTELLAR OVERDRIVE

BARRETT *guitars, lead vocals (verses 2, 4, and 5)*
WATERS *bass guitar, backing vocals*
WRIGHT *Farfisa organ, piano, lead vocal (verses 1-4)*
MASON *drums*
RECORDED *16 March, 1967, Abbey Road Studio 3*
PRODUCED BY *NORMAN SMITH*

A young Dave Gilmour.

THE GNOME

BARRETT *acoustic guitars, double tracked lead vocal*
WATERS *bass guitar, backing vocals*
WRIGHT *celeste*
MASON *drums*
RECORDED *7 May - 16 July 1967 Abbey Road Studio 3*
PRODUCED BY *NORMAN SMITH*

The Gnome

(BARRETT)

A song inspired by J.R.R. Tolkien's fantasy tale of hobbits, elves and epic crusades, *Lord Of The Rings*. Published in 1954, the book had taken on a second wind during the late 60s as 'trip literature'. The name Tolkien gave to his mythical underground kingdom, 'Middle-Earth', was later adopted by one of the psychedelic clubs of the time. Without the subsequent flood of imitations to devalue its charm, *Lord Of The Rings* was much admired at the time. Syd's song loosely describes the journey of Frodo, the hobbit (gnome) who "has a big adventure". "There's also a touch of Kenneth Grahame too," says Andrew King, "The gnome is also the mole from *Wind In The Willows* - perhaps, I dunno."

***J.R.R. Tolkien, author of* Lord Of The Rings.**

CHAPTER 24

BARRETT *guitars, lead vocal*
WATERS *bass guitar, backing vocals*
WRIGHT *Farfisa organ*
MASON *drums*

RECORDED *7 May - 16 July 1967*
Abbey Road Studio 3
PRODUCED BY *NORMAN SMITH*

THE SCARECROW

BARRETT *acoustic and electric guitars, lead vocal*
WATERS *bass guitar, backing vocals*
WRIGHT *Farfisa organ*
MASON *percussion*

RECORDED *15 April 1967, Abbey Road Studio 3*
PRODUCED BY *NORMAN SMITH*

Chapter 24

(BARRETT)

When LSD first hit the streets, the culture that followed was an empirical one. It was defined by those who were using LSD and there was little or no literature to explain the experience. Instead trippers looked to the mystic cultures of the past for guidance. In America, Timothy Leary had taken the *Tibetan Book Of The Dead* and revised it into *The Psychedelic Experience*, the first tripper's manual. Another informal guide was the *I Ching* - the 5,000 year old Chinese 'Book of Changes'. One of the five classics of Confucianism, and a common source for both Taoist and Confucian philosophy, it is used as an ancient poetic horoscope of prophecies based on the casting of randomly thrown coins. Its use became widespread among the underground community of the late 60s, and at one point Apple, The Beatles' business empire, was being governed by decisions made using the I Ching.

The title of the song and most of its lyrics come directly from Chapter 24 of the *I Ching*. This chapter is titled 'Fu', meaning change/success. Syd owned a copy of the now famous Richard Wilhelm translation, first published in 1924, having discovered the book through his love of the esoteric Chinese board game 'Go', which he would often play long into the night with girl friend Lyndsey Korner. Syd himself was searching for some kind of explanation for the psychic upheaval he was experiencing through his growing fame and his LSD revelations. He apparently homed in on this chapter, believing it to represent the constant evolution, death and resurrection in nature. As the Wilhelm translation puts it, "To know this means to know oneself in relation to the cosmic forces." 'Chapter 24' is virtually lifted word for word from one page of this section of the book.

The Scarecrow

(BARRETT)

Telling the tale of a sad scarecrow, who wants a little more from life but realises that he can't move, then becomes resigned to his fate, as the mice churn up the ground beneath him, this song is Barrett at his most enchantingly simple. Syd had been writing songs of one kind or another since 1963, storing his lyrics in a ring binder marked "Roger's songs" (Roger being his given Christian name). His early attempts often amounted to little more than snatched ideas, verses and the odd melody over guitar chords. By 1965, he had developed a strong style, simple, brisk and inspired by his love of Edward Lear, traditional English

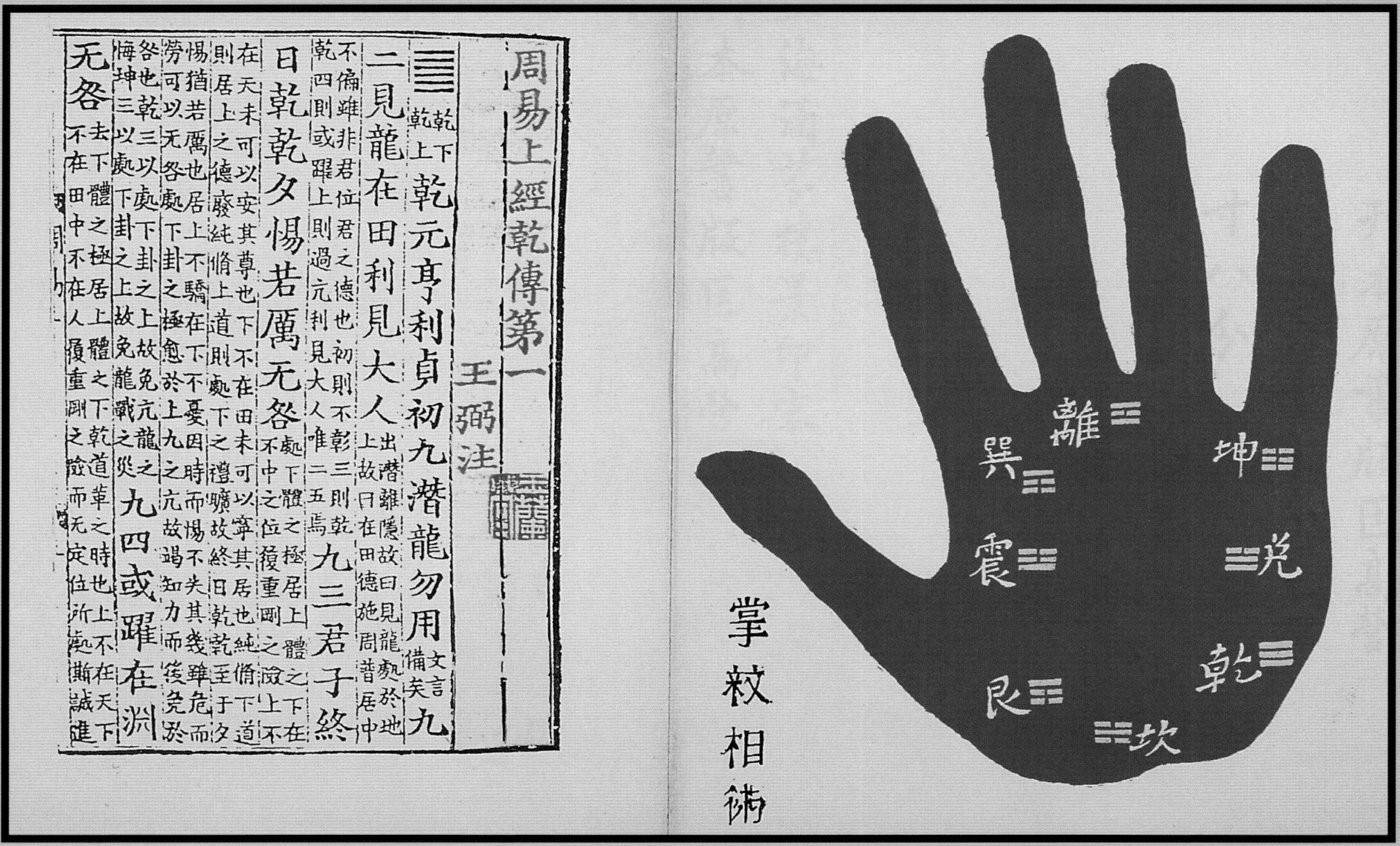

***Chapter 24: the* I Ching.**

folk ballads and the storytelling tradition of the American delta bluesmen. All of these elements fused together with LSD to produce Syd's unique new narrative style. One of the tracks that would later appear on his solo album *Barrett* in 1970, 'Effervescing Elephant', dates from this early period, as does this song. "Syd's songs of that period were a real cornucopia," says Storm Thorgerson. "He was always coming up with these whimsical songs with a nursery feel, that were rooted in the things he had read as a child, overheard or seen. Mix all that up with drugs and The Beatles and you have Syd."

Peter Jenner recalls the lyrics being taken from Syd's ring binder and laid over the simple AEGD chord progression. "Syd wasn't a great one for complex lyrics. I'd say to him, we need a song, Syd, and out would come a song. He would see things like a scarecrow in a field and write a song about it. 'That's nice,' he'd say, and the next thing it was a song. It's tempting to say it has no meaning, but it's very possible that Syd was the scarecrow. Like 'Vegetable Man', that disturbing song where he just described what he was wearing, I think he was writing, albeit subconsciously, about himself."

It's also possible that Syd took the idea for the song from *The Scarecrow*, a children's book by June Wilson which has roughly the same storyline as the song. The simple tune was sung and played live by Syd on his Fender Telecaster guitar, over which Mason overdubbed wood block and Wright contributed serpentine motifs on his Farfisa organ. The track was chosen as the B-side to 'See Emily Play'.

Syd wrote* Bike *for Jenny Spires.

Bike

(BARRETT)

This could easily be seen as a prime slice of 60s psychedelic whimsy, if it wasn't for the extraordinary complexity of the arrangement and the oddly romantic lyrics. The working title was simply 'The Bike Song', and it might be considered Syd's approximation of a love song. The tune is a shy and endearing attempt on the part of the singer to share those things which are special to him - his bike, his cloak, his pet mouse and his gingerbread men - with the girl he decides "fits in" with his rag-tag world. The song starts out straightforwardly enough, but each subsequent verse becomes more bizarre. The tempo changes at the end of every verse. The rising glissando note that finishes each chorus was achieved using a crude oscillator and varispeeding the tape down while the track was running. Written for his girlfriend of the time, Jenny Spires, at the Earlham Street flat where Syd was living with Peter Wynne Wilson, the Floyd's lighting man, it is a classic example of Syd's descriptive style. "He would see things like a bike or cloak and immediately come up with a little alliterative couplet. It was very Edward Lear, actually. He was just looking for funny words that rhymed," says Peter Jenner.

At the end of the song, Syd invites his girl into the "other room" and the song segues into a collage of sounds which may be intended to represent various sexual escapades, or the turbulence of love. "It's the most fantastical muddle of sounds and time signatures, yet somehow Syd makes it all make perfect sense," says Smith. "'Bike' was one of the last tracks where Syd was truly in control. In many ways I think it was a reflection of how simple things were in his world."

Smith was anxious to prove himself the equal of George Martin, and three days were spent making tape loops after a raid of the Abbey Road sound effects library for the sound of the clockwork toys for the end section, overlaid on top of one another before having reverb added. The track ends with repeated speeded up high-pitched laughter taken from a sound effects disc of a seaside mechanical laughing policeman and looped.

This is one of the songs that Barrett is supposed to have mixed for the mono release. "It's not like mixing today with hundreds of channels to consider. There were only four knobs to play with but he seemed to perform these effortless mixes. His hands would fly across the faders, in Studio 3 at that grey gun-metal desk; Syd doing a mix-down without actually looking at it, just feeling. It was spontaneous. You'd think it was random, but it wasn't. It looked effortless when he did things, but there was great grace to it."

BIKE

BARRETT *guitars, double tracked lead vocal, tape effects*
WATERS *Rickenbacker bass guitar, backing vocals*
WRIGHT *Farfisa organ, piano*
MASON *drums*
RECORDED *21-22 May, 1967, Abbey Road Studio 3*
PRODUCED BY *NORMAN SMITH*

A SAUCERFUL OF SECRETS

RECORDED *January - April 1968, Abbey Road Studio 3*

PRODUCED BY *NORMAN SMITH (except title track, produced by Pink Floyd)*
UK RELEASE *29 June, 1968*
CHART PLACING *Number 9 in the UK*

A *Saucerful Of Secrets* was a transitional album, whose songs mirror the shift away from free-form psychedelic pop towards the more adult-oriented material that would define their later career. It also chronicles the most emotionally upsetting and testing time the band had yet endured, as Syd's growing estrangement made his place in the band untenable. On the up side, it marked the arrival of Dave Gilmour, which gave them a new musical focus and a crucial boost at a time when they had all but decided to give up. A *Saucerful Of Secrets* was never originally intended to be a full Pink Floyd album, but a collection of oddments left over from the band's beginnings. With Syd incapable of writing and no obvious contender to take his place, the band fell into limbo.

Barrett's descent was swift. It began almost as soon as the band had achieved international notoriety. On a tour of America, Syd had remained almost catatonic: there was a memorable appearance on *The Pat Boone Show* during which Syd stoically refused to answer any of the anodyne host's questions, and didn't even bother lip-synching to the track. He began talking in strange riddles, and was becoming increasingly paranoid. On a package tour with Jimi Hendrix and The Amen Corner, Davey O'List from The Nice had to deputise, because Syd simply vanished before shows, or would stand playing one note all night. The crunch came at a gig in Brighton, when Syd simply couldn't be found. Nigel Gordon, the 'Acid King', called Dave Gilmour, then in Cambridge, and told him that the Floyd needed a guitarist for that

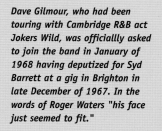

Dave Gilmour, who had been touring with Cambridge R&B act Jokers Wild, was officiallly asked to join the band in January of 1968 having deputized for Syd Barrett at a gig in Brighton in late December of 1967. In the words of Roger Waters "his face just seemed to fit."

1968

A Saucerful Of Secrets

night's show. Both band and managers had tried to take Syd to see noted psychiatrist RD Laing, an exponent of the idea that madness is in the eye of the beholder. Laing heard a tape of Syd in conversation and pronounced him 'incurable'. The band resisted going to see more conventional psychiatrists, fearing that Syd would be placed in a mental institution, and never emerge again.

"We had a deep mistrust of trick cyclists (psychiatrists)," says Peter Jenner. "I'd read a little Irving Goffman, and I knew what these institutions did to people's minds. Syd wasn't in pain or distress, he was just barking mad, so we struggled on, but it was very difficult for everyone."

There was talk of trying to get Syd to become the

Brian Wilson of the Pink Floyd, a writer who would not play live. "I think that idea lasted about five minutes. None of us really thought it could work, Syd was just not functioning properly," says Andrew King. "I think Syd thought it could work, but he was very unhappy."

The Floyd struggled on, and tried recording together, but eventually realized that it was impossible to continue with Syd in the band. Waters in particular, though very fond of Syd, had had enough of the insanity, and told Syd that he was no longer welcome at the sessions. "Things got very nasty at the studio," says Andrew King. "It would literally be Syd in one corner and the rest of the band in the other. There had always been conflict between Roger and Syd but it had made the group what it was. Waters was conventionally forceful, and Syd had the power because he was writing the songs, so it worked. But Syd always thought he had a better way of looking at things - he felt a revolution of the mind and the heart was flowing through him, and that the others were not open to that." Once Waters and Barrett were at odds, their petty differences became magnified into full blown disagreements. "Syd could be very cruel, making fun of how straight-laced they all were. It got very unpleasant, like a very acrimonious divorce. They couldn't have a conversation with each other, because everything they said was loaded with hidden meaning."

Meanwhile, life at the Cromwell Road flat was making Syd's behaviour even more bizarre. With acid on the menu every day, things got increasingly out of hand. "My wife and I had a lot of cats and we gave one to Syd because he liked them, and it seemed to comfort him," recalls Jenner. "He gave the animal LSD as a joke, can you believe it? He used to be a genuine joy to be around, but now he made no sense, and the spark that had given the world 'Emily' was gone." Syd was rescued from the flat and taken in by Storm Thorgerson and Po Powell, but it was too late. Syd was lost for ever.

"Syd just couldn't cope with the drug or his life as a pop star," says Nigel Gordon, a flatmate from 101 Cromwell Road. "Pure liquid LSD was very strong and not to be taken for fun. It was for religious revelation. We wanted to touch God. Syd didn't have the intellect to cope. He was caught in childhood. To him, things were simple. There were no complexities. The LSD world is complex, overwhelmingly so, and he was always fighting it, fighting himself. It destroyed him."

Through all this the band were attempting to make their second album. Syd took to sitting in the reception area at Abbey Road, clutching his guitar, waiting to be invited into the sessions. Eventually he stopped waiting. There were a few strained moments when he took to following the band around the country in his Mini-Cooper, but by April 1968 Syd had disappeared. The band simply stopped calling him up. Jenner and King didn't believe the Floyd were viable without Syd, and stopped managing the group.

"To be honest I think we just wanted out of a very emotionally damaging situation. We were young, it had all been so exciting, and now it had all gone so terribly wrong," says King. "No one involved with that situation will ever get over the way it happened. I used to say to Syd, 'why can't you write another 'Emily' and we'll all be rich and happy again?' but I knew I was only trying to make him feel better. I think we may have pressurized him into a state of paranoia about having to come up with another hit single."

As Syd embarked on his sabbatical from reality, his behaviour became violent and unpredictable. No one wanted to be around him, and in his absence Waters assumed control of the band. The songs that dated from Syd Barrett's brief six month window of creativity had all been used, either as singles or as album tracks. Since he hadn't written anything releasable since 'See Emily Play' the rest of the band became unwilling songwriters. With this came a new sound and new approach to recording.

"All the things that interested us in a studio were not involved with improvization. Very quickly we found that we were aiming to try and perfect things and build them up - particularly in the early days when we were working with four tracks," says Nick Mason of the band's change in direction. "There was a hell of a lot of layering that went on, where things had to be sort of set in stone. It was better if it was simpler and correct than a bit fancy and wrong. I think that started us on something else. Then, when we'd take those recordings into live performance, to work with staging and with lights and all the rest of it, it made life a lot easier and a lot better if we stopped being too free."

With the disappearance of Syd, EMI took to marketing the band in a new way too, as the press release for the album indicates: "Unlike Cornelius Cardew or even Stockhausen, whose futuristic dabblings seem erratic and uncoordinated, the Pink Floyd have managed to blend sounds - all sounds - so that they convey deeply felt convictions with a clarity and directness whose authority is unmistakable."

Another notable first was Storm Thorgerson's trippy cover design on which he attempted to visually convey the psychedelic experience. "I was trying to represent the swirling dreamlike visions of various altered states of consciousness, induced by religious experience, pharmaceutical additives (cough, cough), or Pink Floyd music. Or all three. The cover design consisted of three main ingredients, the marbled work of a friend of ours called John Whitely, the ominous presence of Dr Strange from Marvel Comics, and the use of very trendy infrared colour film."

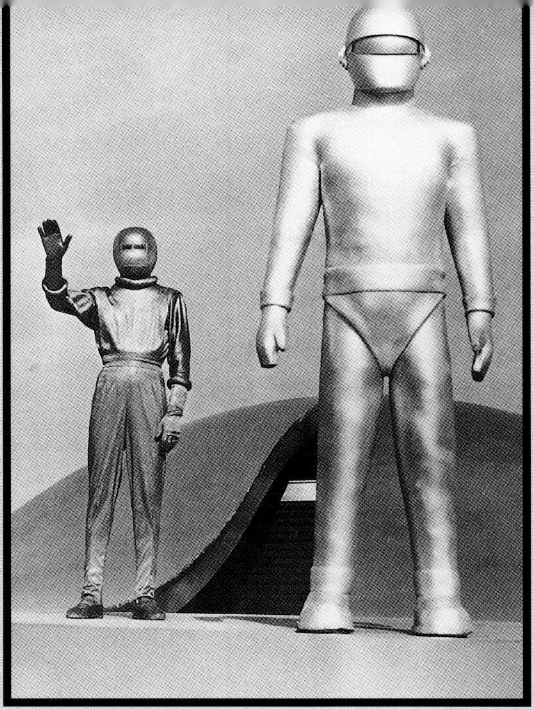

The Day The Earth Stood Still ***soundtrack (with Theremin) influenced Rick Wright.***

Let There Be More Light

(WATERS)

'Let There Be More Light' was the fifth song recorded for the album (March 1968), and the first with no contribution from Syd Barrett. One of the few true science fiction tunes produced by the group, this song includes a few obscure sci-fi references (such as to John Carter of Edgar Rice Burroughs's Mars books), as well as lyrics that seem to be there just because they fit. There is even a joking reference to a well-known Beatles tune - this time Lucy appears in the sky without her diamonds. 'Let There Be More Light' also features an especially good intro and outro, the latter a Johnny-one-chord improvisational-*cosmische* jam, something the Floyd did better than anybody.

Roger Waters: "I hardly ever read science fiction. I used to read a lot, but only very occasionally now. I suppose that the reason that I liked it was because it gives the writer the chance to re-examine important ideas. If you remove an idea from its familiar surroundings, it allows you to look at it in a new light. Also, some of the books offer bloody good yarns, and I like a good yarn." The song mixes the metaphors of the LSD trip with the science fiction world, and tells of an alien craft landing at RAF Mildenhall, revealing to the world a new and exciting reality for humankind. It was typical sub-acid fantasy fare.

LET THERE BE MORE LIGHT

GILMOUR *guitars, lead vocal (verses 2, 4, 6, and 8)*
WATERS *bass guitar, backing vocal (verses 1, 3, 5, and 7)*
WRIGHT *Farfisa organ, piano, lead vocal (verses 1, 3, 5, and 7)*
MASON *drums*

RECORDED *2 November, 1968, Abbey Road Studio 3.*
PRODUCED BY *NORMAN SMITH*

Edgar Rice Burroughs, whose **Mars** ***trilogy inspired*** **Let There Be More Light.**

Careful With That Axe, Eugene

(WATERS, GILMOUR, WRIGHT, MASON)

The band went into the studio at the beginning of November to record this piece, which had been played live since the spring. This was the fourth recorded version of the song, but the first to be officially released. Originally known as 'Keep Smiling, People', the track soon became known by its nickname 'the one chord wonder' on account of its persistent and unchanging C drone bass around which the band weave their melodies. First performed live on 31 May, 1968, the track was written as part of the commissioned score for the film, *The Committee*. Though it didn't survive onto the soundtrack it was heard when the film was premiered, at the Fantasio Club in Amsterdam. That version, recorded in half a day at a cheap demo studio, was so limp that the band immediately disowned it. It appeared next as 'Murderistic Woman' when it was recorded and performed for BBC Radio 1's *Top Gear* show on 11 August, 1968. From then on, the 'one-chord wonder' continued to evolve, becoming tighter, more sinister and spooky, but ultimately more dynamic than all earlier versions.

CAREFUL WITH THAT AXE, EUGENE

GILMOUR *guitars*
WATERS *bass guitar, vocal*
WRIGHT *Farfisa organ, piano*
MASON *drums*

RECORDED *2 November, 1968, Abbey Road Studio 3.*
PRODUCED BY *NORMAN SMITH*
Released on B-side of single 'POINT ME AT THE SKY' 17 December, 1968

REMEMBER A DAY

GILMOUR *guitars, backing vocals*
WATERS *bass guitar*
WRIGHT *piano, lead vocal*
BARRETT *guitar*
MASON *drums*

RECORDED *9 May, 1967, Abbey Road Studio 3*
PRODUCED BY *NORMAN SMITH*

The final title came from the A-side of the single it accompanied - 'Point Me At The Sky', where the name Eugene is mentioned. The song itself is, according to Waters, a reflection of pent-up aggression that builds to a moment of insane, manic, murderistic release. Gilmour delivers some of his best early guitar work with the Floyd on this track, which soon became a live favourite, as 'the scream' was panned around the quadraphonic surroundsound system using the 'azimuth co-ordinator' joystick.

Remember A Day

(WRIGHT)

'Remember A Day' was an outtake from *The Piper At The Gates Of Dawn* and may have gone under the working title of 'Sunshine', although a different backing track of the same name exists at Abbey Road. Ostensibly, it's another of Rick Wright's odes to childhood. Encouraged by Syd to write ("He said that if he could do it anyone could"), Wright composed 'Remember A Day' when he was about to turn 22. Having been educated at the expensive Haberdasher's prep school in London, and enjoyed an idyllic and uncomplicated youth, Wright was aware that the sudden pressures of being in a rock band had robbed him and the others, particularly Syd, of some of their youth, and replaced it with unnecessary and strength-sapping obligations. Although Wright dismisses his two contributions to *A Saucerful Of Secrets* as 'quite atrocious', they are probably the closest anyone in the band came to equalling Syd's plaintive evocation of untainted youth. Syd plays some beautiful slide guitar on this song, which was virtually complete, although it needed to be "touched up a little" for release, with Dave Gilmour adding two minor guitar overdubs.

Rick Wright wrote **Remember A Day** *for the Piper sessions, when it was rejected for being too downbeat.*

SET THE CONTROLS FOR THE HEART OF THE SUN

GILMOUR *lead and rhythm guitars, backing vocal*
WATERS *bass guitar, lead vocal*
WRIGHT *Farfisa organ, piano*
MASON *drums*
BARRETT *lead guitar*

RECORDED *January 1968, Abbey Road Studio 3*
PRODUCED BY *NORMAN SMITH*

Set The Controls For The Heart Of The Sun

(WATERS)

The first song recorded specifically for the LP, rather than a mere leftover from previous sessions, 'Set The Controls' was Roger Waters's first truly effective composition. He was determined, having come this far, to make the band work. Focused and anxious to prove to Jenner and King that he was capable of writing exciting music, Waters worked on the song for four months until he felt it was ready to record, completing it in September, 1967. At the time, all the band were being encouraged to write more, as Jenner, King and Norman Smith were having problems agreeing on anything as a viable third single. While the final result wasn't as frantic or unpredictable as Syd's extemporaneous mayhem, it successfully evokes a sensation of spooky isolation and detachment in the dark reaches of space.

The track builds from Waters's opening repetitive bass motif, while Nick Mason contributes a delicate wash of cymbal and percussive effects using soft beaters. The arrangement also includes a xylophone. It's a subtle masterpiece of dynamics, the choruses lifting off with a mighty surge of Hammond organ. The lyrics, Roger admits, were 'ripped off' from a book of Chinese verse, translated by Arthur Whaley, dating from the late T'ang period, and were simply cut up and rearranged without much thought for what they might mean, a technique probably borrowed from William Burroughs, from whose book *The Soft Machine*, Roger lifted the title. Waters was very aware of the phonetic sound of words and lyrics, and would often write with this as his first and most important criterion. Like much Chinese poetry, the words deal with awakenings of human understanding, the profound wonder of existence and the cycles of nature. In this way, it's reminiscent of the ideas that Syd held

William Burroughs, seen here at his typewriter in 1962.

dear. "It's about an unknown person who, while piloting a mighty flying saucer, is overcome with solar suicidal tendencies and sets the controls for the heart of the sun," offered Roger at the time.

This is one of two songs on the album which more or less represent Pink Floyd as a five piece (as it was indeed envisaged, briefly, with at least one five-man photo session being shot), with the guitar playing shared between Syd and Dave. Syd recorded his guitar first, in January, and Gilmour overdubbed his parts at the end of February. The two were not together in the studio as Gilmour, one of Syd's oldest friends from Cambridge, found it upsetting that Syd often failed to recognise him. The two did, however, play the track together live, at least six times. There are even a few bootleg recordings of the song that briefly feature the five piece Floyd, and include some breathtaking Barrett guitar. The song remained a cornerstone of the Floyd's live set until 1973.

Corporal Clegg

(WATERS)

This was not the last time that a song with sobering lyrics would be set to music that seems jolly and upbeat - see also 'Free Four' from *Obscured By Clouds*, where Waters again tackles the subject of soldiers and death. Nor would it be the last time Roger Waters wrote about a casualty of war. This was his first, albeit slightly comedic, attempt to deal with the death of his father, killed in Anzio in 1944, in a song. It was a theme he'd return to again and again, eventually expanding it into a full album, his last with the group, *The Final Cut*. Corporal Clegg returns from World War Two suffering from shell shock ("He's never been the same"), and imagines receiving medals for his suffering.

This was the last recorded Floyd song to feature any contribution from Syd Barrett. As on 'Set The Controls', Syd recorded his sprawling and sinewy lead guitar work for the song first, and Gilmour added overdubs later. The track was only recorded for fun, originally as an interesting B-side. If you listen closely, you can hear the band, performing backing vocals, erupt into laughter while trying to sing 'Corporal Clegg', towards the end. After the last chorus, what sounds like an insane band of kazoo freaks takes up the melody, over which come a variety of sound effects depicting war. An air raid siren closes the track, before a rather hurried fade-out.

CORPORAL CLEGG

GILMOUR
rhythm guitar, lead vocals
WATERS
bass guitar, lead vocals
WRIGHT
Farfisa organ,
piano, backing vocals
BARRETT
lead guitar
MASON
drums, spoken words

RECORDED *February 1968, Abbey Road Studio 3*
PRODUCED BY *NORMAN SMITH*

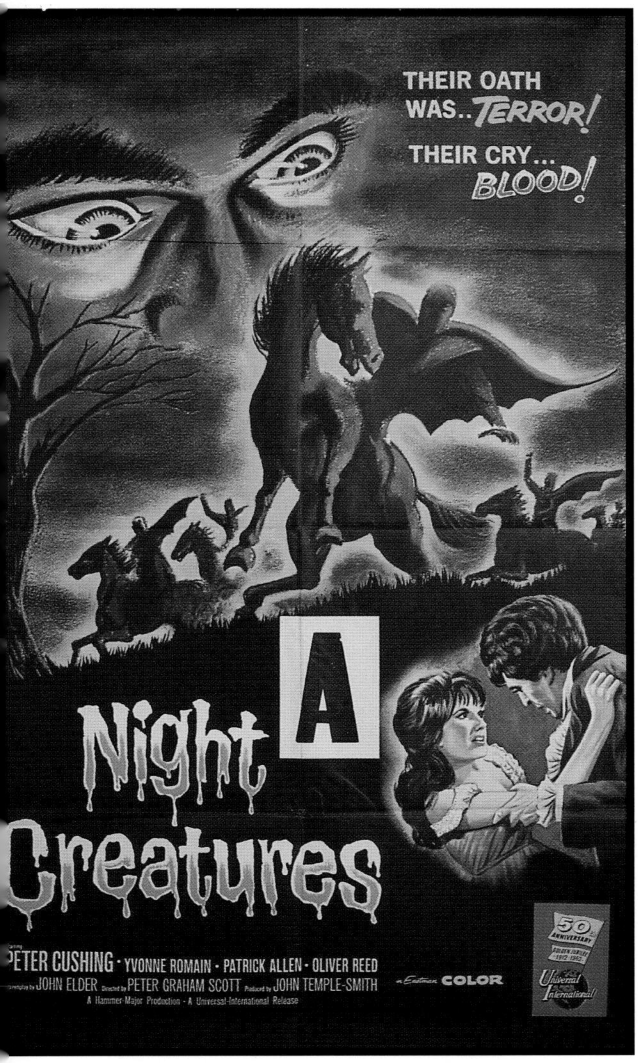

Night Creatures - ***a source for*** **Clegg*?***

A SAUCERFUL OF SECRETS

(INSTRUMENTAL)

GILMOUR *guitars, vocals*
WATERS *bass guitar,*
WRIGHT *Farfisa organ, piano*
MASON *drums*

RECORDED *April 1968, Abbey Road Studio 3*
PRODUCED BY *NORMAN SMITH*

SEE SAW

GILMOUR *guitars, backing vocals*
WATERS *bass guitar, lead vocals*
WRIGHT *Farfisa organ, piano, lead vocals*
MASON *drums*

RECORDED *April 1968, Abbey Road Studio 3*
PRODUCED BY *NORMAN SMITH*

A Saucerful Of Secrets

(WATERS, WRIGHT, MASON, GILMOUR)

By the time this track was recorded, Syd had stopped showing up at Abbey Road and had disappeared on a crazed, uncoordinated zigzagging tour of Britain in his Mini-Cooper. EMI wanted potential hits and less of the psychedelia, which was seen as a passing gimmick that hadn't taken off. The band agreed to an album of shorter pop tunes on condition that they could have one track on the album that was entirely free of any A&R directives and would reflect their developing interest in a more progressive and structured sound. "It was given to us by the company like sweeties after we'd finished. We could do what we liked with the last twelve minutes of the record."

With this track the Floyd made their first departure from Barrett's spectral presence and began to forge a new musical identity. The track is compiled from three separate musical sections segued together, a new composing method that the Floyd would refine through *Atom Heart Mother, Meddle* and *Dark Side Of The Moon*. Though credited to all the band members, the track owes much of its shape to Waters's strong structuralist tendencies. A chart was drawn on graph paper, with timed peaks and troughs, representing the track's dynamic progress. Syd's only comment on his former bandmates' new working practise was, "Their choice of material was always very much to do with what they were thinking as architecture students."

Norman Smith simply couldn't understand the track. "He was into the songs," recalls Rick Wright. "He said, 'I think it's rubbish . . . but go ahead and do it if you want.'" Smith's lack of interest allowed the Floyd free run of the studio. With just an engineer to help them patch effects together and get sounds, they learned a studio craft that would soon become their standard way of working. From this moment onwards, producers were really only a formality for the Floyd.

As to what the music was intended to invoke, the theme was, apparently, war. According to Gilmour, "The first part is tension, a build-up, a fear. The middle, with all the crashing and banging - that's the war going on. The aftermath is a sort of requiem." Gilmour recalled playing guitar on the second section with the instrument "turned up real loud and using the leg of a microphone stand like a steel bar, running it up and down the finger-board. I remember sitting there thinking, 'My God, this isn't what music's all about.' I had just come straight out of a band that spent most of its time rehashing early Jimi Hendrix songs to crowds of strange French people. Going into this was culture shock." The third section is funereal, dominated by Rick's organ and leading into a choral requiem. In a clever touch, echoes of the battle section can be heard buried in the mix. The piece ends slightly abruptly with a cut, deemed necessary to keep it under the allotted twelve minutes.

Reviewers drew highbrow comparisons to *musique concrete* and *avant-garde* musicians such as John Cage and Stockhausen. The largely positive reception pointed the way forward for the struggling Floyd, and gave them confidence that they could make worthwhile music without Syd.

See Saw

(WRIGHT)

The band's opinion of this Rick Wright track is best summed up by its working title, 'The Most Boring Song I've Ever Heard Bar Two'. The sixth song to be recorded for the album, 'See Saw' is definitely a contender for the worst, or at least the most uninspiring, song Pink Floyd ever released. Wright regarded it with particular disdain, branding one of his first attempts at song writing as, "A sort of an embarrassment. The lyrics are appalling. But it was a definite learning process . . . I learned that I'm not a lyric writer." 'Lucy In The Sky With Diamonds' was the lyrical model for this track, a

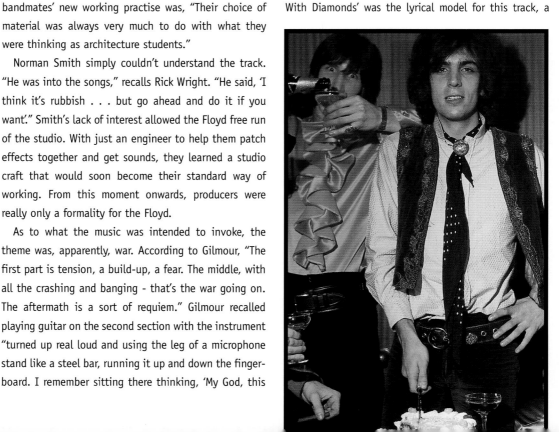

Syd, celebrating **Arnold's** *success.*

narrative song with a large helping of surreal imagery and dreamy reverie. Ironically for Wright, who would rather that the track had been abandoned altogether, it was 'See Saw' that stirred up controversy on the album's release. Suggestions were made that the lyrics dealt with incest, sex and drugs, though its author denied it all, saying it was merely a fairly pedestrian attempt to describe a moment from his own childhood when he and his sister were playing in the garden of the family home.

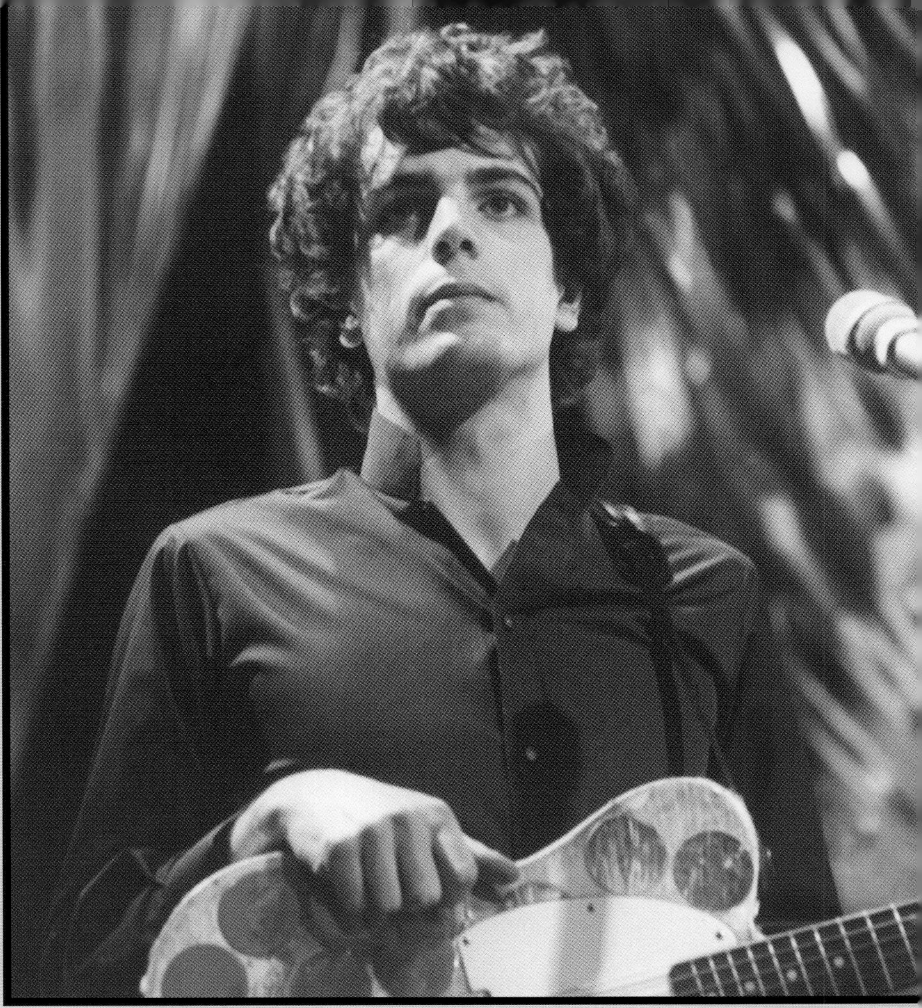

Syd in late 1967, pictured with his trusty mirror disc Fender Telecaster guitar.

Jugband Blues

(BARRETT)

Jugband Blues' is a poignant coda both to the album and to Syd's tenure as leader of the Floyd. The track itself was recorded long before work on *A Saucerful Of Secrets* began in October 1967, at a time when Syd had already begun the slide into schizophrenic exile, becoming less and less interested in recording or writing. Having exhausted the fund of potential singles, Barrett was asked to write new songs with an eye to chart success. Two songs were duly recorded, 'Scream Thy Last Scream' and 'Vegetable Man', but when EMI heard them, tipped off by Norman Smith that they were little more than lunatic ravings, their release was denied.

Barrett had one last song in reserve, this extraordinary hybrid, part jaunty singalong, part melancholic love song, part insane dadaist freefall. When Andrew King heard Syd play it for the first time he was awestruck. It was, in his view, one of the finest things Syd had ever produced and he petitioned for its release as the next single. EMI, via Norman Smith, had the final say, and rejected it as too downbeat to trouble the charts. It was passed over in favour of 'Apples And Oranges', a good song poorly realised, which promptly disappeared without trace.

Barrett wanted the Salvation Army band to play randomly.

Recorded in two sections at De Lane Lea Studios, the first with the full band, the latter Syd alone with an acoustic guitar, the gap between them was bridged by another aural collage section, constructed by the band. In a moment of sublime clarity Syd Barrett encapsulated the pain of his own deteriorating mental condition in lines like "I'm most obliged to you for making it clear that I'm not here/And I'm wondering who could be writing this song". Though each line seems to be a *non sequitur,* they come together into a impression of Syd's advancing schizophrenia. "Syd knew exactly what was happening to him, but was powerless to stop it. He knew he was going wrong inside," says Andrew King.

The middle section features the Salvation Army Band of North London, who recorded their albums at Abbey Road. Syd had asked Norman Smith for a brass section to play through the bridge, and wanted them to play spontaneously, without music. Smith, on the other hand, felt the bewildered musicians should be properly scored. It was the only time Syd had a vociferous disagreement with Smith, who finally agreed to record two versions, one with his scored section and one with Syd's instruction to "play whatever you want". After half an hour Syd grew tired of arguing and walked out, leaving Smith to finish the track his way. Syd Barrett left the building, and all but left The Pink Floyd, too.

JUGBAND BLUES

BARRETT *acoustic, electric guitars, lead vocals*
WATERS *upright bass, backing vocals*
WRIGHT *Hammond organ, penny whistle*
MASON *drums, kazoo*
SALVATION ARMY BAND OF NORTH LONDON *brass section*

RECORDED *October 1967, De Lane Lea Studios, London*
PRODUCED BY *NORMAN SMITH*

More

1969

RECORDED *March 1969, Abbey Road, London*
PRODUCED BY *PINK FLOYD*
RELEASED *July 1969*
COVER BY *HIPGNOSIS*

Still struggling for direction following Syd Barrett's departure, Pink Floyd were anxious to explore any avenue that might potentially provide them with the impetus for change. They weren't certain they could continue as conventional rock band, and so jumped at director Barbet Schroeder's (later to direct *Barfly*) offer to record the soundtrack for his hippie-flick-with-a-message, called *More*. While the band had previously contributed an improvized short score for Peter Sykes's film *The Committee* (which starred Paul Jones in a vehicle, never formally released, that crudely attempted to explore the fashionable theories of R.D. Laing, the psychiatrist who maintained that schizophrenia was the only logical response to an insane world), the recordings were poor, and the band were deeply disillusioned by the whole episode. Waters, in particular, was anxious to establish the band's multimedia potential, and always regretted not approaching Stanley Kubrick to score *2001: A Space Odyssey*, in late 1968.

Schroeder approached the band with a finished edit of the film, explained the themes to them and drew up a written brief for the scenes in which he would use their music. He agreed to let the Floyd produce themselves and offered them the kind of freedom in the studio they had hitherto only experienced at the recording of the track 'A Saucerful Of Secrets', a year before. In fact, EMI agreed to classify the *More* soundtrack as a special project, and gave the band a higher royalty than on their previous albums. The other incentive, of course, was the large sum of money that Schroeder was offering - £600 each for 8 days' work, and complete ownership and rights to all the material once it had been used in the film! This was substantially more lucrative than touring around the country's less salubrious venues.

Work began in late March and was completed an astonishing eight days later, making it the shortest session for any Pink Floyd album. Barbet Schroeder supervised, helping the band to understand the scenes and the flow of the film. "(Soundtracks are) contract

Post-Barrett Pink Floyd in 1969. Barbet Schroeder (above), was fascinated by liberal hippie ideals.

Cirrus Minor was the name the Floyd gave to the imaginary place where everything felt good, relaxed and secure. Schroeder wanted a track that would evoke the feelings of escape through Heroin.

work," commented Dave Gilmour at the time. "You start in the studio without anything . . . you chuck things down, and ask, 'How about something like this?' Then you work on it a bit. It's not the same process as making your own music for yourself - much more hurried, and less care tends to be taken."

Gilmour's considered comments belie the fact that he approached the whole process by getting righteously stoned, then simply letting the tapes roll. Certainly, some of the more way-out tracks like 'The Nile Song' indicate that *More* was also a chance for the band to rock out. Sixteen tracks were completed over five all-night sessions, of which 13 would be released on the album. The three additional songs, 'Seabirds', 'Hollywood', and 'Theme (Beat Version)' appeared in the film only.

The music and the lyrics loosely follow the action of the film. There was a strong parallel between Pink Floyd's music and the film's subject matter. Though the frenetic psychedelic edge had gone from their music with the departure of Syd Barrett, the band were still perceived as every Head's cosmic avatar - ideal music to trip to, get stoned to or even nod out to. Popular culture had certainly caught up with the Floyd by 1969. The age of psychedelia was passing, but LSD and marijuana were now firmly assimilated into the musical culture in the form of long progressive tracks and the fabled rock-outs of bands like Deep Purple and Led Zeppelin. When the psychedelic age dawned in the mid-60s, LSD was seen as the sacred drug, the key to a new consciousness. By the end of the decade, however, the casualties were rolling in, and this forced many people to reappraise their ideas on drugs. This gave rise to a strong distinction between the so called positive drugs - the psychoactives, the revelatory drugs - and the bad drugs, like heroin, which were considered spirit-sapping.

More was a hip morality tale that crudely explored the divide between these so called good and bad drugs, through a doomed love affair. The band felt that the film said the right things about drug culture, having themselves experienced first hand the damage that abuse of drugs could cause. Despite their image, post-Barrett Pink Floyd were more into alcohol abuse than drugs, though all smoked marijuana.

The action takes place in Paris and Ibiza, off the Mediterranean coast of Spain, in 1964-5, and follows the story of an idealistic but naive German graduate Stefan (Klaus Grünberg), desperate for new experience and adventure. He hitch hikes to Paris and falls in love with an ex-junkie, Estelle, before becoming deeply involved with a radical drug-oriented scene. The pair run away to Ibiza, where they encounter Dr Wolf who, it turns out, is the local supplier of heroin to the island's growing population of addicts. The couple's relationship is numbed by drugs, so Stefan decides they must escape to a villa on the other side of the island. After a blissful period where the two explore themselves and the bright sun-kissed landscape, Stefan discovers that Estelle is again doing heroin. Instead of refusing, he decides to try the drug, and so begins his slow descent. The pair eventually take LSD to break their addictions, and succeed until a violent break-up ensues, Stefan, paranoid and jealous, believing that Estelle is being unfaithful. He seeks solace in poor quality street heroin, overdoses in a back alley and is buried in a pauper's grave, the locals believing that he has committed suicide.

The plot is simple, but the characterisations are very strong, and in many ways it is still a powerful counterpoint to the late 60s drug experience. However, despite the sensitivity and maturity with which the drug issue is explored, the film was savaged by the critics. The most stinging criticisms were directed at Schroeder's script. Unfortunately the director had not employed a script editor who understood English well enough to prevent clichéd youth speak from creeping into the dialogue. "They were saying things like 'Groovy man, let's get high'," commented Gilmour at the time. "Schroeder was a foreign director. . . he didn't know the subtle difference between what slang was acceptable and hip and what wasn't." In France, where the dialogue didn't appear so clichéd, *More* achieved cult status comparable to *Easy Rider*, and is still regularly shown at film festivals and colleges.

The cover is the second Hipgnosis classic for Pink Floyd. Using a still taken from a scene in the film, in which Stefan is playfully attacking a windmill near the summer cottage on Ibiza, Thorgerson changed the registration of the colours, creating a psychedelic infrared solarised effect, designed to show how the dream can be corrupted and distorted. The back cover is another still taken from the emotional centrepiece of the film, the scene where Stefan and Estelle are on their LSD trip, sharing a deeply spiritual experience atop the cliffs, watching the setting sun, and chanting the Om.

Though the Floyd themselves have always sought to distance themselves from the album, believing it to be flawed and hurried, *More* did provide several tracks which would continue to be played in their live set over the next three years. It was also a chance for the band to experiment unhindered in the studio with their own sound and production ideas. It also proved an important lyrical stepping stone in the band's move towards a new sound for the 70s.

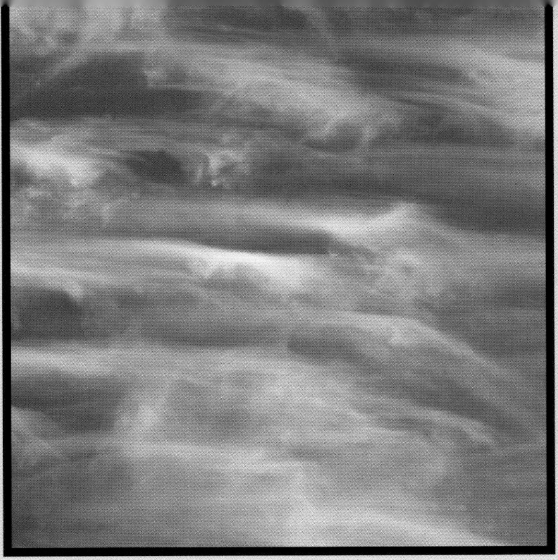

Cirrus Minor

(WATERS)

Schroeder wanted a song for the film that would mirror the sensation of escape through both marijuana and heroin. A minute of the song appears in the film, in the scene where the main character, Stefan, is under the influence of marijuana and also of heroin, to which he is rapidly becoming addicted. Though Waters hadn't taken heroin, its effects were known to him - Syd Barrett had taken heroin when he was just 19 and had described to Waters, during the year when they lived together, exactly what the sensation was like.

Along with The Beatles, Pink Floyd pioneered the use of sound effects in their recordings. The proximity of the Abbey Road sound effects library to Studios 2 and 3 meant that both The Beatles and the Floyd would regularly raid the shelves for 'atmospherics'. The sound of birdsong that runs prominently through the track, and that would later find its way onto the next three Floyd albums, was taken from the infamous 'dawn chorus' tape. With Gilmour's lilting acoustic guitar and double tracked vocals, and Wright's ethereal spectral organ, the track immediately conjures the image of a lazy, soporific dream-like summer idyll. It then metamorphoses into a heavily reverbed and quite disturbing outro that was intended to parallel the dislocation and reverie that both drugs produce. Rick uses both a Hammond and his favoured Farfisa organ, overdubbed across one another. The Hammond provides the rumbling deep undertow, the Farfisa the twittering cadences.

CIRRUS MINOR
GILMOUR *double tracked vocals, acoustic guitars*
WRIGHT *organ*
WATERS *bird song*

The Nile Song

(WATERS)

The Floyd's first venture into the arena of 'heavy metal', this track was the result of a late-night stoned jam at the studio, and marries Gilmour's saturated powerchord Stratocaster thrash and hoarse vocals with Waters's lyrical tale of a man dragged down by a beautiful goddess. 'The Nile Song' is a classic siren tale, its title referring to the Nile maidens who are said to lure unfortunate men into the water, where they drown. The song is featured in the party scene early in the film, when Stefan and Estelle first meet. Schroeder wanted the song to reflect the fact that the union is doomed, that Estelle would eventually drag the hopelessly besotted Stefan down, resulting utimately in his death. Indeed, the lyrics make ominous reference to the events that are to follow in the film, with the evocation of the siren "summoning my soul to endless sleep", referring to the heroin that eventually kills Stefan. This track would also provide the inspiration for 'Young Lust' on *The Wall*, a decade later.

THE NILE SONG

GILMOUR *vocals, electric guitars*
WATERS *Fender bass*
MASON *drums*

Crying Song

(WATERS)

Late in the film, this song is played on a portable tape recorder by Estelle in her apartment, back in Ibiza town. Stefan acknowledges that he has to take on Estelle's burden, to save her from becoming beholden to the dealer, Dr Wolf. He agrees to start selling drugs himself to pay off her debts. The song echoes Stefan's resignation to his new fate as a slave to love. This is made manifest in the Sisyphean reference to "rolling away the stone" - the symbol of that burden.

CRYING SONG

GILMOUR *double-tracked vocals, acoustic guitar, double-tracked electric slide guitar*
WRIGHT *Farfisa organ*
WATERS *Fender bass*
MASON *drums*
UNKNOWN *vibraphone (possibly Wright)*

Stefan and Estelle relax on their Ibizan balcony in the old town.

UP THE KHYBER (JUKE BOX) (INSTRUMENTAL)
MASON *drums*
WRIGHT *piano, Farfisa organ*
WATERS *Fender bass*
GILMOUR *tape effects*

Another quiet, acoustic song written by Roger and sung by Dave with double-tracked voice, notable for the atmospheric lazy vibraphone and Rick Wright's quiet, strained organ harmonies in the background. Gilmour performs some lazy slide cadences, double tracked as the track closes.

Up The Khyber (Juke Box)

(MASON, WRIGHT)

GREEN IS THE COLOUR

GILMOUR *vocals, acoustic guitar*
WRIGHT *piano, Farfisa organ*
WATERS *Fender bass*
MASON *drums, percussion*

This comes directly after *Crying Song* in the film, when Stefan turns over the tape and plays the other side. The fast, repetitive drum rounds, overdubbed with Wright's demonic, free jazz, reverbed piano stabs are playing when Stefan discovers Estelle has been doing heroin again without his knowledge. Nick Mason was fond of repetitive drum patterns and would eventually adapt this idea on his suite on *Ummagumma*. There is also copious use of saturated tape echo and some of Wright's most aggressively psychotic organ. This is free jazz, and very reminscent of the band's origins as a structuralist psychedelic act back in 1966. Rick Wright in particular had always maintained that he was, first and foremost, a lover of modern jazz - Coleman, Coltrane, Kirk - and that rock was something he played almost by default. The sole composition by Mason and Wright together, the track ends with the tape being sped forward with the machine still in the play mode. The Khyber Pass is a dangerous mountain pass connecting Afghanistan and Pakistan, and was route the heroin trade took en route to Turkey and eventually Europe. 'Khyber pass' is also Cockney rhyming slang for 'arse' making the title of the track in Cockney-speak 'Up The Arse'!

The Khyber Pass.

Green Is The Colour

(WATERS)

This gentle acoustic song accompanies a sequence at Estelle and Stefan's idyllic cottage, when everything seems perfect and the symbolic idealism of the pair is still intact, as they wander around naked, swim in the azure sea, smoke hash and make love. The piece is reprised later in the movie when Stefan and Charlie, his acquaintance from Paris, meet at the coffee shop where Stefan is dealing drugs. Charlie tells Stefan he must leave Estelle and come back to Paris with him or else fall victim to her curse, adding that Estelle has already destroyed two men to his knowledge. Stefan is told in no uncertain terms that he is slipping down and his biggest mistake would be to think that he would be the exception to the rule - hence the reference to the "hopeful and the damned" in the final lines of Waters's lyric. Stefan takes it all on board, but proclaims that he is caught hopelessly by the golden haired siren, and can't live without Estelle, whatever the consequences to himself.

This is the first time Waters uses the images of sunlight and moonlight in a song to depict good and bad aspects of the human psyche. Stefan can see the good in Estelle but knows that her beauty, idealism and goodness will eventually be eclipsed by her own darkness - and, with it, his, too. This image would become one of the major lyrical strands running through *The Dark Side Of The Moon*. Gilmour sings in a higher register normally associated with Roger's voice, and is accompanied by his own acoustic guitar and a beautiful Ibizan flute played by Nick Mason's wife at the time, Lindy. 'Green is the Colour' became a concert favourite for the next two years.

CYMBALINE

GILMOUR *vocals, acoustic guitars*
WRIGHT *piano, Farfisa organ*
LINDY MASON *penny whistle*

Cymbaline

(WATERS)

The high point of the album, Roger Waters has said that 'Cymbaline' derived from a nightmare he had some time before work began on the album (the track would become incorporated into the suite *The Man* later in 1969 under the title 'Nightmare'). In Syd's absence, and with Dave Gilmour still very much the New Boy, Waters found himself fronting the group by default. With that power came responsibility and pressure - which this lyric obliquely explores. Waters thought of himself as an artist or facilitator first and a musician second, and, by 1969, he was beginning to understand

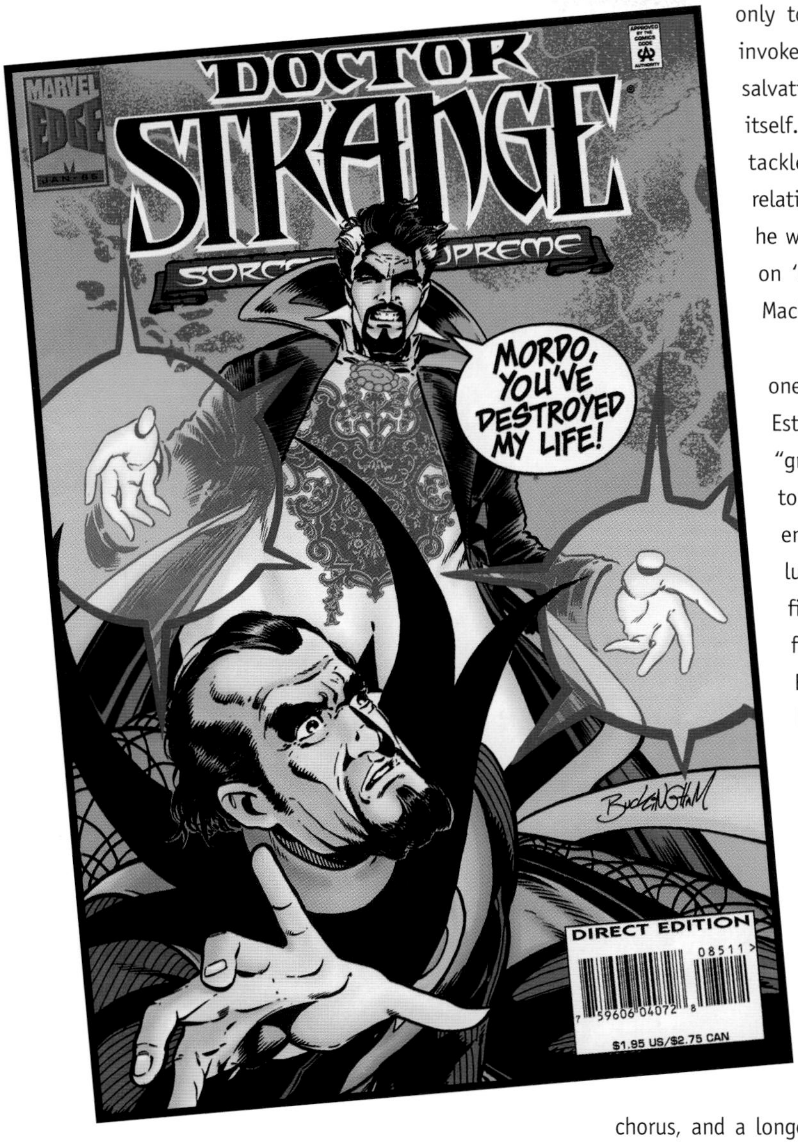

Dr Strange, Marvel *superhero.*

for himself how the music business places the artistic temperament under strain to create for gain. This was obviously brought into stark relief by the events surrounding Syd Barrett's departure from the band a year earlier.

Waters uses the dark images and symbols of his nightmare, from which he "begs to be woken", as a subconscious metaphor. He inverts the song lyrics in on themselves, and likens the frantic effort to find a rhyming couplet for the song to walking a cliff edge, while "the ravens" - those who feast off the artist's success and laugh if he happens to fail - circle overhead. As the ravens are "closing in", his manager and agent are busy selling the pictures to the papers "back home". The lyrics of the third verse are more oblique; Dr Strange was a Marvel comics superhero, particularly popular with Heads, who, through his mystical powers rooted in ancient magics, could change shape and transport himself into other dimensions at will. Waters, who had taken LSD, albeit only once at this point, understood only too well the dislocated reverie, and invokes Dr Strange as a possible form of salvation, rescuing him from the nightmare itself. This was Waters's first attempt to tackle the subject of the artist's relationship with the music business, one he would later expand on more explicitly on 'Have A Cigar' and 'Welcome To The Machine' from *Wish You Were Here*.

'Cymbaline' is used to accompany one of the film's key sequences, when Estelle puts the track on, declaring it "groovy!", before showing Stefan how to smoke grass using a pipe. The song ends abruptly as Stefan, consumed by lust, tears off Estelle's underwear. The film then cuts abruptly, in classic fashion, to the post-coital afterglow. Estelle then admits to Stefan that she has taken heroin. He makes her promise never to touch it again, and she agrees, although we can guess that this is a promise that will be soon broken. Waters's lyric helps evoke the darkness to come.

The version of 'Cymbaline' used in the film was recorded earlier in the sessions than the album version. It is in a higher key, has different verses, an extra chorus, and a longer organ solo from Rick Wright. The live performances of the piece, which lasted into 1971, were different again. The track became something of a centrepiece to the band's concerts, as it very effectively demonstrated the band's quadraphonic sound system. Near the end of the song, the music would stop, and a tape of footsteps would be introduced into the mix. Using the 'azimuth co-ordinator' the footsteps would appear to walk round the auditorium, with doors opening and closing as they went. Travelling through one final door triggered an huge explosion, at which point the remaining verse of the song would be played.

Party Sequence

(WATERS, WRIGHT, GILMOUR, MASON)

Fittingly enough, this track is played at a party, on Stefan's arrival in Ibiza, where he smokes marijuana, drinks and becomes paranoid that Estelle has been sleeping with the middle-aged hotel owner Dr Wolf.

PARTY SEQUENCE

(INSTRUMENTAL)

MASON *bongo drums*
UNIDENTIFIED MUSICIAN
Ibizan flute

MAIN THEME

(INSTRUMENTAL)
GILMOUR *electric slide guitar*
WRIGHT *Farfisa organ*
WATERS *Fender bass, gong*
MASON *drums*

IBIZA BAR
GILMOUR *double tracked lead vocals, rhythm and slide guitars*
WRIGHT *backing vocals, Farfisa organ*
WATERS *Fender bass*
MASON *drums*

MORE BLUES

(INSTRUMENTAL)
GILMOUR *electric guitar*
WATERS *Fender bass*
MASON *drums*

In desperation he hits Estelle - they make up and fall into each other's arms. Cue dissolve into post-coital afterglow. A simple piece, utilising different bongos and hand drums, with flute laid on top, it is played in the film by a motley collection of ragged-arsed stoned Ibizan heads and hippies. The film version of 'Party Sequence' is different, with a guitar rounding out the ensemble.

Main Theme

(WATERS, WRIGHT, GILMOUR, MASON)

This moody improvization, reminiscent of the early impressionistic work such as 'A Saucerful Of Secrets', is first heard over the opening credits of the film as Nestor Almendros's refracted photography of the sun blossoms onto the screen. As the sun rises, the track fades in, with Waters's gong and spooked Farfisa chords from Wright, over which comes Mason's heavily reverbed hypnotic, metronomic drum pattern and Gilmour's disturbing slide guitar. It is reprised briefly near the end of the film, bringing things full circle, as Stefan contemplates his misery and desperation, having lost Estelle to the drug dealing Dr Wolf. Here the message of the film is made explicit by Stefan as he contemplates his fate, "The psychedelic revolution excludes degrading drugs, such as alcohol and heroin. The changes we have been through, our plunge into egotism and alienation, are the opposite of the liberation I can read on the faces of these people who have reached the other side." He then promptly breaks on through to the other side himself, by overdosing.

'Main Theme' is one of the most evocative pieces on the album, and it was improvized by the band at one of the first sessions for the film. It survived in the Floyd set for some time, played by the band, as a short instrumental, into 1970.

Estelle gives **Main Theme** *a spin.*

Ibiza Bar

(WATERS, WRIGHT, GILMOUR, MASON)

A reprise of 'The Nile Song', this has most of the same riffs, as well as the same vocal style, except on the chorus, which is almost inaudible, possibly because the lyrics are gibberish. The recording and mix are also significantly cruder than 'The Nile Song' itself. This is the second song to appear in the film. After Stefan has arrived in Paris, he goes to a bar where the song is playing, and meets Charlie - his crooked but streetwise friend.

More Blues

(WATERS, WRIGHT, GILMOUR, MASON)

This short, mellow electric blues piece never quite manages to get going - but this is deliberate. Gilmour starts out with his guitar and Nick's reverbed 4/4 drums fade in, then stop dead, leaving the guitar to meander on. This continues periodically throughout the tune and makes it a candidate for the most frustrating piece the band ever recorded. Estelle is kidnapped by Dr Wolf's men who tell her she must return the heroin she has stolen, and that Stefan must work at the bar at his hotel, dealing drugs, in order to pay for the money and smack they've already used up. The only alternative is jail, so Stefan and Estelle move back into town and he begins working at the bar where the track is played.

Quicksilver (Water-Pipe)

(WATERS, WRIGHT, GILMOUR, MASON)

For many the album's highlight, this is one of Pink Floyd's most accomplished and evocative sound collages, deep, spacey, impressionistic and reminiscent of the epochal *Games For May* set back in May 1967 at the Queen Elizabeth Hall. Beginning with the sound of Rick Wright scraping his hand across the piano strings, the tape was then sped up and slowed down manually, at random, while the tape machine was still in the 'play' mode to produce a uniquely disturbing section that segues into an epic improvization of the kind the Floyd still specialised in during this period. With its gong, meandering spectral organ, vibraphone and use of tape effects, courtesy of Dave Gilmour's

Stefan and Estelle in contemplation.

Binson Echorec, the sound was, for once, specifically designed to evoke the drug sensation, accompanying a section in the film when Stefan and Estelle are at their summer cottage, smoking cannabis through a water-pipe. They get to discussing heroin, and Estelle convinces Stefan to try it for the first time. The piece reprises later in the film, during their LSD trip, in which they are symbolically trying to shake their smack addiction. Elements of this piece formed the basis for the later tune 'Sleep' in the suite *The Man*.

QUICKSILVER (WATER-PIPE)

(INSTRUMENTAL)
GILMOUR *slide guitars, tape effects*
WRIGHT *piano effects, Farfisa organ*
WATERS *Fender bass*
MASON *percussion, vibraphone*

A Spanish Piece

(GILMOUR)

Gilmour's first sole writing credit on a released song, this track features some highly accomplished flamenco style guitar over which the guitarist performs a truly ridiculous 'drunken Spaniard' impression. Schroeder originally told the band that he needed some music for use in a bar scene in which the radio is broadcasting a dire Spanish radio station. "In the middle of it, David tried to make the sort of speech noises you'd expect to hear," recalls Waters. One of the Floyd's most unintentionally comical pieces, it is worth panning your stereo over to the right channel, just to hear what must rate as the worst Spanish accent in recorded history. Embarrassment at this might explain why Gilmour chooses to dismiss *More* as relatively unimportant in the Floyd canon.

Contrary to Schroeder's initial idea, 'A Spanish Piece' ended up being used in a scene that takes place in the lobby of Dr Wolf's hotel, when Stefan, having just arrived in Ibiza, is trying to track Estelle down. He finally locates her at Wolf's residence, and is immediately suspicious of their relationship, Wolf being many years her elder. It is interesting to note that Gilmour's vocals are omitted from the mix used in the film - his lothario impressions clearly too much even for Schroeder!

A SPANISH PIECE

(INSTRUMENTAL)
GILMOUR *vocalisations, flamenco guitars*

Dramatic Theme

(WATERS, WRIGHT, GILMOUR, MASON)

A variation on 'Main Theme', this piece appears in the film just as Stefan begins to enjoy his job at the bar, and, though his idealism is gone, feels secure enough to leave Estelle at the hotel with Dr Wolf. That night, Estelle does not return home until late and Stefan takes another fix to cope with his jealousy, as he imagines Estelle having sex with Dr Wolf. Having been free of the heroin itch since his LSD 'cure', Stefan's descent back into junkie limbo comes just when things look as though the two might escape the degrading heroin spiral. But this moment of weakness proves to be the beginning of the end for Stefan and the film itself. 'Dramatic Theme' picks up where the original 'Main Theme' leaves off. Once again, the music arose from improvizations at the first of the *More* sessions. Rhythmic from the beginning, it includes more of Gilmour's soaring slide guitar. It is these long cadences that provide the element of drama the title implies.

DRAMATIC THEME

(INSTRUMENTAL)

GILMOUR *electric slide guitar*
WRIGHT *Farfisa organ*
WATER *Fender bass, gong*
MASON *drums*

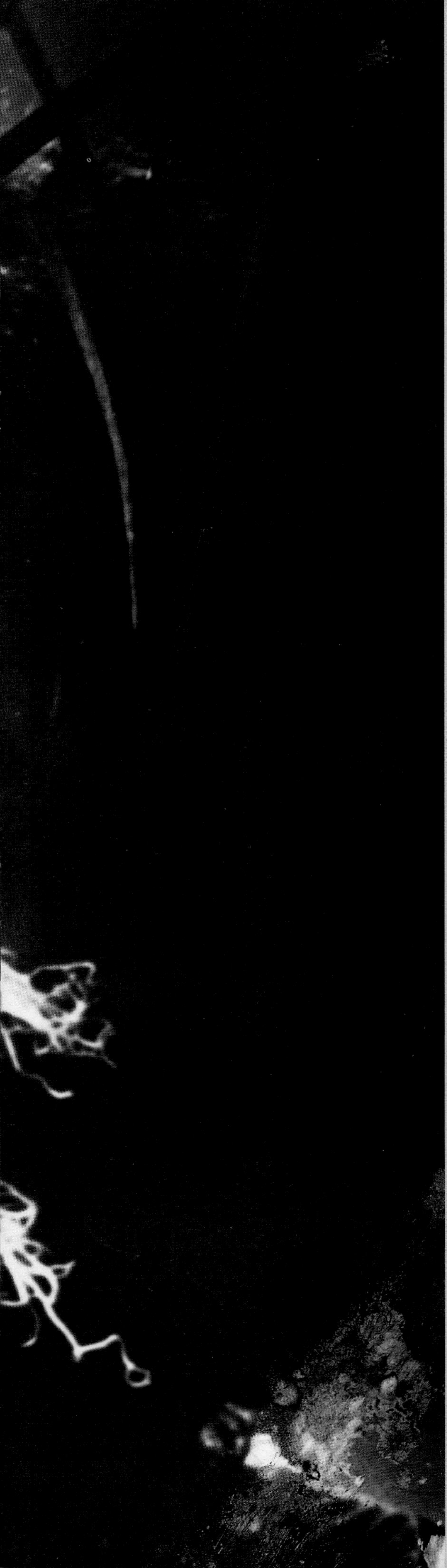

Ummagumma

1969

Half live album, half solo studio experiments, *Ummagumma* was designed to publicly close the door on one part of Pink Floyd's career and open the door on another. The second half of *Ummagumma* (Cambridge schoolboy slang for having sex, and chosen as the album's title because it 'sounded like something you could chant') was conceived first. Originally, the band planned to release a single album showcasing the more experimental side of the group. The impetus for these solo cuts came, surprisingly, from the usually reticent Rick Wright who was, as the band's only classically trained player, fed up with the limitations placed on him by the conventional rock'n'roll format of drums, bass, organ and guitar. Early in 1969, he told the rest of the group how he felt they had forsaken and betrayed their experimental manifesto, and had become just another band on the rock'n'roll treadmill. Wright had been listening to the newly instigated and highly contentious Tuesday evening broadcasts on BBC Radio 3 devoted to new electronic composition, and he had begun taking a renewed interest in the avant garde, attending concerts by Cornelius Cardew and Terry Riley. He wanted to write 'real music' and once told the press his ambition was to hear his own symphony performed at the Festival Hall.

LIVE PERFORMANCES RECORDED *at Mother's Club, Birmingham, on 27 April 1969, and at Manchester College of Commerce, Manchester, 2 May, 1969*
PRODUCED BY *PINK FLOYD*

SOLO STUDIO SEGMENTS RECORDED *at Abbey Road, Studios 2 and 3 on 27 April, 2 May, and June 1969*
PRODUCED BY *NORMAN SMITH*
SLEEVE DESIGN AND PHOTOGRAPHY BY *HIPGNOSIS*
RELEASED *25 October, 1969*
CHART PLACING *Number 5 in the UK. Number 74 in the US.*

Above: Rare interior shot of Mother's Club Birmingham at which one half of the* Ummagumma *live set was taped on 27th of April 1969.

Left: While the Pink Floyd sought to officially close the door on the Barrett era of the band with* Ummagumma *Barrett himself was readying himself for his first solo album. Later that year, as* Ummagumma *appeared in the stores, Syd started demoing songs for* The Madcap Laughs*, one of the finest albums of its time. This rare publicity shot from the period shows Syd in his favourite Hawaiian shirt with daffodils taped to his forehead.

"The band had studio time booked for June, and I remember they turned up in the studio with Norman Smith and said, 'We've got to make a record. What are we going to do?'," recalls engineer Peter Mew. "There was much heated discussion, and at the end of it they decided to go with Rick Wright's idea of each of them doing a quarter of the album. I think the main criterion at that point was that it was weird and different. I remember them really pondering about how they could get it to sound new and different."

Work began on the solo pieces, some of which were taken from work-in-progress ideas that each member had demoed at home during the first few months of 1969, and the main recording commenced, during June, at Abbey Road, Studios 2 and 3.

The band approached the record with the specific intention of road-testing the new 8-track facilities at Abbey Road Studio 2 (A new 3M recording machine and a transistorised state of the art mixing desk), to try and create a new sound. Waters in particular had learned a lot about studio craft and tape manipulation, having worked with experimental composer, and friend of Nick Mason, Ron Geesin. The two had together scored the soundtrack to a film called *The Body*, the year before, in which sounds from the body were manipulated, on tape machines and primitive effects processors, to produce music.

Ummagumma was also the Floyd's first release on the newly formed EMI offshoot Harvest (set up by the 23 year old Malcolm Jones as a label to foster the less mainstream 'progressive rock' acts). Originally *Ummagumma* was to have been a single album, but Jones was wary, fearing that an album of experiments might alienate the fans, so he came up with the suggestion of a double album. Double albums were then a relative rarity. The Beatles had released the *White Album* and Dylan *Blonde On Blonde*, but these were very much the exception to the rule. Jones suggested adding the live album into the package. This was eagerly embraced by the band, who, by late 1968, had grown weary of their set. The live performances of old favourites that make up the first disc of the double set were meant to be the formal goodbye to songs of which the Floyd had grown tired, a gift from the band to their fans.

Although some recordings were overdubbed with minor 'patch-ups' back at Abbey Road, they are otherwise totally live and showcase the band at the height of their late 60s power (originally the album included an extraordinary version of 'Interstellar Overdrive', which was only dropped because of space problems). Despite the obvious strengths of the performances, however, the band still felt they hadn't managed to capture on tape the full impact of the live show. Rick Wright: "We all believed it was going to be one of the best things we'd ever put onto record, which I think it was at that time, but the stuff on the album isn't half as good as we can play."

The front cover is a Hipgnosis classic - four different variations on the same picture set inside the same image, producing the visually arresting composite image of the band members receding into infinity! It was clever and stylish, setting the tone for many of the progressive rock covers of the 70s, including those of Led Zeppelin. On the US issue of *Ummagumma*, the *Gigi* soundtrack album cover that features in the shot was airbrushed out, after RCA records threatened a copyright infringement lawsuit. The rear cover is a classic period piece. Shot at Biggin Hill airstrip in the south of England, it features the band's Commer van, all their equipment and two of their roadies (Pete Watts and Alan Stiles), laid out on one of the runways.

ASTRONOMY DOMINE

GILMOUR *guitar, harmony vocals*
WRIGHT *Farfisa organ, lead vocals*
WATERS *bass guitar, backing vocals*
MASON *drums*

CAREFUL WITH THAT AXE, EUGENE
WATERS *scream and assorted vocalisations*
GILMOUR *guitar, falsetto*
MASON *drums*
WRIGHT *Farfisa organ*

SET THE CONTROLS FOR THE HEART OF THE SUN

WATERS *lead vocals, bass guitar*
GILMOUR *guitar*
MASON *drums*
WRIGHT *Farfisa organ*

Astronomy Domine

(BARRETT)

To many this is the classic version of 'Astronomy Domine'. The piece had developed since its inception back in 1967, when Syd began translating his LSD experiences into impressionistic sound collages. This version proves that Gilmour was as adept as Syd at experimental guitar noises. Indeed Gilmour has often noted that he taught Syd a lot of the techniques that would become Barrett's trademark

Ever since the Games For May concert at the Queen Elizabeth Hall in May of 1967, the band had augmented their musical line up with various pieces of percussion. Waters often played incidental gong during some of the more esoteric moments in the set.

sound, in particular the use of slide and echo. Gilmour had also been a keen advocate of The Binson Echorec and it is arguable that, though heavier and more structured, this version is more accomplished and spacey than the Barrett version. It includes an extended muted organ solo in the middle, highlighting Wright's previously under-rated contribution to the tune. Despite this, however, 'Astronomy Domine' was one of Wright's least favourite tracks and he would often complain bitterly at having to perform it.

Careful With That Axe, Eugene

(WATERS, WRIGHT, MASON, GILMOUR)

Incredibly, though the song was only formerly available to Floyd-obsessed punters as the B-side to the 1968 single 'Point Me At The Sky', this is the sixth version of 'Careful With That Axe, Eugene' recorded, though only the second to be released. Again the piece had developed during its time in the Floyd live set and was now significantly longer, and frighteningly intense. Waters's scream, denoting the band's exit from the spacey middle section and into the heavy drum-led freakout at the end, had become even more harrowing, and was now one of the highlights of the Floyd set.

Manchester College of Commerce where the second portion of the Floyd live set was taped on the 2nd of May.

Set The Controls For The Heart Of The Sun

(WATERS)

Another piece that had gone through noticeable development since the original version was recorded, it opens with Mason's cymbal roll, and his drumming plays a much greater role, overall, than previously. He uses beaters instead of drumsticks, and his fills add a lot to the song. The piece reaches a much higher climax than on the original, and the guitar is much more pronounced. The extended instrumental section before the third verse also includes an 'effects' section, with Gilmour creating strange ascending and descending feedback-type patterns with his guitar. There are also a couple of lyric changes.

Wright had always been fond of Arabic-sounding modal organ phrases of the kind heard here. The band used to refer to them as Rick's Turkish Delight riffs, after the soundtrack to a TV ad for Fry's Turkish Delight.

A Saucerful Of Secrets

(WATERS, WRIGHT, MASON, GILMOUR)

PART I **'SOMETHING ELSE'**
PART II **'SYNCOPATED PANDEMONIUM'**
PART III **'STORM SIGNAL'**
PART IV **'CELESTIAL VOICES'**
(ALL FOUR PARTS INSTRUMENTAL)

The *Ummagumma* version of 'A Saucerful Of Secrets' divided the piece up into four titled parts which relate to the concept of a war. Though you wouldn't know it, this is a composite version, the first half taken from the 27 April Mother's gig, and the second from the 2 May concert in Manchester.

The breakdown of 'A Saucerful Of Secrets' into its component parts enabled the band to get more PRS performing royalties when the track was played on the radio, and from sales. It was a habit the band, always with an eye on the £sd, got into during *Atom Heart Mother* and employed again on *Dark Side* and *Wish You*

A SAUCERFUL OF SECRETS

GILMOUR
lead vocals,guitar
WRIGHT
Farfisa organ
WATERS
bass guitar
MASON *drums*

SYSYPHUS

RICK WRIGHT *piano, drums, timpani, Mellotron, tape treatment and all other instruments*

GRANTCHESTER MEADOWS

WATERS *lead vocals, acoustic guitar, all other instruments and tape effects*

Detail from a Grecian urn depicting Sisyphus, condemned to roll a stone up hill for all eternity only to have it fall back just as he reaches the top. Rick Wright was the first to employ the image although Waters would appropriate it in his later lyrics.

Were Here. This version is wildly improvizational, and puts the original studio version into sharp relief, with Gilmour providing some truly inspired manic guitar feedback effects that equal anything Syd performed live.

Sysyphus

(WRIGHT)

Sysyphus', Rick's solo piece, was named after the mythical Greek king of Corinth called Sysyphus (more usually spelt 'Sisyphus') who was condemned to Hades (Hell) for imprisoning the god of death, Thanatos, in order to prevent his own death. Sysyphus's punishment was banishment to Hell, where he had to roll a heavy stone up a steep hill, only to have it repeatedly (and perpetually) roll down again just as he got to the top.

Part I **(Instrumental)**

Wright wanted the piece to parallel the tale of Sysyphus; his exit from the firmament and descent into Hades. Dark and majestic, a grand, semi-orchestral wash, created using the Mellotron, gives way to free jazz piano - something Wright always claimed was his first musical love. The Mellotron was a new instrument for the Floyd, and one that rapidly found a niche within their sound. It can now be seen as an early form of sampler that used tapes to store sounds, rather than a digital memory. Each key on the keyboard triggered an individual tape loop, which would play, sounding that particular note. You could change the tapes to include pre-recorded choirs, flute, string sections and brass sections. The machines were, however, notoriously unpredictable, always going out of tune and frequently breaking down altogether, making them virtually useless on long tours. In the studio, however, the machine was used to add sound effects to the tapes, for the occasional string chorus and for bass parts.

Part II **(Instrumental)**

The second part is a piano piece, heavily influenced by Stockhausen and John Cage, two names of which Wright was more than aware, having studied for a year at The Guildhall School of Music in London, just as Stockhausen was pioneering the use of plucked piano strings, ball bearings rolled down the strings, stark dissonant chords and general piano abuse. The Floyd's adoption of these composers was part scholarly pretension, part youthful enthusiasm for the new. Underpinning all of this are some arhythmic cymbals and backwards tape effects.

Part III **(Instrumental)**

Part III is entirely 'experimental', mixing Mellotron, Farfisa organ, birdsong, gongs and Wright's only attempt to play slide guitar on any Pink Floyd album, reverbed in the background. This may sound like a random assortment of sounds, but it is a highly organised piece, some of which was scored, that Wright hoped would reflect his aspirations towards serious late 20th century electronic composition.

Part IV **(Instrumental)**

After an organ introduction, birdsong and the onset of ever stranger discordant chords on the organ, the piano motif from Part I is revived, bringing the piece full circle.

Wright claims that this piece helped clarify his thoughts on his approach to music. From this point onwards, his compositions became simpler and more emotionally based, Wright realising that the impact derived from his playing rather than the sophistication of the piece itself: "It was tremendously important in that respect, and I learned a lot about what constitutes good music, or rather music that people really want to hear."

Grantchester Meadows

(WATERS)

The Man and *The Journey* were two song cycles that comprised an album-length piece, performed live in concert on 14 April, 1969, at the Royal Festival Hall, London, under the title of *More Furious Madness from the Massed Gadgets of Auximenes*. This was the first attempt by Pink Floyd to create an extended conceptual piece, and included two tunes that would be recorded in the *Ummagumma* sessions two months later: Gilmour's 'The Narrow Way' and Waters's 'Daybreak', which evoked the image of a peaceful dawn, beginning the 'day in the life' theme of *The Man*. 'Daybreak' was the basis for 'Grantchester Meadows', differing only slightly in melody, lyrics and the fact that Gilmour's high harmony vocal on the choruses does not feature on the latter.

Inspiration came from the poet Rupert Brooke, who lived in Cambridge, near Grantchester Meadows, and whose pastoral early poems Waters was taught while attending Cambridgeshire High School For Boys. This piece was Waters's own pastoral tribute to his childhood home. He began work on 'Grantchester Meadows' in January of 1969, at home, and finished it in early April at Abbey Road. Playing the acoustic guitar, something he had not previously done on any Floyd track, and would not do again until *Animals* seven years later, Waters sings a fragile double-tracked harmony vocal over the top. The track is notable for its use of sound effects and prominent natural ambient sounds; this would become a consistent feature of Floyd albums from this moment onwards. In the second verse, the lyric mentions the "dog fox gone to ground", and Waters was able to find a tape of a barking fox to mix into the piece. He does the same thing when the lyric mentions the kingfisher, using the sound of the bird's wings catching the water as its pursues its next meal. These all came from the tape library. At the end of the song, a fly or bee can be heard buzzing around, followed by the sound of footsteps entering the room, and frantic attempts to swat the unfortunate creature. The footsteps were recorded in Studio 2, and belong to Storm Thorgerson, who was sent walking down the stairs and around the studio wearing a pair of clogs! The fly was then panned, so it appeared to follow the footsteps. This track became a legendary piece of Head music when headphone culture hit the world of hi-fi in the early 70s.

Grantchester Meadows on the banks of the river Cam just outside Cambridge.

Several Species Of Small Furry Animals Gathered Together In A Cave And Grooving With A Pict

(WATERS)

SEVERAL SPECIES OF SMALL FURRY ANIMALS GATHERED TOGETHER IN A CAVE AND GROOVING WITH A PICT

WATERS *double-tracked vocals, all instruments, tape loops and effects*

One of the most unusual pieces ever to appear on a Floyd album, this track embodies the experimental era of the Floyd and other such bands through its imaginative uses of 'animal' vocal sound effects (most of them done by Roger, then sped up or slowed down) to create a multi-layered chorus, functioning very effectively as a rhythm track. This animal section supposedly contains hidden messages, which are revealed when the record is played at different speeds. This is, of course, not possible using CD.

The 'Pict' section (Picts being a slightly derogatory byword used by the English to describe their Celtic brethren north of Hadrian's Wall) is fascinating, comic and strange. At first listen, the rant makes no sense whatsoever. Repeated listening reveals a strange rambling monologue, delivered in a heavy and not altogether convincing Scots accent. Peter Mew claims the monologue was improvized live in the studio, which is borne out by the occasional descent into nonsense as Waters loses

Poet Robert Burns is parodied by Roger waters who adopts an over the top scottish accent for the nonsense spoken interlude.

Jimi Hendrix track the 'Wind Cried Mary' is the final element of the parody rounding off waters section with the words ' and the wind cries Mary.'

THE NARROW WAY

GILMOUR *vocals, acoustic and electric guitars, bass, piano, drums, Farfisa organ, Mellotron and VCS-3*

the thread of his narrative.

This 'poetic monologue' appears to parody the style of the renowned Scots poet Robert Burns and does, if you can be bothered to listen to it and translate the Scottish, tell a story. Narrated by the 'Pict', it appears to concern itself with the civil unrest amongst the Scots during the reign of Mary, Queen of Scots, in the mid-1500s, as the Catholic supporters of the Queen warred against the Protestant opposition. Bizarrely, the narrative ends up with a tongue-in-cheek reference to the Jimi Hendrix track 'The Wind Cries Mary'! Many Floyd fans still think that Scottish experimental musician Ron Geesin, who Waters was friendly with at the time, following their collaboration on the soundtrack for *The Body*, supplied the bizarre narrative vocalisations for the piece. "It certainly wasn't me," says Geesin. "I can understand why they thought that. I was doing a lot of experimental compositions, very way out stuff, on John Peel's radio programmes at that time, and a lot of it involved tape and vocal experiments. It was probably coincidental actually. Roger's mother, Mary, was Scottish like mine." Geesin later recorded a parody of this track called 'To Roger Waters, Wherever You Are'.

The Narrow Way

(GILMOUR)

Gilmour admits that he "bullshitted his way through" his own solo contribution to *Ummagumma*, feeling that the idea was at best, misguided, at worst a pretentious waste of time that would alienate their fans.

Part I **(Instrumental)**
The basis for part one of Gilmour's contribution was an instrumental written for the suite *The Journey*, a pleasant acoustic blues guitar piece, 'Baby Blue Shuffle in D Major'. The track was recorded for a BBC Top Gear session on December 2, 1968. According to Peter Mew, Gilmour added the strained and not entirely pleasant sounding guitar overdubs to the studio version believing that acoustic guitar on its own was not 'weird' enough.

Part II **(Instrumental)**
Based around a repetitive electric riff, created using saturated fuzz guitar that was double, then triple-tracked, and with Farfisa organ added just for luck, this was a throwaway bridge designed simply to segue into part III. Gilmour also plays drums.
Part III
Gilmour originally wrote this track for inclusion in the

Originally written to acompany 'The Man' section of **The Man and The Journey** *suite in 1969, 'The Narrow Way' was Gilmour's guitar led contribution which he embarked on reluctantly , describing the results as ' a pretentious waste of time.'*

The Grand Vizier was the chairman of a group of viziers who ruled over the Ottoman empire.

suite *The Man*, and decided, in the absence of anything else, to rework the song for his solo contribution. He had never really addressed, before, the problem of recording lyrics for release on an album, and found the prospect terrifying. "I just went into the studio and started waffling about, tacking bits and pieces together. I got desperate at one point, rang Roger up and said, 'Please help me write the lyrics,' but he said, 'No, do 'em yourself.' Consequently the song was recorded using almost all of the original lyrics." The song was written to accompany the part of the show in which the man makes the transition from childhood to adulthood - a rites of passage tale.

The centrepiece of Gilmour's solo contribution, 'Narrow Way Part III' opens with Mellotron tapes of the male voice and guitar sent through a rotating Leslie speaker, usually used for organ. The live version was rougher than the version on *Ummagumma*, and the bootlegs from the time attest to the fact that Gilmour was unsure of the lyrics - they change every time he performs it. On this studio version, Gilmour was apparently so embarrassed by them that he insisted they be set so low in the mix as to be almost inaudible.

The Grand Vizier's Garden Party

(MASON)

Part I: Entrance **(Instrumental)**
Intended to be the grand introduction to the 'entertainment' that is about to come, the piece begins with tom-toms sent through tape delay, as the speed of the tape machine was varied using an oscillator. This provided an ascending repeat over which is heard the improvized flute playing of Mason's wife Lindy.

Part II: Entertainment **(Instrumental)**
Part II was pieced together in Studio 3 at Abbey Road, using fragments of tape recorded at Abbey Road and at Nick's home in Islington, where he had several Revox quarter inch tape machines. Mason took sections of sound and drum patterns he had recorded, mixed them onto quarter inch tape and cut them into 1, 2 and 3 inch sections. He then randomly edited the segments of tapes together, some sequenced backwards, into the curious backing for this section of his solo piece. "EMI was very hidebound in those days. It was still run by guys in white coats. I was prevented from editing my own tapes by a studio manager who told me I wasn't a union member." Mason also processed his own drums and cymbals electronically using the highly sensitive Neve EQ sections on the new mixing desk. The result was a truly experimental sound collage that in the academic sense, at least, comes closest to the true spirit of *musique concrete* prevalent in electronic composition at the time. Mason, though one of the more down to earth members of the band, eagerly embraced the *avant-garde* - regularly attending concerts and listening to the work of experimental groups like Joe Byrd and BBC Radiophonic workshop enfants terribles White Noise. Mason even uses a cash register in the composition, though, unlike the register that would make up the 'Money' loop on *Dark Side Of The Moon*, this one was actually recorded at Abbey Road by Mason himself (incidentally, the cash register, purchased by the sound effects library, is still in the cupboard under the stairs at Studio 2).

Part III: Exit **(Instrumental)**
Part III is a drum freakout of the old school variety, eventually giving way to a reprise of the flute motif from 'Entrance'.

The Grand Vizier was the title given to the 'chairman' of several viziers in the Ottoman (Turkish) Empire. Mason coined the title at the last minute, having seen a reference, in the newspaper the day before, to the Queen's garden party and married it with his knowledge of the Ottoman courts.

THE GRAND VIZIER'S GARDEN PARTY

MASON *drums and all tape treatments*
LINDY MASON *flute*

Zabriskie Point

1970

RECORDED
December 1969, Rome, Italy
PRODUCED AND MIXED BY
PINK FLOYD
PRODUCTION SUPERVISED BY
MICHELANGELO ANTONIONI
RELEASED *March 1970*

In mid-November of 1969, Pink Floyd flew to Rome to begin work on their third film soundtrack - Michelangelo Antonioni's *Zabriskie Point*. Antonioni, a fashionable, respected Italian semi-underground director, had made a string of cult classics, including 1966's 'Swinging London' thriller, *Blow Up*. With his reputation at its zenith, MGM had offered the 56 year-old director a big budget deal to direct a conceptual film that would tap into the anxiety and disenfranchisement of young America. The result was a meandering, unfocused film whose precise message is vague and open to varied speculation. Loosely however, *Zabriskie Point* can be said to deal with the ways in which society systematically destroys the idealism of the young, their inevitable estrangement and the subsequent pursuit of an alternative. In other words it's a typical hippie flick.

Produced by Carlo Ponti, and written in part by cult playwright Sam Shepard, the film stars Mark Frechette and Daria Halprin as two disillusioned teenagers. He is a student, caught up in campus riots, who becomes suspected of shooting a cop. She is the young secretary of a greedy property mogul seeking to build a rest home on sacred desert land. Mark disappears, steals a light aircraft and flies out to the desert, where he meets Daria. Together they decide to break free, and discover themselves by rolling around naked under the desert sun. They paint the plane pretty psychedelic colours, he returns it to the place he stole it from and is promptly shot. The film ends with a symbolic explosion of Daria's boss's home to the sounds of the Floyd's reworking of 'Careful With That Axe, Eugene'.

Pink Floyd's involvement came when Antonioni heard 'Careful with That Axe, Eugene' on the *Ummagumma* album in 1969. He had first seen the Floyd at the IT launch gig at the Roundhouse in October, 1966 but was particularly taken with their latest album. Deciding it

***Italian Director Michelangelo Antonioni's anti consumer hippie movie* Zabriskie Point *reflected the revolution in popular culture that had taken place. Although deeply flawed as a movie it was nevertheless an important musical milestone in the run up to* The Dark Side Of The Moon.**

ALCOLM X

Hippie flick: **Zabriskie Point *poster.***

would be perfect for the climactic final scene of *Zabriskie Point*, which had already been shot, he commissioned the band to record a new version of 'Eugene', then to score further music for the film while the final editing was being completed.

Installed in a five star hotel in Rome, the band settled into a comfortable routine. "Every day we would get up at about 4.30 in the afternoon. We'd pop into the bar and sit there till about seven, then stagger into the restaurant where we'd eat for about two hours and drink," recalls a faintly amused Waters. "By about halfway through the two weeks, the bloke there was beginning to suss out what we wanted; by the end he was coming up with these really insane wines. Anyway, we'd finish eating - the *crêpes suzettes* would finally slide down by about a quarter to nine . . . then stagger drunkenly to the studio."

The band would work until seven or eight in the morning, eat breakfast at the hotel, go to bed, get up and walk back into the bar. The only disturbance to this otherwise idyllic routine was Antonioni himself, who insisted on supervising the sessions personally. As rushes of the movie played on a small screen, Antonioni would attempt to direct the band's music - to the growing frustration of Waters in particular. "We did some great stuff, but he'd listen and go - and I remember he had this terrible twitch - he'd go, 'Eet's very beautiful, but eet's too sad,' or, 'Eet's too strroong.' It was always something that stopped it being perfect. You'd change whatever was wrong and he'd still be unhappy. It was hell, sheer hell." Nick Mason sums up the two weeks of sessions with Antonioni thus, "Unbearable. . . a fucking crazy man to work for."

Despite Antonioni's meddlesome supervision, the director decided to use just three of the eight tracks the band recorded. The remainder of the soundtrack was taken up with snatches of The Grateful Dead's 'Dark Star', Patti Page's 'Tennessee Waltz', Kaleidoscope's psychedelic country rock gem 'Brother Mary', The Youngbloods' 'Sugar Babe', the detached solo guitar of John Fahey and the bizarre pinetop mountain yodelling of Roscoe Holcomb!

While the three tracks on *Zabriskie Point* are not among the Floyd's best known, they are a fascinating snapshot of a band undergoing a very profound transformation. Though in concert they were still playing the material from *A Saucerful Of Secrets* and *The Piper At The Gates of Dawn*, they were clearly looking for a new sound, and already thinking of new themes, and approaches to writing and recording their music. The ambient sections, the use of atmospherics and the technique of intercutting sections of film and TV, in particular, would become a constant feature of the Floyd's future work. Indeed, 'The Violent Sequence', written by Rick Wright to accompany the riot sequences that open the film, in which UCLA campus students are beaten by police, though rejected by Antonioni, would get a new lease of life, three years later, as 'Us And Them' on *The Dark Side Of The Moon*.

Heart Beat, Pig Meat

(WATERS, GILMOUR, MASON, WRIGHT)

What David Gilmour now describes as "awful, rubbishy, echoed stuff" is, in the context of the late 60s at least, an extremely effective sound collage. 'Heart Beat, Pig Meat' appears over the opening credits of the *Zabriskie Point* film. One of the Floyd's finest excursions into the realm of ambient atmospherics, it mixes random dialogue and pieces of music with Rick Wright's meandering reverbed Farfisa organ, which surfaces from the mix throughout the song, only to be borne away again on the rapidly moving tide of ghostly falsetto vocals from Gilmour. The only constant element is the heartbeat, a rhythmic undercurrent that underpins the track and propels it along. Nick Mason recorded a small tape loop, using a tom-tom drum played with beaters, to which he then added a short delay, to create an approximation of an arhythmic heart beat.

Antonioni expressed the need for a piece which would reflect the transient and inconsequential nature of consumer-driven existence, while also incorporating a

HEART BEAT, PIG MEAT

WATERS *bass, screams, tape effects*
GILMOUR *guitar, falsetto vocals*
WRIGHT *Hammond organ*
MASON *heartbeat*

RECORDED *December 1969, Rome, Italy*
PRODUCED AND MIXED BY *PINK FLOYD*
PRODUCTION SUPERVISED BY *MICHELANGELO ANTONIONI*

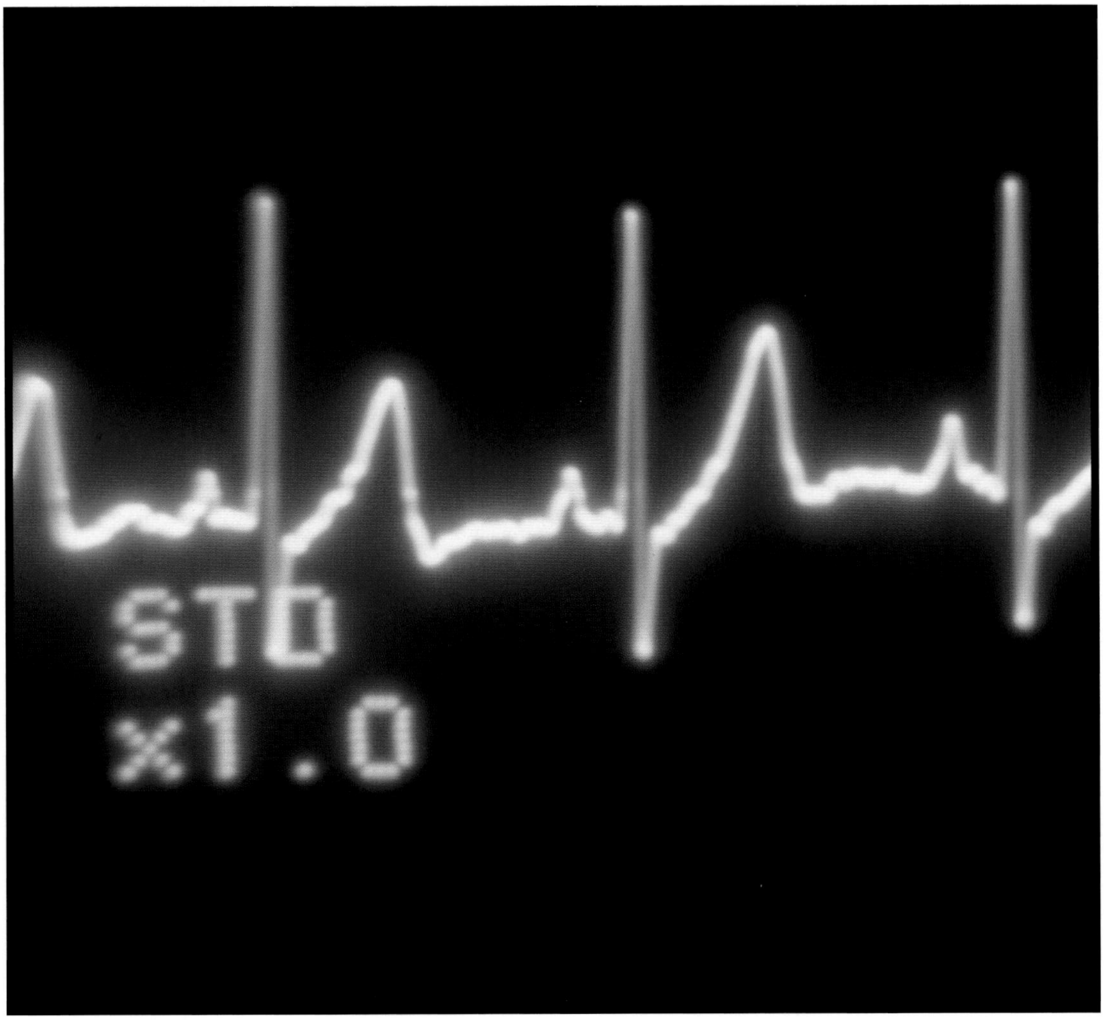

Waters's heartbeat obsession: a human ECG.

sense of the alienation that many young people were feeling as a result. The extracts of dialogue that fade randomly in and out of this ambient track were suggested by Antonioni and were recorded directly from American TV. The tapes were originally intended for a scene in the film where the Mark character watches a succession of bloated consumer ads for holidays in Florida and for dry cleaners, along with grim pronouncements on the menace of teenagers on drugs, taken from a news broadcast. There's even a snatch of Rachmaninov included in the mix!

The title is an obvious play on the two central themes of the piece - the term 'Pig Meat' referring to the term American kids used to describe those who were brutalised by the police at Kent State. Two years later the band would make the heart beat an important recurring aural theme in their most famous song cycle, *Dark Side Of The Moon*. The pig, invoked as a repulsive symbol of consumerism and corruption, would also resurface as major lyrical theme on 1977's *Animals* album. Soundly ecological, Pink Floyd clearly believed in the recycling of good ideas.

CRUMBLING LAND

WATERS *Fender bass, scream*
GILMOUR *lead and rhythm guitar, lead vocals*
WRIGHT *Farfisa organ, backing vocals*
MASON *drums, tape effects*

RECORDED *December 1969, Rome, Italy*
PRODUCED AND MIXED BY *PINK FLOYD*
SUPERVISED BY *MICHELANGELO ANTONIONI*

Crumbling Land

(WATERS, GILMOUR, MASON, WRIGHT)

Taking its title from the landscape, and the sandy deposits that form Zabriskie Point itself, which literally crumbles beneath one's feet, this unusual track proved a real departure for Pink Floyd. Sounding almost like a parody of the other country-influenced songs on the soundtrack, provided by Kaleidoscope, *Crumbling Land* is a jaunty picked acoustic guitar piece with airy doubled harmony vocals. The upbeat country style was at Antonioni's insistence. "He could have got it done ten times better by numerous American groups but he used ours. Very strange," commented Gilmour at the time. Antonioni wanted "a happier song" for the section of the film where the hero and heroine wander through Death Valley and up to Zabriskie Point itself, before the soundtrack gives way to Jerry Garcia's 'Love Theme' and . . . well, you can guess the rest. Though reticent about this stylistic departure, the band agreed, if only to get Antonioni to leave them alone. Working to Antonioni's rough cut of the film, they wrote a song that incorporated references to both the action taking place in the film and Waters's wider concerns about the pollution and destruction of nature by the uncaring corporate concerns of the consumer society. Waters, struggling with his socialist principles, held from youth, found the process by which society corrupts everything it touches, leaving dispossessed and alienated people in its wake, fascinating. It would become a major lyrical obsession for the next ten years.

Here, in an echo of his reading of Rupert Brooke, Waters uses the image of an eagle to embody the spirit of nature and at the end of the song, having witnessed the resources of the world being squandered, the eagle simply escapes to freedom and flies off into the sun. In a sly reference to Antonioni himself, Waters includes a reference to a man who appears "like a mirage on the sand", who "made a moving picture of the crumbling land". The closing section of the track was actually recorded on the Rome streets by Nick Mason. A cacophonous mix of hooting car horns, noisy engines, Vespa scooters and street clatter, it was intended to depict the pointless polluting rush of the modern world. This was put through heavy reverb, then rapidly panned before being cut abruptly, providing the track with a powerful, if surprising, ending.

COME IN NUMBER 51, YOUR TIME IS UP

WATERS *Fender bass, scream*
GILMOUR *lead and rhythm guitar, falsetto vocals*
WRIGHT *Farfisa organ*
MASON *drums*

RECORDED *December 1969, Rome, Italy*
PRODUCED AND MIXED BY *PINK FLOYD*
SUPERVISED BY *MICHELANGELO ANTONIONI*

Come In Number 51, Your Time Is Up

(WATERS, GILMOUR, MASON, WRIGHT)

Yet another version of 'Careful With That Axe, Eugene', the track that first attracted Antonioni to the music of Pink Floyd. Unlike the rest of the music used in the film, which is, by and large, merely incidental, this track was very much integral to the explosive finale of the film. Indeed Antonioni had earmarked it for use before shooting had begun. That finale, in which the female lead character imagines her exploitative boss's house, in the desert, detonated in slow motion, was supposed to be the film's violent climax - a symbolic explosion of the American dream (yawn). In this way, the structure of 'Careful With That Axe, Eugene', building from a whisper to a climax, and followed by a violent frenetic freak out, mirrored precisely the tensions inherent in the film itself. Antonioni synchronises Waters's bloodcurdling primal scream with the first explosion of the scene, in which a vast fridge explodes sending its pre-packaged plastic contents radiating out in slow motion arcs through the sky.

A little shorter usual, and lacking any of the standard 'Eugene' lyrics, this is one of the best

recorded versions of the track, in both intensity and power. Gilmour's lead guitar at the finale is inspired and frenzied, reaching a demonic intensity that none of the preceding versions quite manage to capture. This alone makes it worth tracking down.

The Floyd took the rather bizarre title from influential surrealist comedian Spike Milligan's first *Q* TV series for the BBC. Huge fans of British comedy programs like *Monty Python*, the Floyd often interrupted recording sessions back in England to watch TV. Milligan would regularly end his surreal sketches with a megaphone, through which he'd shout, "Come in number 51, your time is up!" Originally, such a phrase would be heard around boating lakes, when the boat owner on the shore would shout through his megaphone, informing his client that it was time to return the boat.

Absurdist comedian Spike Milligan.

Picnic, A Breath Of Fresh Air

1970

During the late 60s and early 70s the cut-priced compilation album, or 'sampler', proved a popular promotional strategy for record companies. Funky young labels, such as Island Records, popularized these rangy compilations, seeded with tracks by the label's more successful bands as a lure to try the less commercial or newer bands. This was a particularly useful tactic in the newly emerging progressive rock arena, which found its radio play confined to the late night corners of the John Peel show. A double album for about thirty shillings provided an inexpensive point of entry, and many nascent music fans of the time fondly remember these albums as the first in their collections.

Picnic, A Breath Of Fresh Air was the lavish double sampler for EMI's new progressive rock imprint, Harvest. It featured established acts Deep Purple and The Pretty Things next to more obscure delights, such as The Battered Ornaments and Quatermass. Syd Barrett's 'Terrapin', a track from his *Barrett* album of 1970, was also included. In fact, many of the acts, including Syd, were managed by Jenner and King's Blackhill Enterprises, who struck a deal with the 24 year old Harvest A&R director Malcolm Jones, allowing their artists, Syd, Kevin Ayers, Roy Harper, The Battered Ornaments, Forest, Edgar Broughton and The Third Ear

Floyd live on stage.

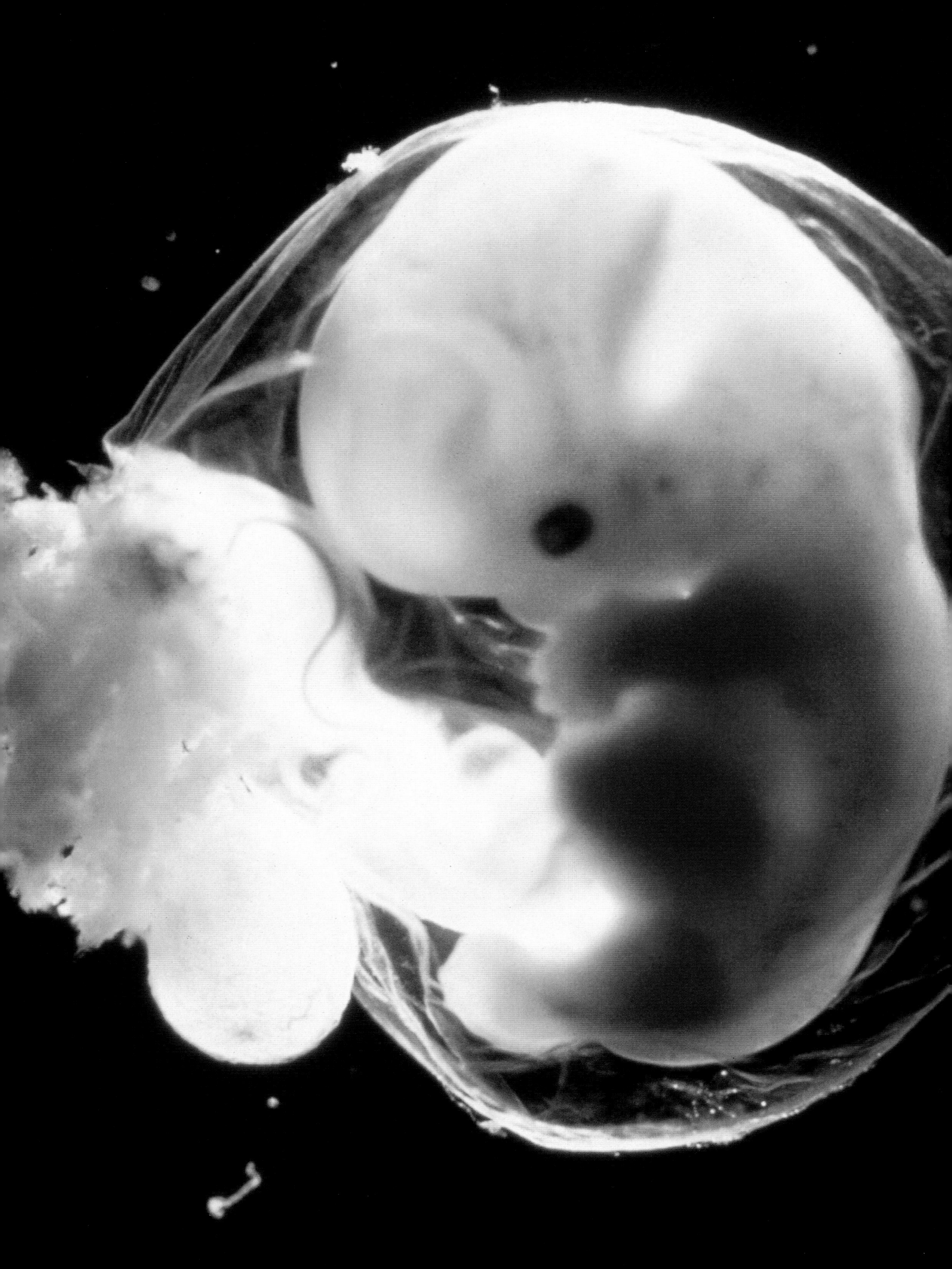

Band unlimited studio time at Abbey Road, as well as a guaranteed LP release, regardless of how extreme their offerings were. The result, according to John Leckie, then a trainee engineer at the studio, was that "suddenly the place was overrun by hippies with long greasy hair, and the whole place reeked of dope. It was a great period".

With a suitably surreal Hypgnosis cover, depicting young seaside revellers dressed in gas masks, *Picnic* would have become a big seller had it not been for a mix-up over Pink Floyd's contribution. Malcolm Jones, looking for a tempting nugget from his premier progressive act, went to the Abbey Road tape library and found the previously unreleased 'Embryo'. With the band on a three week holiday, and the release date of the album looming, Jones took a chance that they'd have no objections to its inclusion on the sampler. Unfortunately, they had objections. On returning from holiday, all four Floyds wrote to both Jones and Beecher Stevens (who'd signed the group to EMI), insisting that the track wasn't finished, wasn't up to their normal standards and would give their fans a false impression of their future output. They demanded that the album be immediately withdrawn. By this point *Picnic* had been in the shops for just ten days. Many of the copies pressed were recalled and destroyed, and their covers pulped. "EMI got Norman Smith to mix it," recalls Dave Gilmour. "We'd lost interest in it." Gilmour had yet to overdub his electric guitar parts, and they hadn't got round to utilising a tape effect known as "the labyrinth" - whereby five Revox tape machines ran in conjunction to create a cavernous tunnel of echo - to suggest a womb-like ambience. "There isn't much unreleased stuff in the vaults. That's one of the very, very few tracks that we never actually finished . . . I think we released just about everything that we worked on for any length of time."

Embryo

(WATERS)

During 1968, Pink Floyd began assembling a set of reworked old songs and new sketches under the collective title, *The Massed Gadgets Of Auximines*. Designed originally to be played live, the set was divided into two suites, *The Man* (your common or garden 'day in the life' concept - Daybreak, Work, Afternoon, Doing It!, Sleeping, Nightmare, Daybreak revisited) and *The Journey*, a musical voyage from birth to death which, naturally, included 'Embryo'. Later plans to record the set as a concept album were abandoned, in favour of the *Ummagumma* double album concept of one live LP and one studio selection comprising four individual solo contributions from each band member.

'Embryo' was first recorded for the BBC *Top Gear* show on 2 December, 1968, but, despite being a favourite part of their live set, it remained unrecorded for almost a year until it was unexpectedly dusted down during the *Ummagumma* sessions of June 1969. Concerning the thoughts of a foetus, wondering what the world outside has in store, 'Embryo' is an early glimpse of the obsessions Roger Waters would later develop fully on *Dark Side Of The Moon, Wish You Were Here* and *The Wall*: fear, alienation and uncertainty. Through the embryo's speculations, Waters explores the untainted hope of the unborn and his hankering for the purity of infancy, and crystallises the idea that the world begins its systematic corruption of that purity from the moment of birth. This sense of pre-ordained betrayal would dominate *The Wall*.

Dave Gilmour's almost whispered vocals provide the wavering melody with a sublime melancholy. Underpinned by Waters's repetitive octave bass notes, Wright's single note piano and a meandering flute mellotron replicate the tranquil ebb and flow of amniotic fluid. The song ends with the reverbed chirruping squeaks and gurglings of the emerging baby, sounds created by slowing the tape machine down to 15ips (inches per second), recording Nick Mason laughing, and repeating the word 'yippee', then playing the results back at the usual 30 ips. In its (ironically) unfinished state it is one of the Floyd's most eerily evocative tracks.

In the live set, during the 1970-1971 tour, 'Embryo' was embellished with a haunting Gilmour guitar solo, atmospheric VCS3 synthesiser textures and some of Rick Wright's trademark modal organ runs. However, it bore little relation to the starkly beautiful version on *Picnic*.

EMBRYO

GILMOUR *lead vocal, acoustic guitar*
WATERS *Fender bass, tape treatments*
WRIGHT *Farfisa organ, flute Mellotron*
MASON *drums, percussion, tape treatments*

RECORDED *28 and 29 June, 1969, Abbey Road Studio 3*
PRODUCED AND MIXED BY *NORMAN SMITH*

UK RELEASE: *June 1970 on the Harvest compilation* PICNIC - A BREATH OF FRESH AIR. *Later issued on the* WORKS *compilation in US, 1984, and CD, 1995.*

Gilmour in his home studio, 1973.

Atom Heart Mother

A*tom Heart Mother* is an album without a concept or focus. Coming at a time when rock music was attempting to escape its protracted adolescence in search of something altogether more serious and satisfying, it reflects the changes within the British rock scene as much as it does the transition of the Floyd from psychedelic space rockers (a label they abhorred) to serious progressive contenders. More a collection of loose ideas in search of direction than a cohesive album, it nevertheless succeeded in redefining the band for the 70s and proved to be a milestone in the development of the methods and approach that reached their apotheosis two years later on *Dark Side Of The Moon*.

RECORDED *March-August 1970, Abbey Road*
PRODUCED BY *PINK FLOYD*
EXECUTIVE PRODUCER *NORMAN SMITH*
COVER DESIGN & PHOTOS BY *HIPGNOSIS.*
RELEASED *10 October, 1970*
CHART PLACING *Number 1 in the UK; Number 55 in the US*

Pink Floyd's first recording in the 70s reflected the band's quest for a new sound, a new approach and a new image. They had, to put it simply, exhausted every avenue and recycled every stray scrap of music from their illustrious past, and knew the time had come for something radically different. But inspiration proved to be a problem: the band were exhausted from the constant touring and, not for the first or last time, found themselves contemplating giving up altogether. "There was a sense that everyone was just coasting along, waiting for someone else to become inspired," recalls Gilmour.

Bereft of ideas, the band decided that they should rehearse together, jam up some music and then link the resultant pieces together, as they had done with 'A Saucerful Of Secrets'. The track they came up with, called 'The Amazing Pudding', formed the basis of the band's most ambitious, if flawed, piece to date. If songs were not forthcoming (and they were not), the lateral thinking Floyd would approach the recording process from a completely different angle.

Ron Geesin, Jazz fanatic, experimental electronic composer and general thorn in the side of the early 70s musical establishment, wrote the orchestral score for* Atom Heart Mother *after the Floyd had laid down the basic backing tracks. Seen here in his Notting Hill studio in 1967.

The album consisted of two lengthy group compositions, between which were sandwiched three

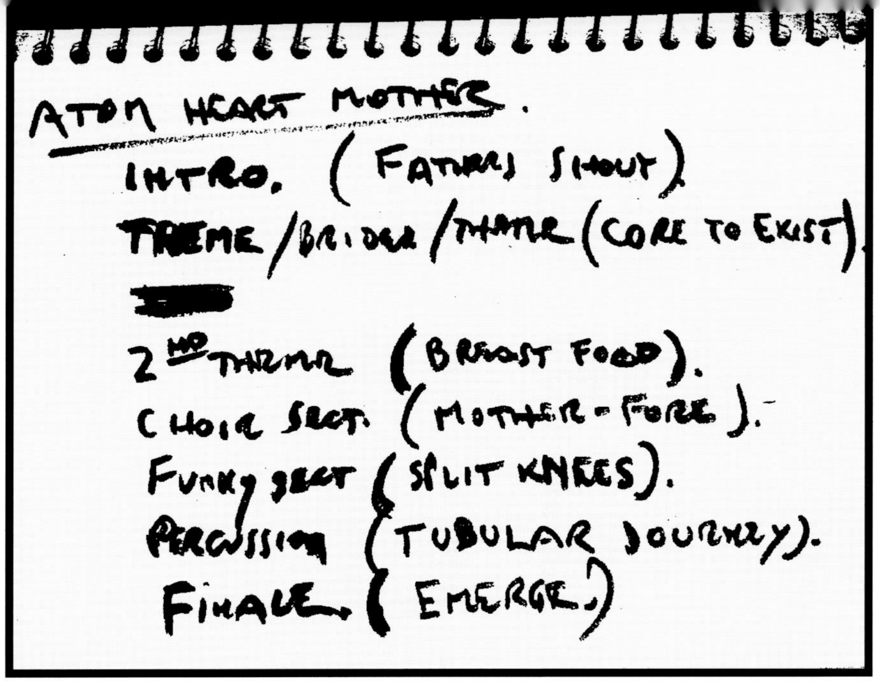

Geesin's original title suggestions.

more traditional sounding 'songs'. The track that eventually became the title piece of the album, 'Atom Heart Mother', was originally intended as a simple drums-bass-guitar-organ and sound effects piece, of the kind they had been playing for the last two years. Only when they had segued all the various ideas that had made up 'The Amazing Pudding' with those jammed together in the studio did the idea of orchestration raise its head. Simply, the band felt their track was too dull as it stood, and felt it "needed a lift". Ron Geesin, the experimental composer, and friend of both Mason and Waters - the latter having worked with Geesin on the soundtrack to the Anthony Battersby/ Tony Garnett film *The Body* back in 1968 - was an obvious choice for the salvage attempt. Young, hip and considered one of the great pioneers of experimental music in Britain, his work with electronics, tape and traditional instrumentation had won him many fans from John Peel to the respected *avant-garde* composer Cornelius Cardew.

Technically, however, the album is a *tour de force*, eagerly embraced by the Head fraternity at the time. It was, to use the slang of the day, a 'head fuck', especially if listened to on headphones, with its use of ambient sounds and stereo panning. Peter Bown, who had worked on the Floyd's first album *The Piper At The Gates Of Dawn* was assisted by a junior engineer by the name of Alan Parsons, later of course to distinguish himself on *Dark Side Of The Moon*. It was also the band's first album to be recorded using the new 3M eight-track tape machines and customised transistorised mixing desks installed at Abbey Road. This opened new vistas of complexity, which in part led to the idea of the heavy orchestration. "Their attitude was, 'there are three tracks left on the master tape, what can we do to fill them up'?" recalls Peter Bown.

The band were not altogether happy with the results. Having laid down the backing track to 'Atom Heart Mother' they had been forced to hand the project over to someone else when they went on tour, simply in order to fulfil the record company deadline. The finished product was, in their view, rushed and shoddy, betraying the band's lack of real direction. "We'd like to think about it a lot longer next time," said Mason. In recent interviews Gilmour is more candid in his condemnation of the album: "A load of rubbish, to be honest with you. We were at a real down point. We didn't know what on earth we were doing, or trying to do at that time, none of us. I think we were scraping the barrel a bit." Perhaps inevitably, the band blamed record company and managers for forcing them to release sub-standard Floyd product.

The album's title, *Atom Heart Mother*, came from the track of the same name, which itself was a typically last minute example of Floydian serendipity. The band were recording a session for John Peel's BBC *Sunday Concert*

DJ John Peel indirectly, prompted the track's (and album's) title.

show, the first broadcast premiere of the album. The studio manager needed a title for his running order. The band had been referring to the track under its working title of 'Untitled Epic' and, latterly, 'The Amazing Pudding', but they felt this was too 'jokey' and undergraduate to warrant sticking with it. It was during a break during recording, when the band sloped off to a pub opposite the BBC's Maida Vale studios, that the new name came. As they sat outside, nursing their pints, Ron Geesin suggested that the band look through a copy of the Daily Mail for a possible headline title. On one of the inside pages, Nick Mason found a story about a pregnant woman who had undergone heart surgery, and had an atomic pacemaker fitted to her heart. You can guess the headline.

The cover was equally casual. Another Hipgnosis commission, the cover of *Atom Heart Mother* is one of Storm Thorgerson's greatest sleeves. Initially, however, it was thought that he had lost his mind when he suggested the striking picture of the cow, on its own, in a field, with nothing on the cover to indicate that this was a record by Pink Floyd. His brief from the band, who had no overall concept mapped out for the album, was simply to come up with a cover that was as un-psychedelic and as un-Floyd-like as he could. The Floyd were trying to distance themselves from their psychedelic space rock past and move into more serious adult oriented rock territory. Taking his lead from Andy Warhol's infamous cow wallpaper, Thorgerson drove around the countryside of southern England on the lookout for a suitable candidate for bovine immortality. He selected a pedigree Friesian called Lulubelle III, and the photo is, as Thorgerson immodestly puts it, "The ultimate picture of a cow, it's just totally *cow*."

The sleeve was also a bold commercial step in a new direction. It was among the first albums by a major label band not to feature the band's name anywhere. Not only that, but the cover, like the album title itself, had absolutely nothing to do with any of the tracks on the album. Mason later claimed there was a spurious connection between the Atom Heart Mother and the cow - both were symbolic of the earth mother. Hmmmm.

Despite the band's reservations about the album, the great Floyd experiment paid dividends. As Nick Mason put it, *Atom Heart Mother* was "the beginning of an end". That end was the end of the image of the Floyd as dithering anachronistic subspace psychedelic rockers. The album, against all expectation, reached number 1 in the UK and made a breakthrough in the US, where it achieved a healthy 55 on the Billboard charts (thanks in part to the enormous billboard picture of Lulubelle III that adorned Sunset Strip and had DJs asking "what the hell it was all about"). But its success was also down to the paradigm shift that was occurring within rock. The arrival of the album neatly coincided with the end of rock'n'roll's protracted pop adolescence, and the emergence of the first wave of serious progressive AOR. *Atom Heart Mother*, for all its formless origins, succeeded in catalysing the merging progressive scene with a work that dared to mix classical and rock sensibilities. Like Soft Machine, who played The Proms at the Albert Hall, Emerson Lake and Palmer who had successfully melded aggressive progressive Hammond-driven rock, classical and jazz into their epochal live reworking of Mussorgsky's *Pictures At An Exhibition* and Deep Purple, whose album of rock concertos with The Royal Philharmonic had the music establishment up in arms and the Heads crying that the revolution had finally come, the Floyd were now seen as figureheads of the progressive rock scene. The irony is that their most lethargic and directionless work to date had somehow taken on a life of its own. This, too, was a hint of things to come.

Atom Heart Mother

(MASON, GILMOUR, WATERS, WRIGHT, GEESIN)

It was one of the cruel ironies of the record industry at this time that bands only got paid royalties and performance payments on the number of tracks listed on an album. This was bad news for progressive rock acts whose complex conceptual suites of music, though worthy, often made them less money than if they had simply churned out twenty simple three chord hits. In an attempt to ensure that they maximised the financial reward, the Floyd cunningly split 'Atom Heart Mother' into six sections, which, as far as the Performing Right Society people in Ganton Street were concerned, warranted six individual tracks. They did the same thing with 'Alan's Psychedelic Breakfast'.

Work on the title track of the album began in late November, 1969, when the band decided to try to work up a new piece of music for their forthcoming tour. It was Gilmour who wrote the main theme for the suite, the recurring melodic motif that forms the basis of the piece. Gilmour named this chord sequence 'Theme From An Imaginary Western' at the time, because it evoked the grand scores of Elmer Bernstein in westerns such as *The Magnificent Seven*. Waters was intrigued by the motif, in particular its heroic plodding quality, which he claimed reminded him of "horses silhouetted against the sunset".

ATOM HEART MOTHER

WRIGHT *piano, Mellotron strings, Hammond organ, orchestration*
WATERS *bass, tape collage and effects*
GILMOUR *guitars, backing vocals, acoustic guitar*
MASON *drums, percussion, tape collages*
GEESIN *orchestration*
ABBEY ROAD SESSION POPS ORCHESTRA *brass and orchestral sections*
DIRECTED BY *RON GEESIN AND JOHN ALDISS*
THE JOHN ALDISS CHOIR *chorus*
RECORDED *at Abbey Road Studio 2, intermittently between February and July, 1970*

This theme triggered an extended piece which the band called 'Untitled Epic'. Ideas were thrown about by various people, until five distinct parts had developed, connected by the main theme which was woven in using Gilmour's guitar or Wright's chords on the piano. The piece was played live for the first time on 18 January, 1970, at Croydon Town Hall, as an 18 minute work-in-progress under the title 'The Amazing Pudding' (this title came about because the piece was a kind of 'pudding' of everyone's different ideas mixed together). Five days later, it was played again, in Paris, and it was refined still further over the next two weeks, before the band eventually convened to begin recording at Abbey Road Studio 3, at the end of February. Having laid down a backing track, the band then added in four new segments, which they had jammed together in the studio. Some sections of the old piece were discarded in favour of the new additions, before the whole mess was cut into the final backing track. This process was completed at the end of April.

It had not been the Floyd's original intention to include a full choir and orchestra, but on listening back to the results of their studio handiwork they realised that the backing tracks were lifeless - even with copious overdubbing of more guitars and keyboards, the track would have sounded leaden. With an American tour looming there was no time to re-record the track or get a replacement together. Enter Ron Geesin, a challenging and well respected member of the experimental *avant-garde* who, while not always received with enthusiasm by the musical establishment, was something of a counterculture icon, regularly performing sessions for John Peel on BBC Radio 1, and on Radio 3's early shows exploring electronic composition. It was Mason who had first met Geesin, having been introduced by a mutual acquaintance. From 1968, he became a frequent visitor to Ron's subterranean studio in Ladbroke Grove, where he'd watch Geesin creating complex sound collages, and they'd listen to obscure jazz albums - a passion they shared. Geesin knew how to score music, and after a few discussions with the band it was decided to orchestrate this 'Imaginary Western' in the grand tradition.

Before handing over the reigns to Geesin and heading off, in May, on their tour of the USA, the band held a series of musical powwows with him to establish a few ideas for the score. He had been given a rough quarter-inch tape of the backing, from which he had noted the chord progressions and scored the backing track. "The tape was very shaky and the tempi were all over the place, because it had been made up from so many different sections of music. It would have been better if they had actually re-recorded the whole thing once it was edited together, just for continuity. Rick Wright came around for an afternoon and suggested an idea for the start of the choir. It was actually a motif like an English folk song - what Vaughan Williams might have taken as an English folk song and done variations with."

Soon after, Gilmour appeared and played the central melody that had triggered the piece in the first place. Geesin dutifully transcribed this, before writing his own variation on Gilmour's original theme. "Roger couldn't read music, and just kind of accepted that I was getting on with it. There was no great creative input from them at all. They were tired, and just wanted someone to come in and sort it out for them."

Geesin worked on his score during May. Working with the band's sparse backing track, he created a multi-layered orchestral piece that had its own internal melodies and motifs, but which relied on the backing track for counterpoint and dynamics. Only when Geesin came to start overdubbing his score on top of the Floyd's backing track did the problems begin.

Using the Abbey Road Session Pops Orchestra, a group of hardened second division players hired by EMI to provide cheap backing for pop sessions, Geesin set to work. The orchestra consisted of a solo cello, three trumpets, three horns, three trombones and a tuba, two violins and two woodwind. In addition there was the twenty-voice John Aldiss Choir. With the session players being paid by the hour, the pressure was on, and the first of many problems was encountered as the band ran through Geesin's score. It became apparent that the session players could not adhere to the wavering tempi of the Floyd's backing track. "It was crippled from the start really. There were tempo variations between sections that weren't due to any progression, dropping back a beat here or surging forward half a beat there. I had tried to even it out as best I could. Because of my passion for, particularly, black jazz music, I tend to like things ahead of the beat. Because Mason played so far behind the beat, it made scoring things very difficult. But the juddering was so extreme with the tempi that they had to normalise it. I've always maintained that classical musicians just can't swing."

Some of the musicians, sensing that Geesin was young and green, grew restless, and deliberately began trying to make his life difficult. One particular member of the brass section made a point of querying everything Geesin said, in a disparaging tone. "Brass players, they're a hard fuckin' bunch of heartless people sometimes. One or two of this lot were particularly jaundiced, and they thought, 'well, we'll have this bastard'. Add to that the fact that I was with these jumped-up long haired rock musicians and it was war. I was used to working with the lead players in The Philharmonia Orchestra, a better class of people, who actually gave something, rather than these hardened bitter pros, just there for the money." The denouement came when the ringleader of the dissenting horns asked one stupid question too many. "I said something like, 'Listen mate, are you going to play, or am I going to go for you and we'll sort this out man to man'?"

By mid-June Pink Floyd were back in the UK, and anxious to get involved again with their album. Geesin, on the other hand, had reached breaking point. The sessions had hit an impasse, and the pressure of months of intense work finally took its toll. "I couldn't cope any more. It wasn't foaming on the floor or anything, but I just had to give it up. I dare say the group, in the box, were tearing their hair out, thinking, 'Christ, is this bloke going to get through this? I hadn't gone berserk, I wasn't screaming and beating my fists on the wall. I was just slightly overwrought," says Geesin. John Aldiss took over, and supervised the remaining sessions.

The track was wrapped up in the last week of June, before the piece had its official live premiere in its orchestrally-embellished form at the Bath Festival. Minor adjustments were made, and a final mix was performed in July. Though not separated into sections until the album sleeve went to press, the bandings are as follows.

A: Father's Shout

The introduction, in which the recurring melodic motif is established with Geesin's 'stuttering' brass, was designed, he maintains "to smack the public in the face, before the public could smack the piece back. It is like one of Schoenberg's last works, *String Trio*, that starts off with the most fantastic wipeout of total energy, it flattens you, and it says, 'Look out, I'm coming through'. It was meant to be far more stuttery, but it proved pretty well impossible for those second-rate players. They had to regularise that stutter to become a syncopation they could understand." It contains elements of musical parody on the original Gilmour theme of an imaginary western. The title came from Geesin. "I love opposites, and I thought if there is this 'Atom Heart Mother' there should be a father too. And what do fathers do? Well, mine bellowed a lot. It's also because my favourite pianist, Earl Hines, was nicknamed 'the father' ('Fatha') and it's the kind of thing he'd call a track down there in Harlem or something."

Mason, conductor.

" 'Breast Milky' was a nod back to the body soundtrack", says Geesin, "Lots of titties and nipples. I thought if you have a father you have to have a mother too."

John Aldiss directs the choral ensemble in studio 2 Abbey Road late June 1970. The Floyd's backing tracks were played back through giant Tannoy speakers so the choir didn't have to wear headphones.

B: Breast Milky

Beginning with a duet for organ and cello, the other instruments of the band slowly fade in. The title was another of Geesin's trawlings of the subconscious. "I'd been working on *The Body* (soundtrack) with Roger, and there were a lot of babies and titties and things, and the whole thing was just a play on the 'Atom Heart Mother' aspect again."

C: Mother Fore

Geesin was anxious to create some dynamics within the piece, and he worked hard to make it look as if there had been some interplay between the orchestra and the electric instruments, although they had been recorded in very different circumstances. In this case, Wright's organ and a solo member of the choir do battle, before giving way to a surging choral section. The chords for this section came from Wright, who himself had been influenced by Purcell. Wright also shared Geesin's love of jazz and *avant-garde* classical music, and was making a conscious attempt at the time to expand his musical horizons. He was, in many ways, frustrated by the confines of the rock format. In an effort to find new inspiration, Wright became fanatical about emotional or 'Romantic' music – Berlioz's *Symphony Fantastique* and *Te Deum*, Mahler, Bruckner, Carl Orff, Messaien and Aaron Copeland - although he has claimed that this interest led him into what was also an arena of self-indulgence.

D: Funky Dung

Geesin's original title for this section was 'Split Knees'. The band changed it to 'Funky Dung' at the last minute, a play on the fact that the track is funky and dung comes from cows! "I'd scored it so that beat number one was in a certain place, and had written the whole section calibrating the inflections from there," says Geesin. "As it turned out, from Nicky's (Mason) point of view, beat number one was one beat off that - and he insisted that everything I'd written for the section had to be moved one beat. So that whole part has all my writing one beat away from where it should have been, and it all got very confusing. I should have just rubbed out the bar lines and moved them one beat up, but I wasn't clever enough."

E: Mind Your Throats Please

Reminiscent of John Lennon's *Revolution No. 9*, this sound collage was assembled by Waters and Mason from pieces both had been working on in their home studios. According to Geesin, the title was inspired by the *The Body* soundtrack, in which he and Waters had used similar techniques to create the collage

of sound which accompanies a scene about the human mouth and oesophagus.

F: Remergence

Bringing a reprise of the main themes from the previous sections, this final section also introduces what Ron Geesin believes is the best melodic theme in the whole piece. "It is a musical joke. At the last chorus I said to myself, 'We are not going to repeat this bloody melody again,' so I thought I'd write another one to go over it. That second melody was never exploited, but it sends you off down a completely new road, doesn't it? It just starts to fly, then the piece ends which is a shame."

If

(WATERS)

Unusually gentle, this is Roger Waters's most heartfelt song to date, expressing regret at some of the more confrontational traits in his character, that may have caused others pain. Some have suggested that this is one of Waters's first attempts to deal with the guilt he had been feeling about the way Syd had been dropped from the band. It was he who had taken the lead and finally broken the news to Barrett that the band no longer needed his input. Ron Geesin, a close friend of Waters at the time, claims that this is "a real insight into the man's soul. He was funny, really. He'd call you up and you'd arrange to meet, then he would simply not turn up, or you'd find he'd gone off shopping or something. He found people difficult to be around sometimes, I think, but he was a deep thinker and a man who really felt things - even though he knew he sometimes wasn't the nicest of people to be around - very confrontational."

Summer '68

(WRIGHT)

If Rick Wright could be said to have a recurring theme through his songwriting with the Floyd, it is that of being in a band itself. Like 'Paintbox' and 'Stay', soon to appear on *Obscured By Clouds*, the lyrics deal with Wright's disillusionment at the whole rock'n'roll circus. A mournful lament, concerned with the transient romance and emotional emptiness of a sexual encounter with a groupie, the track was based very firmly in Wright's experiences during the heady Pink Floyd US summer tour of 1968. "There were groupies everywhere; they'd come and look after you like a personal maid, do your washing, sleep with you and leave with a dose of the clap." In the cold light of the morning after the night before, Wright reflects on how empty the experience has been, but can see his own loneliness is

IF

WATERS *acoustic guitar, bass*
GILMOUR *bass, electric guitar, double tracked lap steel guitar*
WRIGHT *Hammond organ, piano*
RECORDED *August 1970, Abbey Road Studio 2.*

SUMMER '68

WRIGHT *lead vocal, piano, Hammond organ, orchestration*
WATERS *bass*
GILMOUR *guitars, backing vocals, acoustic guitar*
MASON *drums, percussion*
ABBEY ROAD SESSION POPS ORCHESTRA *brass section*
RECORDED *July 1970, Abbey Road Studio 2*

Above: Ron Geesin's tape machine malfunctions, home studio Notting Hill 1970.

Geesin found Waters "very deep indeed".

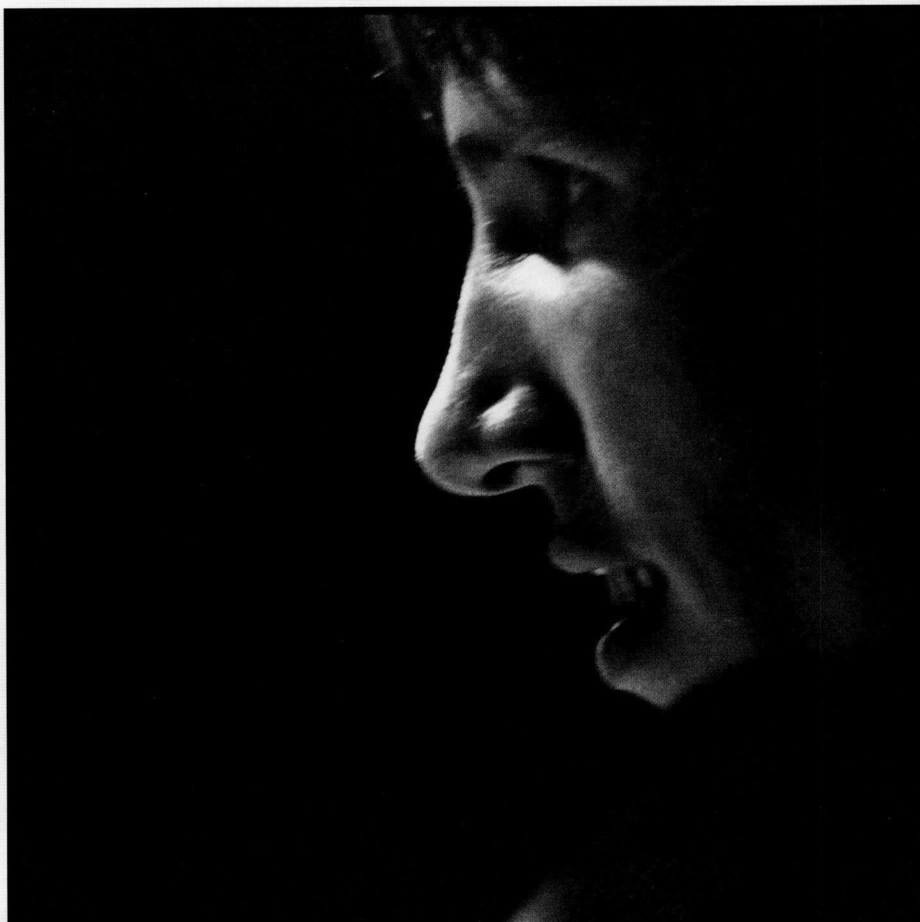

Wright and Gilmour leaning over the console of Abbey Road studio 2 anxiously listening to playbacks, 19th June 1970.

FAT OLD SUN

GILMOUR *lead vocal, acoustic and electric guitars, lap steel guitar*
WATERS *bass*
WRIGHT *Hammond organ*
MASON *drums*
RECORDED *August 1970, Abbey Road Studio 3*

at the heart of his feelings of reproach. Married to longtime girlfriend Juliette Gale since 1965, the song was partly a confession to her of his on-the-road antics and, in a strange way, a love song about missing her familiar comfort.

Wright felt embarrassed about most of his attempts to write lyrics, feeling them crass, simplistic and possessed of little comment on anything of any importance. 'Summer '68' was one of the only songs he felt happy with - not because he thought the lyrics were great, but because they expressed a very heartfelt and genuine emotion.

The Kinks: Gilmour may have unwittingly borrowed elements of their track 'Lazy Old Sun'.

Fat Old Sun

(GILMOUR)

Inspired by Roger Waters's childhood reverie 'Grantchester Meadows', Gilmour set to work on his own rose-tinted evocation of his early childhood in Cambridge. The church bells of Evensong ease you into this gentle acoustic evocation of youth spent swimming in the river Cam, laying under blue skies and smelling the sweet scent of newly mown grass from youth's endless summer.

The song also chronicles, as would many of Gilmour's future songs, the passage from that idyllic childhood to the harsher adult world. The setting sun is employed as the symbol of that transition, and it would reappear in Gilmour's late 80s and 90s work.

This is the second of three Pink Floyd songs about Cambridge, the home town of Waters, Gilmour and Syd Barrett, and it could almost be seen as a blueprint for the track 'High Hopes' on *The Division Bell* over twenty years later, when the same territory was revisited from a middle-aged perspective.

Some commentators suggest that both the lyric and

the mood of the piece were additionally influenced by The Kinks' song 'Lazy Old Sun', and Gilmour, uncharacteristically, does sing in the same high register as Ray Davies. On the same album, a track called 'Big Black Smoke' opens with the bells of Evensong! Gilmour explained this further coincidence by claiming that there were only two commercial sound effects libraries in existence at the time, so naturally people would end up using the same sound effects, in this case those from Abbey Road. When quizzed, the guitarist acknowledged that he had heard the track, and perhaps was subconsciously influenced by The Kinks. "They've never sued me," he added wryly.

Alan's Psychedelic Breakfast

(GILMOUR, MASON, WATERS, WRIGHT)

Pink Floyd's interest in *musique concréte* was well established by the time they began work on 'Alan's Psychedelic Breakfast'. If it has any specific origins at all, however, it is in a legendary performance the band gave during the autumn of 1967, at The Roundhouse in London. The Pink Floyd were pushing the rock envelope with a devastating set of impossibly loud psychedelic free form rock music. Syd, though teetering on the brink of terminal psychedelia, was nevertheless at the chaotic height of his powers. In the middle of a long wayward version of 'Interstellar Overdrive', swathes of echo and feedback strafing around the room, Syd dropped his Telecaster to the floor and coolly walked off stage. Barrett's behaviour was, at best, unpredictable, so the band played on, bringing the swirling hypnotic music to an ear splitting crescendo, at which point the errant guitarist reappeared on stage, carrying a small camping stove, sat himself down on a chair and proceeded to nonchalantly fry an egg. In a moment of crazed inspiration he pulled a microphone over the sizzling pan, cackling gleefully as a surreal snap, crackle and pop was added to the psychedelic maelstrom.

The sound effects for this expanded exercise in *musique concréte* were recorded in the kitchen of Nick Mason's Islington home, on a Revox quarter-inch machine that the drummer used to make experimental tape loops. While Mason recorded events, faithful Floyd roadie Alan Stiles (who used to cook the band's breakfast while they were on tour) gave a running commentary on the breakfast he was preparing. Each section of tape was then edited and labelled by Mason under its component title: frying eggs 1, bacon frying 2, cornflakes 3, washing up 4 etc. The final montage was split into three parts, 'Rise And Shine', 'Sunny Side Up' and 'Morning Glory'. In between the sections of music (which Gilmour admitted were thrown together at the last minute and "absolute rubbish") Stiles is heard cooking breakfast, providing a running commentary that leads into 'Sunny Side Up', in which Alan eats breakfast and jokes about macrobiotic food in LA. This, in turn, leads into a simple acoustic number in which Dave duets with himself. The sounds of Alan cooking breakfast are reintroduced, and we segue into 'Morning Glory', referring to morning glory seeds, which are powerful psychedelics, and of which Stiles was extremely fond - hence the title of the piece. The song ends with the washing of dishes and a dripping tap (if you listen carefully you can also hear cars passing outside Mason's kitchen window) which, on the original LP, was cut into the run-out groove, continuing on into eternity: a Floydian variation on the Chinese water torture.

Though the band felt the idea had been a good one in principle they realised, when they heard the final result, that the experiment was deeply flawed and tried to keep it off the album. As Wright observed, it was pretentious, and only succeeded in making people laugh - not the desired result at all. Despite this setback, the Floyd did not abandon their interest in *musique concréte*, making sound effects and spoken interludes an integral part of the theme and content of *Dark Side Of The Moon*.

ALAN'S PSYCHEDELIC BREAKFAST

WATERS *bass*
GILMOUR *acoustic and electric guitars, double tracked lap steel guitar*
WRIGHT *piano, Hammond organ*
MASON *drums, tape edits and home recordings of Alan Stiles*
ALAN STILES *spoken commentary*
RECORDED *August 1970, Abbey Road Studio 2 and Nick Mason's kitchen in Highbury*

Relics

1971

A compilation, released on the budget Starline label in 1971, *Relics* was intended to cash in on the unexpected number 1 success of the *Atom Heart Mother* album. The band were back in the studio at Abbey Road, recording the music that would become the *Meddle* album, when EMI proposed a compilation of the band's early material. Tapes were dug out of the Abbey Road vaults and the *Meddle* sessions suspended, while the band listened through their recent past and earmarked the tracks for inclusion. Originally it was decided that *Relics* should include previously unreleased tracks from the Syd Barrett period, most notably the two proposed singles recorded at De Lane Lea studios in August and October of 1967: 'Scream Thy Last Scream' and 'Vegetable Man'. These bizarre records show Syd teetering precariously on the brink of insanity, and while they proved amusing to the band, prompting a hysterical laughing fit in the control room as they listened to a playback, they also prompted a reawakening of the profound sadness that surrounded Barrett's slip into insanity. It was decided that they should remain in the vaults, for Syd's sake if no one else's. The Barrett myth was already building, and Gilmour, in particular, Syd's teenage companion and guitar guru from the Cambridge days, was anxious not to fuel further prurient interest in Barrett's madcap life. Barrett himself had settled down in seclusion and was living a less troubled but still deeply haunted and disturbed existence.

Instead, it was decided that *Relics* should be an album of oddments, singles, B-sides and tracks from their soundtrack album *More* that would sound acceptable when taken out of context. The only Floyd track unique to the compilation is 'Biding My Time'. Nick Mason designed the cover of the album, a strange line drawing of a Heath Robinson-like machine with the label "A bizarre collection of antiques and curios". This just about sums it up.

Early 1971 Pink Floyd were ensconced in Abbey Road studio 2 preparing material that would later become the track **Echoes**. *The Success of* **Atom Heart Mother** *had prompted EMI to compile an album of rarities, early singles and unreleased material for the budget EMI offshoot Starline. The band interrupted the* **Meddle** *sessions to listen to old tapes including Barrett's fractured* **Vegetable Man** *and* **Scream Thy Last Scream.**

Biding My Time

(WATERS)

The sound of a band in transition, this unjustly overlooked Floyd track, written by Waters and originally recorded at the end of the *Ummagumma* sessions, remained unreleased for almost two years, until its appearance on *Relics*. Like 'Embryo' it failed to fit the album's format and so was shelved. As the Floyd desperately sought to find a new style and approach in the absence of Syd Barrett, they toyed with several themes in an attempt to give old tunes a new lick of conceptual paint. 'Biding My Time' began life under the title of 'Worktime', a Waters song written for the suite *The Man*. Along with *The Journey*, this formed part of the *Massed Gadgets Of Auximines*, of early 1970. *The Man* suite, not one of the Floyd's finest conceptual ideas,

dealt with the working day of the average man, taking you from his rising in the morning to his return to bed at night.

The song is also a veiled reference to Waters's own situation. Having always thought he would eventally become an architect, Waters had come to terms with the fact that music was now his career. In an early hint at one of the central themes on *Dark Side Of The Moon*, Waters's lyrics deal with the various ways in which we distract ourselves and waste time, as life passes us by. With Gilmour's lazy, sliding, chromatic Memphis guitar motif giving it momentum, the track starts slowly and builds, eventually giving way to a sleazy sounding follies chorus line brass, then to a blistering guitar freakout. Not known for his abilities as a multi-instrumentalist, Waters plays the swaggering, lascivious trumpet break. The feel was prompted by an article Waters had read that stated that men at work think about sex ten times every hour.

When the song was perfomed live, the band would take a tea break on stage. During some later performances, roadies would bring on a pot of tea and a radio. A mike would be placed in front of the radio and the entire audience would listen to whatever was on at the time.

BIDING MY TIME

WATERS *bass, lead vocal, trumpet*
GILMOUR *lead and rhythm guitar*
WRIGHT *piano*
MASON *brushes and drums*
RECORDED *9 July 1969, Abbey Road Studio 3*
PRODUCED BY *NORMAN SMITH*
UK RELEASE *May 1971 on the* RELICS *compilation*

Meddle

RECORDED
January, March, April, 1971 at Abbey Road, Studio 3 May at Abbey Road and Morgan Sound Studios, Willesden ; July at Morgan Sound Studios; August at AIR Studios, Oxford St; September at Command Studios for the Quad mix.
PRODUCED BY *PINK FLOYD.*
RELEASED *13 November, 1971.*
ALBUM COVER DESIGNED BY *PINK FLOYD.*
INNER SLEEVE PHOTO BY *HIPGNOSIS.*
CHART PLACING *Number 3 in the UK; Number 70 in the US*

Meddle marks the beginning of what proved to be the most productive and creatively innovative period of Pink Floyd's career. Though the studio experiments had been underway since *A Saucerful Of Secrets*, through *More* and the deeply flawed *Atom Heart Mother*, *Meddle* was the first album on which the trademark Pink Floyd sound, with the Waters-Gilmour partnership at its heart, was in perfect balance. No longer seen as the new boy, Gilmour had risen to become the most important musical force in the band, while Waters, who had been saddled with the lyric-writing by default following Barrett's departure, was beginning to escape the minor poetic aspirations and pastoral obsessions that had dogged his earlier lyrics.

Following *Atom Heart Mother*, Pink Floyd became aware that they had become slack and complacent, churning out the same patented variety of pseudo-academic rock and post-psychedelic AOR to the same stoned punters. "We had run out of ideas. There was nothing left to explore and we were creatively bankrupt," as Nick Mason succinctly put it at the time. "Until very recently we were in acute danger of dying of boredom, but now this depression has lifted a bit because we have finally got a very rough basis for this new project. We want to make people experience something new, something that's going to make them think and feel new things."

Following the final date of the *Atom Heart Mother* tour, the band held a meeting at Dave Gilmour's London home, where it was decided that the band's next album should be a radical departure - an all or nothing record - on which they would pioneer a new way of making music. "We never really considered either what the record company or our fans wanted. We were always quite arrogant in that way, believing that we knew best and that everyone else would catch up sooner or later," said Rick Wright.

The basis for the band's new sound was to be a track created from segments and recorded moods, segued together to form one long piece. This would eventually become 'Echoes' and take up the whole of the second side of the album.

Recording began early in January 1971 in Studios 2 and 3 at Abbey Road, with relaxed sessions, the Jack Daniels flowing and various Blackhill artists who were also working at Abbey Road dropping by to see what was going on in the Floyd camp. During three early sessions, each three days long, the band laid down the various fragments and musical ideas that would eventually fuse together to form 'Echoes', the centrepiece of the album. These ideas developed throughout March, April and early May when the track (which was originally titled simply 'Nothing: Parts One to Thirty Six') underwent a name change to 'We Won the Double' (a reference to Waters's favourite football team, Arsenal, who had won both the League title and the FA Cup that May).

Echoes ***was still routinely played in the Floyd's live set into 1974 by which point (thanks in no small part to the success of*** **Dark Side Of The Moon*****) the track was acompanied by a stunning son-et-lumiere display of pulsating lights and morphing globular projections. It became the highpoint of the 1st half of the Eclipse performances.***

By the end of May it finally reached a cohesive form. Pink Floyd's lengthiest single recording ever continued throughout the month, amidst a gruelling tour schedule, when the track received several cautious airings as a work in progress called 'Return Of The Son Of Nothing'. Work on 'Echoes' finally wrapped in July, when the tapes were segued, at Morgan Sound in Willesden and George Martin's Air Studios in Oxford street. It was almost unheard of at the time for EMI recording acts to be allowed to work at independent studios, but the precedent had been set by The Beatles, who worked at Trident and Air Studios in 1969 and 1970, a time when Abbey Road was not yet using state of the art 8 track equipment. By 1971, 16 track was establishing itself as the latest standard, making 8 track - the format used in all Abbey Road studios at the time - outdated. Because the studio had become such an integral part of the Floyd's approach to making albums, they were always anxious to ensure that they had access to the latest techniques and technology. "Morgan in particular was very cramped, a bit smelly actually, above this tailor's shop on the Willesden High Road," recalls engineer John Leckie. "You had to go up these tiny stairs to get to it and it certainly didn't have the creature comforts of Abbey Road, but the Floyd were willing to put up with that because it had the technology they wanted. To them the studio was crucial, and the whole of 'Echoes' was really as much about studio techniques and precision sounds as it was about their playing. It was a very technical record in that respect, but it had soul in the playing. That's why it works so well. You don't sit there thinking, 'I wonder how they did that' - it just sounds right." To insiders at the time, Abbey Road - for a short time nicknamed Shabby Road - was simply not keeping abreast of developments in recording technology. Within six months, Abbey Road was refitted with new machines and desks for 16 track - just in time for the recording of *Dark Side Of The Moon*.

Under pressure from EMI, and Capitol in the US, to complete on time, the band recorded material for the other half of the album in a relative rush during July and August, having spent almost six months working on 'Echoes'. While they acknowledged that these other tracks were somewhat half-hearted affairs, both in content and in production values, mixing of the album was finished in September, and the band had barely decided on the titles for all the songs when the album was rushed into production to be in the shops for Christmas.

Meddle, though it received a mixed reaction from the critics at the time, was monumental leap forward for the Floyd. While it confused their old fans it won them a new audience who knew little of their psychedelic origins in the UFO days. In short, *Meddle* was the album that finally blew them free of the psychedelic tag. It is debatable whether Pink Floyd ever were truly psychedelic - their music was always too structured for that - but the legacy of Barrett and his LSD excursions had clung to the band who, despite being a band of boozers rather than trippers, had been crowned the kings of psychedelic space rock. *Meddle* delivered a new manifesto to Floyd fans and prepared the ground for the next five years of the band's career. To both the band and their fans, it served as the musical and conceptual blueprint for *Dark Side Of The Moon*. As Gilmour astutely points out, 'Echoes' was the musical progenitor of *Dark Side*, while the remaining songs on the album hint at many of the themes and obsessions that would drive Waters's lyric writing from then on. For Gilmour, though the album veers from the enduring excellence of 'Echoes' to the throwaway 'St Tropez' and 'Seamus', he felt that it was the first truly rounded Pink Floyd album. "*Meddle* was the first sign of really having a direction and knowing, and trying to achieve something. It was the first real Pink Floyd album as far as I was concerned."

Like the music it contained, the album sleeve was also a major departure for the Floyd, who decided, for the first time, that they would design it themselves. This was not entirely successful, though it did keep Floyd fans guessing about what exactly it purported to show. Though they executed the photography, Hipgnosis were only brought in as design advisors, working from the brief supplied by the band - most notably Gilmour and Waters. True to form, once the recording sessions were complete, the Floyd disappeared off on tour, this time to Japan. With pressing plants on standby waiting to get the record into the shops for Christmas, the cover concept had to be thrashed out over the phone. The band called Storm Thorgerson with their initial brief, who then passed it on to the photographer, who dutifully tried his best to work around the garbled instructions. A first set of roughs were then shuttled by courier to Japan, amended and returned to London with further instructions. "It was not the ideal way to work, and it shows," said Storm Thorgerson.

The cover design featured a tinted picture of an ear, over which were superimposed some concentric ripples in clear water, with the result that the ear looked like it was under water. The concentric ripples in the water, being a physical manifestation of a sound wave, were there to signify the idea of the 'Echoes' track itself - at one point considered as the title for the album.

The inner photo spread was stark and arresting in its simplicity, shot on high contrast black and white film for added detail and clarity. The band felt it was time to show themselves and their faces to their public. With no frills and no gimmicks, it marked a brief period of visual simplicity for the band. For their next album, *Dark Side Of The Moon*, they reverted to form and let the imagery do the talking for them.

As for the title of album, once again a last minute decision after *Echoes* itself was dropped, Gilmour admitted that this was a play on words - a medal being a prize for achievement and meddle meaning to interfere unnecessarily with something. It was, apparently, just another word they liked the sound of.

One Of These Days

(WATERS, WRIGHT, MASON, GILMOUR)

A track that grew directly from a chance experiment in the studio, when Waters decided to plug his bass through Gilmour's Binson Echorec tape delay system. Engineer John Leckie observed its genesis, "The track was based around that bass riff which Roger worked out using the Binson. He had the straight bass through one amp and the Binson signal coming out of another, and a DI line into the mixing desk. He fiddled around with the tape speed on the Binson until the echo was in exact double time with the bass line he was playing." The result was the clipped, hypnotic groove-laden bassline to this track. Dave Gilmour then double tracked Waters's original riff, and the two tracks were panned to opposite sides of the stereo spectrum. Originally this dual bass sound was so arresting that the piece was going to be made up using the sound of the bass only. It was Gilmour who eventually suggested that they add in the other instruments to flesh it out, eventually splicing a second improvized section - the vibrato section - into the track, before cutting back to the final heavyweight freakout, over which Gilmour plays some of his most demonic lap steel guitar. Fans of *Dr Who* will notice that, during this section, the 'melody' from the sci-fi TV show's theme tune can be heard. This was Waters's idea of a joke, and is played on the VCS-3 Putney synthesizer, a relatively small and primitive 3 oscillator mono synthesiser, controlled via a joystick and a patch bay! The wind effect that opens and closes the piece also came courtesy of the VCS-3.

The 'lyrics' to the track, if you can call them that, "One of these days I'm going to cut you into little pieces", were created by Nick Mason, whose voice was slowed down and put through a guitar amplifier with a fast tremolo and a Coloursound distortion pedal. The title itself came from Waters's fractured imagination. The person who he wanted to cut up was none other than the benign, happy-faced BBC Radio 2 disc jockey Jimmy Young! Waters had already created a tape collage for Pink Floyd shows that featured snatches of Jimmy Young's oldies show (which was full of 60th birthday dedications and cozy golden wedding anniversaries) that had been cut up and rearranged randomly into a disturbing surreal monologue. Waters felt that Young epitomised a disturbing breed of babbling, inane broadcasters, and the title itself refers to the fact that Waters had, in his own way, cut Young up into little pieces . . . of tape! These sound collages, used to introduce 'Alan's Psychedelic Breakfast' on the *Atom Heart Mother* tour, right through to performances of 'Raving And Drooling', two years later, were one of the most amusing and surreally disturbing sound effects the band ever used.

Originally the track was much longer, and was edited down into its final length at Morgan Sound, on 16 track.

Dr. Who: ***Ron Grainer's exceptional theme tune provided a melodic motif used on*** **One Of These Days.**

ONE OF THESE DAYS

WATERS *bass (including echo repeat), VCS-3 synth*
GILMOUR *bass, Stratocaster guitar, Lewis electric guitar, double tracked Fender lap steel guitar, backwards tape effects*
MASON *vocal treatment, drums, tape treatments*
WRIGHT *piano, Hammond organ*

A Pillow Of Winds

(WATERS, GILMOUR)

A PILLOW OF WINDS

WATERS *bass*
GILMOUR *fretless bass, lead vocal, acoustic and slide electric guitars*
MASON *drums*
WRIGHT *Hammond organ*

The band felt that 'One Of These Days' was such a powerful and, to many who heard it, overwhelming track, they needed to bring everyone down with something gentle. One of the last things to be recorded for the album, 'A Pillow Of Winds' segues from 'One Of These Days', as the VCS-3 wind fades out.

The song, which at the time was almost seen as filler material, is dominated by Wright's subtle Hammond undertow and Gilmour's overlaid acoustic and electric slide guitars. It also features a beautiful, if inconsequential, lyric by Roger, another of his sub-Rupert Brooke musings on nature, designed to evoke the warmth and comfort of home.

Fearless

(WATERS, GILMOUR)

FEARLESS
WATERS *bass, electric rhythm guitar*
GILMOUR *vocals, Stratocaster lead guitar*
MASON *drums*
WRIGHT *piano*
'THE KOP' (FANS OF LIVERPOOL FOOTBALL CLUB) *chorus*

Fearless' actually owes much of its sound and feel to Syd Barrett, who, despite his prolonged sabbatical from reality, still seemed to exercise an enormous influence on the group. Syd would often de-tune his guitar at random, searching for new and interesting tunings to base his songs around. He had once showed Roger Waters a guitar tuning that he had come across, which, for some reason, the bassist had remembered, and this forms the musical basis for this track (for anyone interested, this is an open G tuning, G-G-D-G-B-B). Waters took this tuning and simply played bar chords at the 6th and 3rd frets, to provide the harmonic changes. Gilmour adds some tasteful ambient tremolo guitar, and Mason the plodding behind-the-beat drums.

Many claim that Waters's lyric, a loose metaphor for the struggle to achieve against overwhelming odds that threaten to drag you down, contains the first, albeit cryptic, references to several of Waters's major lyrical themes on future albums: the notion of time passing, the soundless struggle of man's journey and the tragic decline of Syd Barrett. Barrett, the spectre that seemed to hover over the group at every turn, was resurrected in the mind of the remaining members of the Floyd during the sessions for the album, when EMI decided to compile the *Relics* compilation of early Floyd singles, B-sides and oddments. At Abbey Road, in between the album sessions for *Meddle*, the band had to listen through the old tapes, including the disturbing last gasps of Barrett: 'Vegetable Man' and 'Scream Thy Last Scream'. "They got very nostalgic when they heard the tapes," says John Leckie. "You could tell that it had been a strange time for them and the memories were not all good ones."

The lyrical theme of the song is that of a contented fool whose mind is apparently somewhere else when the judgement of his peers descends on him from on high. Nevertheless, "fearlessly the idiot faced the crowd" and he is spurred on by the humanity of the people who love him - at which point the 'Kop' chorus comes in singing 'You'll Never Walk Alone'.

Recorded at the 'Kop' end of the stadium at a Liverpool v West Ham home match in 1970, this Rodgers and Hammerstein song, originally from *Carousel*, was adopted by the Liverpool F.C., as a theme song of solidarity, after it was re-recorded by Gerry And The Pacemakers, a local Merseybeat outfit who enjoyed hits during the mid-60s.

The 'Kop' end at Anfield, Liverpool.

San Tropez

(WATERS)

Written as filler track in order to have the album ready to go to press for the Christmas market, 'San Tropez' was Waters's cynical, absurdly up-tempo, jazzy response to the band's US label Capitol's insistence that there be a 'happy' radio friendly singalong track on the album, to hook in a few undecided Christmas punters with a buck burning a hole in their pocket!! The track was recorded in August and, yes, Waters had recently been on holiday, though not to San Tropez. This was, however, the place where Syd and Dave Gilmour had been arrested back in the summer of 1965, while busking. Because the track was a last minute addendum to the album, little was done by way of arrangement, and the track is more or less as the original demo version Waters had recorded.

Waters, a sceptic and a cynic, was aware from an early stage of how his own circumstances as a fairly wealthy middle class rock star were at odds with his cherished socialist beliefs. The track is also a strong self parody, and gives the first hint of the feelings of betrayal that would later influence *Animals*, *The Wall* and *The Final Cut*: "Born in a home with no silver spoon/I'm drinking champagne like a good tycoon". Some believe that the song's more purple passages chronicle Waters's first acid trip, in Greece with old Cambridge friend Nigel Gordon.

Seamus

(WATERS, WRIGHT, MASON, GILMOUR)

As Syd Barrett noted in his classic encounter with *Melody Maker*'s 'Blind Date' reviews feature back in 1967, "I like jokes, The Pink Floyd like jokes. Jokes are good." As a coda to the album this aural joke works along similar lines to the final track of the Beach Boys' *Pet Sounds* where Banana, Brian Wilson's pooch, can be heard yelping as a freight train passes by. Wilson, high on grass, thought the joke was hilarious.

This track came about in similar circumstances. The dog responsible, Seamus, belonged to Steve Marriott of Small Faces and Humble Pie fame, who had trained the dog to yowl whenever he heard the blues. The dog was brought into Abbey Road by Dave Gilmour, whose friends were looking after the mutt while Marriott was touring America with Humble Pie. It was late, and the band were hopelessly stoned in the studio. As Gilmour, who had wanted to record just such a blues pastiche for some time, started to jam a slothful 12 bar on his acoustic guitar, the dog started to whine and howl. This triggered a stoned hysterical laughing fit amongst the band, and immediate calls for engineer John Leckie to roll the tapes. "'Seamus' was fun but I don't know whether we ought to have done it in the way we did it on that album really, 'cause I guess it wasn't really as funny to anybody else as it was to us," recalls a rather contrite Gilmour.

Gilmour and his Stratocaster.

Echoes

(WATERS, WRIGHT, MASON, GILMOUR)

Making up the whole of side two of the album, 'Echoes' was a daring experiment, considered by many to be the finest track the band ever recorded. Although the track carries on the long tradition of improvized and segued pieces, that began with 'A Saucerful Of Secrets', there was no real precedent for it, in terms of length or complexity; at least, not in the Floyd's canon. It was folk rock singer songwriter Roy Harper, another of Blackhill's artistes, who gave the Floyd courage to cover a whole side with one suite of music. "They worshipped Roy," says John Leckie. "To Dave in particular he just couldn't do anything wrong. Anyway, when Harper made *Lifemask* that was it for the Floyd. They thought it was amazing that Harper could release an album with one side of the record entirely taken up by a single track. You have to remember this was a time when bands were trying to cultivate serious images. They thought that if Roy

SAN TROPEZ

WATERS *bass, vocals*
GILMOUR *rhythm guitar, Fender lap steel guitar*
MASON *drums*
WRIGHT *piano*

SEAMUS

WATERS *bass*
GILMOUR *vocals, rhythm and slide guitar*
MASON *drums*
WRIGHT *piano, Hammond organ*
SEAMUS *howling*

Steve Marriott - owner of Seamus.

ECHOES

WATERS *bass (including echo repeat)*
GILMOUR *lead vocals, fretless bass, Stratocaster guitar*
MASON *drums*
WRIGHT *backing harmony vocals, piano, Hammond organ*

RECORDED *4-21, 24-26 January 7-28 March, 8 -14 April 2, 9-11 May at Abbey Road Studios 2 & 3 July 19-27 at Morgan Sound August 23-27 at AIR Studios Oxford Street, 1971*

could get away with it, they could too. They never had much time for what A&R men or the EMI bosses would think about it. Their attitude was that they made the records, and EMI sold them. But the Floyd were always something different. There was this aura around them that you didn't question anything they did. It was like the clever kids who are allowed after-hours access to the chemistry labs."

Having decided that they were going to create one long conceptual track, the band convened at the studio in January, and during three three-day sessions, playing to a metronome that was miked up in a broom cupboard, they recorded thirty six segments of music which they entitled 'Nothing, Parts 1-36'. The first of those parts was the now infamous 'Pink Floyd Sonar Ping'. While playing around with his piano, Rick decided to amplify it through a Leslie rotating speaker. One particular note stood out very clearly, a resonant fifth octave concert 'B'. The electronics, the room and the PA equipment being used conspired, uniquely, to produce one single note that carried, and seemed to resonate with an eerieness the band loved. A complete accident of circumstance, this fundamental frequency was a one-off moment. "We said, 'That's great!' and we used it as the start of the piece," commented Gilmour. The irony was that having once got this sound, on the experimental demo sections, the band could not recreate it. The final version was a tape sample from that original demo track!

"We spent ages trying to get the ping, and couldn't," recalls John Leckie. "'Echoes' was the first piece we recorded for the album, and at the time there was no precedent for the way they were doing it, which was to record in sections. I don't think anyone even knew if it was going to work. They wanted to use the studio more creatively, like it was part of the process rather than just the means to an end. It took ages though, even by Floyd standards. On drum kits they wanted very specific sounds, close miked here, distant there, and it would literally take three days to get the right high hat sound or something. It was all in the detail for them. There were a lot of jams in the studio before we even got to thinking about sounds, but it was very considered. They spent a lot of time, Dave and Roger, talking about moods and structure. It's very impressionistic."

"Basically we're the laziest group ever. Other groups would be quite horrified if they saw how we really waste our recording time," commented Gilmour wryly at the time.

At the end of January the band listened back to the thirty six fragments, and started trial edits to establish a flow for the piece. From these edits, the band then re-recorded certain segments as entire pieces of music, to establish better musical continuity. These recordings were then further sequenced and overdubbed during March, April and early May, at Abbey Road. Many of the thirty six ideas were jettisoned or combined together, until eight major musical themes remained, forming a cohesive piece which was ready to be officially performed live for the first time at Richmond College on 22 April, 1971, under the title 'The Return Of The Son Of Nothing'. The show was recorded, and further alterations were made to the structure. The piece was played again at *The Crystal Palace Garden Party* in London, on 15 May, 1971, at which point the band decided they were happy with it.

In mid-May, Floyd decamped from Abbey Road to Morgan Sound Studios in Willesden, to finish the recording of 'Echoes'. Here, the tapes were segued together into their final form, and additional overdubs added, using the 16 track technology. At the time, Abbey Road had not made the transition to 16 track, and the Floyd were the first EMI act, other than The Beatles, to use outside studios. There were then only three studios in London with 16 track tape machines: Trident, George Martin's AIR Studios, on Oxford Street, and Morgan Sound. Morgan was a cramped, shabby studio with none of the comforts of Abbey Road, but its equipment was state of the art: their 16 track machine was linked to one of the new, but already legendary, Neve mixing consoles.

This equipment was put to good use, and allowed the segues and sound effects to blend more smoothly, without resort to reduction mixes, whereby the eight tracks are reduced down to three or four, incurring an inevitable loss in quality. "'Echoes' is rather similar to 'Atom Heart Mother' in terms of it running through various movements," said Mason who, as he would on *Dark Side Of The Moon*, acted as an editor for 'Echoes'. "There are various things in the construction that have a Pink Floyd flavour, but are also very dangerous Pink Floyd clichés. One is the possible tendency to get stuck into a sort of slow four tempo. And the other thing is to take a melody line and flog it to death. Maybe we'll play it once slow and quiet, the next time a bit harder and the third time really heavy, which tends to come a little bit into *Meddle* and in *Atom Heart Mother*, but it's slightly more forgivable with the choir and orchestra, 'cause it's nice building on an orchestra and bringing in extra brass and playing more complex lines."

Recording for the song was finally finished on 2 June, save for a few minor overdubs, such as Gilmour's seagull guitar noises and the sound effects of cawing crows to add that trademark hint of ominous darkness. The vocals were added at a final Morgan Studio session in July, along with a few additional guitar overdubs to flesh out the final section of the piece. For guitar fans, Dave used his Fender Stratocaster and a Lewis guitar for the recording, with fuzz, wah-wah, and vibrato effects, and what he describes as the four part chorused guitar orchestra that brings the piece to a tumultuous climax.

During its early incarnation as 'Return Of The Son Of Nothing', the piece was performed as a work in progress, with lyrics very different from those on 'Echoes'. A science fiction theme was dominant, but interwoven with a romantic theme. Apparently set in the future, the lyrics are vague but evocative. Still very rough at this point, Roger would later rewrite the entire first verse, and part of the third, when he was inspired to change his imagery from space to the ocean depths.

When it came time to lay down the final vocal, Waters opted for a rewrite with a strong humanistic steak. He was anxious to break away from what he saw as the rather meaningless, inconsequential lyrics of old. Waters himself acknowledges that the lyrics for 'Echoes' provide a blueprint for his future exploration of alienation, and of the agents that conspire against freedom. The lyrics refer obliquely to the struggle with authority figures, who purport to know the 'wheres and whys', and to the problems encountered in attempting to establish one's own independent identity. Indeed, it was at this time in his life that Roger was beginning to realise that one has to take hold of one's own destiny and steer it in the desired direction. Waters's concept of freedom is a humanistic one. He had always had problems with authority figures (he was well known at Regent Street Poly for constantly challenging the teaching methods of the lecturers, who would attempt to teach their pupils by making them learn their text books by rote), and he would later personify such people as 'pigs' on the *Animals* album.

As in the case of 'Atom Heart Mother', it was a performance for the BBC *In Concert* show on 30 September, 1971, that eventually prompted the final name change from the 'Return Of The Son Of Nothing' to 'Echoes'.

A weary Floyd, in Hamburg, 1971.

Obscured By Clouds

Though it often goes unnoticed by many casual Floyd fans, *Obscured By Clouds*, an album Nick Mason describes as "a sensational LP", was the Floyd's second major soundtrack project. The film itself continues the middle-aged Barbet Schroeder's obsession with the emerging hippie culture and its spirit-seeking aspirations. Unlike *More*, however, the plot of the film - best described as hippies-go-native-in-search-of-enlightenment-as-they-search-for-a-lost-valley-in-New-Guinea - borders on the farcical and is extremely tedious.

OBSCURED BY CLOUDS
(SOUNDTRACK TO THE FILM LA VALLÉE*)*

RECORDED *23-29 February, 22-27 March, 1972, Chateau d'Herouville, France*
PRODUCED BY *PINK FLOYD*
RELEASED *3 June, 1972*
CHART PLACING *Number 46 in US*

Although the band had had their differences with Schroeder over his 'supervision' of the *More* soundtrack, which they actually saw as interference and meddling, the boundaries were re-drawn for *Obscured By Clouds*. The Floyd were more experienced and confident by 1972 and were able to dictate the rules of engagement to a much greater extent.

The album came at an interesting point in the band's development. They had their first number 1 album, their most accomplished and ambitious work yet, *Meddle*, in the bag; a successful album that had cracked the Top 50 in the US. The Floyd possessed a confidence that they had not had when they made *More*. They were given the opportunity to record for two weeks at the newly refitted Chateau d'Herouville just outside Paris, a studio where Marc Bolan and Elton John had cut some of their most popular albums. Obviously some of these pop and glam sensibilities wore off on the band, as a couple of the tracks are distinctly un-Floydian, verging on the glam-rock sound prevailing in the UK at the time. The studio also provided the band with the chance to experiment with 16 tracks for the first time, in readiness for the *Dark Side Of The Moon* sessions the following year.

The process was the same as it had been on *More*: Schroeder brought in a finished edit of the film, explaining, in the absence of subtitles, the action and the characters. Despite expressing reservations at the content (another hippie-flick yawn), the band enjoyed the sessions. Since it was unlikely that the film, mostly in French, would be shown in the UK or the US and would not therefore tarnish their reputation, they took the money and the studio time as a kind of holiday. Unlike *More,* however, the band made less of an attempt to create music to fit the action itself, knowing from the *More* experience that only segments of the music would end up in the film anyway. Instead they used the studio time in the state of the art French studio as a chance to explore some musical ideas and studio techniques that had no place in any of the formal Floyd projects of the time. Consequently, *Obscured By Clouds* is the unusual sound of the Floyd letting go, and (gasp) having a little fun in the studio.

Chateau d'Herouville, outside Paris.

OBSCURED BY CLOUDS
INSTRUMENTAL

GILMOUR *VCS-3, double tracked electric slide guitar*
WATERS *Fender bass*
MASON *drums*

RECORDED *23-29 February, 22-27 March, 1972 at Château d'Herouville, France*

Like *More*, many of the extracts heard in the film were different from the versions heard on the final album. As the extracts used in the film didn't necessarily have to be complete takes, the Floyd and Schroeder picked the most adept, regardless of whether the rest of the take was up to the same standard. The versions heard on the album represent those with which the Floyd themselves were happiest. As with *More*, the band were given a special royalty for the project by EMI, because, in their eyes, soundtracks were considered more worthy artistically. This rule would, however, be dropped after this album, for all EMI artists involved with soundtrack projects.

Storm Thorgerson created the cover using one of the film stills, of a naked girl seen through the undergrowth, refracting it through a prism lens to give a dappled effect. It is not considered one of his best.

Obscured By Clouds

(WATERS, GILMOUR)

This instrumental piece, produced in the studio and based around the pulsing VCS-3 synthesiser drone played by Gilmour, opens and closes the film *La Vallée*. "When the early synthesizers first came out we learned to use them fairly quickly, but they weren't like the ones you get now which you just plug in and play," comments Gilmour. "You had to patch these sounds together on a small patch bay and create sounds yourself from scratch. It was fun, and we got very good at making drones." Using the 16 tracks, several drones were layered on top of one another before drums and Gilmour's guitar were added.

Mason then overdubbed metronomic drums. One of the favoured new studio toys at the time was the Benson Drum Machine, a teak box of primitive electronics that created early electronic drum machine sounds. The band had long wanted to use one, but were unable to locate one for the recording, so they decided to try and reproduce the clipped dry drum sound of the Benson themselves. It was this sound that formed the basis of the drum track. Mason used tuned toms, played with beaters, which were close-miked and put through a noise gate to give a clipped, precision feel. Finally, Gilmour played some double tracked slide cadences on his Stratocaster guitar. At the time the sound was very new, and recalled the sounds of the 'Krautrock' acts coming out of Germany, such as Neu! and early Kraftwerk.

La Vallée begins on the island of New Guinea, just north of Australia, and as the camera pans over the mountains, setting the scene, 'Obscured By Clouds' is played. Whatever the qualities of the rest of the film, the opening is highly effective. The track reappears at the end of the film, when Vivian, the female lead, crests the last ridge and spots the hidden valley that the group of hippie explorers have been seeking. The sun breaks through the clouds, revealing their destination in all its beauty.

WHEN YOU'RE IN
INSTRUMENTAL

GILMOUR *rhythm guitar and VCS-3*
WATERS *Fender bass*
WRIGHT *Hammond organ*
MASON *drums*

RECORDED *23-29 February, 22-27 March, 1972 at Château d'Herouville, France*

When You're In

(WATERS, GILMOUR, MASON, WRIGHT)

Originally designed as the heavy coda to the title track, this ultra-heavy guitar-led rock-out was not used in the film. The two tracks were performed as one during forthcoming tours. This was a classic Floyd 'jam' written and recorded at the Chateau.

Burning Bridges

(WRIGHT, WATERS)

It is significant that the only other composition in the Floyd canon by Waters and Wright, jointly, other than 'Stay' from this album, was 'Us And Them' on *Dark Side Of The Moon*. This track may be a simple nondescript ballad, but the production sound was a certain blueprint for *Dark Side Of The Moon*. The music was Wright's and the lyrics were another Waters tale of transition from childhood to adulthood - the Floyd's perennial theme.

The film begins in a New Guinean native artefact shop in the Australian outback, where an attractive and wealthy French ambassador's wife, Vivian (played by Bulle Ogier), is trying to buy rare bird feathers which will be the envy of her friends in Paris, and may fetch a good price amongst the couturiers. She is disappointed that the shop has none to sell, but then meets Olivier (Jean-Pierre Kalfon), who has arrived to sell some feathers that he has collected himself. Vivian, toying with an ornamental dagger, drops it on Olivier's foot, wounding him. She accompanies him to the hospital and back to his camp, where he invites her to look at more of his feathers in his tent. 'Burning Bridges' is heard through this scene.

Like many of the tracks on *More*, this benefits from the time constraints the band was under to come up with the material. In their attempt to get the music done on time, they explored avenues of music they would never normally have tried. With little time to change their minds about whether it was right for the Floyd, or even any good, this was recorded and mastered in one short day's work! Gilmour provided the riff, Waters the lyrics.

Olivier explains that he and his friend Gaetan (Michael Gothard) are planning to explore the mountainous area of Papua New Guinea, where he bought his feathers from a missionary. The next expedition will be to a hidden valley marked on the maps as 'obscured by clouds'. Vivian dines with the group, and asks to see Olivier's feathers one more time before she goes home, at which point 'The Gold It's In The . . .' is played.

BURNING BRIDGES

GILMOUR *rhythm guitar through Leslie cabinet, vocals*
WATERS *vocals, Fender bass, tape treatments*
WRIGHT *Hammond organ harmonized with VCS-3, vocals*
MASON *drums*

RECORDED *23-29 February, 22-27 March 1972 at Château d'Herouville, France*

The Gold It's In The. . .

(WATERS, GILMOUR)

This uncharacteristic rocker has a strong element of glam-rock about it. Influenced, possibly, by the fact that glam-rock figurehead Marc Bolan had recorded at the studio, or perhaps a simple reflection of the fact that Pink Floyd rarely got to embrace the more traditional rock'n'roll forms, it is a powerful riff-based rocker, jammed in the studio.

THE GOLD IT'S IN THE . . .

GILMOUR *lead and rhythm guitar*
WATERS *Fender bass*
MASON *drums, percussion*

RECORDED *23-29 February, 22-27 March 1972 at Chateau d'Herouville, France*

Wot's . . . Uh, The Deal

(WATERS, GILMOUR)

The album's unexpected highlight has a strong humanistic element, dealing with the fact that the band were growing up, changing their attitudes to the music business and beginning to see it less as a hobby and more as their job. All were now family men, to a greater or lesser extent, and this was changing their attitude to making music - they started to take it a lot

WOT'S . . . UH, THE DEAL

GILMOUR *double-tracked acoustic guitar*
WATERS *Fender bass, tape treatments*
WRIGHT *Hammond organ, piano*
MASON *drums*

RECORDED *23-29 February, 22-27 March 1972 at Chateau d'Herouville, France*

Top left:* La Valley *was another of Barbet Schroeder's hippie flicks although this one considerably more ludicrous than* More. *Luckily for the Floyd the movie was not widely shown outside of France.

Jean-Pierre Kalfon who plays Olivier and Bulle Ogier as Vivian play the travellers in search of hippie nirvana via the hidden valley of new Guinea.

MUDMEN

(INSTRUMENTAL)

GILMOUR *fuzz guitar*
WATERS *Fender bass*
WRIGHT *Hammond organ, VCS-3*
MASON *drums*

RECORDED *23-29 February, 22-27 March 1972 at Chateau d'Herouville, France*

CHILDHOOD'S END

(INSTRUMENTAL)

GILMOUR *lead vocal, acoustic and electric guitar*
WATERS *Fender bass*
WRIGHT *Hammond organ*
MASON *drums*

RECORDED *23-29 February, 22-27 March 1972, at Chateau d'Herouville, France*

FREE FOUR

(INSTRUMENTAL)

GILMOUR *acoustic guitar, electric guitar through Leslie cabinet*
WATERS *lead vocal, Fender bass*
WRIGHT *VCS-3*
MASON *drums*

RECORDED *23-29 February, 22-27 March 1972, at Chateau d'Herouville, France*

more seriously. In particular, Waters was desperately aware that time was passing him by. "Around that time there was a sense that we had all grown older, we weren't a pop band, we weren't really anything at all," commented Waters at the time.

This track marks the perfect synthesis of Waters's lyrical intropspection and Gilmour's musical aspirations. For the next five years this uniquely creative balance would produce some of the greatest rock music ever heard. In the film, the song plays in the scene when Olivier refuses to sell his feathers, and makes love to Vivian.

Mudmen

(WRIGHT, GILMOUR)

Mudmen' again exploits the 16 track technology, layering Hammond and VCS-3 synthesiser to create another of the album's sublime instrumental interludes. In this case, the music was directly inspired by the action in the film, and fitted the band's muse perfectly. During the journey into the forest in search of feathers, the group visit a native tribe, before going to stay with a missionary in the mountains. The missionary sends Vivian and Olivier to a shaman, who gives feathers only to people he loves. A few seconds of 'Mudmen' is played while Vivien does her best to make a good impression. But she get more than she bargains for when she is handed feathers of the precious *kouman* (bird of paradise) - feathers she has been longing for. She is overtaken by a bizarre vision, the implications of which are not obvious until later, when she takes a psychedelic cocktail brewed by the native shaman, and becomes one with the forest. Vivian feels liberated, powerful and beautiful, identifying with nature, and she symbolically comes to terms with her sexuality via a snake.

***The shamanic 'mudmen'*.**

Childhood's End

(GILMOUR)

Gilmour, not noted for his love of science fiction, is said to have taken the title of this track from Arthur C. Clarke's classic novella. In this case, however, the title is used as a literal description of the passing of youth and the emergence into the 'harsh realities' of adulthood.

There's a humanistic weariness to it, partly precipitated by Gilmour's current state of mind. He too had accepted that rock'n'roll was all about hard work. The innocent folly of childhood had gone, the band had made it through the most trying times, when they had no direction, and they'd cut what they all felt was their first true Pink Floyd album, but they were still broke. It is a song of resignation.

'Childhood's End' accompanies the scene in *La Vallée* where the rich, elegant Parisian Vivian decides to accompany the five-person hippie expedition as they drive by jeep into the heart of New Guinea, searching for the sacred valley that is obscured by clouds. Vivian, however, is hoping to find the rare and valuable feathers she has been after, including the plumage of the precious bird of paradise, to take back to Paris.

Free Four

(WATERS)

Taking its title from the typical rock'n'roll count-in 'one two three four' that begins the track, 'Free Four' provided the Floyd with an unlikely hit on US FM radio. Released as a single in four territories including the US, where it broke into the FM radio top 50, it was crucial in helping prepare the ground for *Dark Side Of The Moon*.

What this jaunty pop-funk backing belies is the fact that this is Roger Waters's first serious attempt to deal with the death of his father. Killed in Anzio,when Waters was just a year old, by a German Stuka dive bomber, his father, a proficient musician, remained just a snapshot in the family album, yet became the most significant lyrical theme in his life. In the light of his later work, in particular *The Wall* and *The Final Cut*, this is the most important and personal lyric he had yet written.

It takes the perspective of an aged and not entirely coherent man in a hospice, looking back on his life from his deathbed. The person concerned is Roger Waters, "the dead man's son", and he is looking back not only on his life but on that of his father, who never had the chance

Anzio, near Rome, 1944.

to get old and senile, because he was "buried like a mole in a foxhole". With references to madness and paranoia, 'Free Four' is the important blueprint for tracks such as 'Breathe' on *Dark Side of The Moon*, in which life is seen as passing by without you really noticing. Indeed, in the film version of the song, in which an extra verse appears, there is even a reference to "taking a slice" of the money pie, a cynical metaphor that would reappear on 'Money' from *Dark Side Of The Moon*, a year later.

Towards the end of the song, the lyric diverts to take in another perennial Waters theme, that of the 'Rock Machine' itself. On numerous occasions, Waters likened playing stadiums with a rock band to being at war. This, of course, would form a very strong lyrical element of *Wish You Were Here* and *The Wall*.

In the film, the track, though completely incongruous lyrically, is heard at the point when the hippie explorers hit mountainous terrain and are forced to abandon their jeep in favour of horses. The group barter for horses from the local bigoted American poachers, until Vivian gives all her money to the cause.

Stay

(WRIGHT, WATERS)

The third of Wright's songs to deal with the pressures of the rock'n'roll lifestyle and the emptiness it can produce, 'Stay' could almost be seen as a love song if it weren't for the cruel rejoinder in the last verse, which makes the true circumstances all too clear. The first verse talks of how he, having downed a bottle of wine, elegantly and romantically persuades a girl to stay with him until the morning. In the cold light of day, dealt with in the second verse, he wishes that the girl, whose name he doesn't even know, would simply disappear. Wright, of all the band, found being on the road the most difficult, not because he couldn't cope, but because the nature of the work entailed constant exposure to those familiar rock'n'roll condiments, sex, alcohol and drugs. In a wider sense, the song also deals with the loneliness and dislocation of touring with a large rock act, with which Wright never entirely came to terms and which he had already chronicled in 'Summer 68' on *Atom Heart Mother*. Since he was happily married to his wife, Gale, at the time, one can only assume he was taking a hypothetical look at the world of groupiedom.

This single was the flip side to the US single release from the album - Waters's 'Free Four' - but did not appear in the film. It's probable that Wright's piano progression was influenced by Elton John's 'Your Song', which was, coincidentally, recorded in the same studio the year before.

STAY

WRIGHT *piano, lead vocal*
GILMOUR *guitar*
WATERS *Fender bass*
MASON *drums*

RECORDED *23-29 February, 22-27 March 1972, at Chateau d'Herouville, France*

Absolutely Curtains

(WATERS, GILMOUR, WRIGHT, MASON, THE MAPUGA TRIBE)

With the luxury of 16 tracks to play with at the 'Honky Chateau', Rick Wright and Dave Gilmour could experiment with the layering and overdubbing of sounds to an extent that they had not hitherto been able, using the 8 track recording system at Abbey Road. They used the additional tracks to build up a sound montage, the foundation of which was the long, swirling rumble of low Hammond organ notes through the rotating speakers of the Leslie cabinet. Over this, Gilmour or Waters layered a low drone from a VCS-3, with all three of its oscillators patched through the same frequency setting. Then Wright's trusty Farfisa was added, and, finally, a 'tack piano', which was in the studio after a 1971 Elton John session, with thumbtacks pressed into the felt hammers to recreate the sound of classic honky tonk piano - though the Floyd decided to use it for an eerie percussive effect, rather than pub rock! Nick Mason overdubbed timpani and cymbal played with beaters. Towards the end of the track Gilmour overdubs pairs of plucked guitar notes to provide a delicate musical motif before the track fades into the chanting of the Mapuga tribe. The words to this song are indecipherable even to those who speak New Guinean. There are approximately 717 native different dialects and, as is the case in India, few of these different dialects can be understood by speakers of any of the others! Needless to say, the Mapuga didn't attend the sessions, and the Floyd dubbed the chant from the sound recordist's tapes, recorded on location in New Guinea.

ABSOLUTELY CURTAINS

GILMOUR *picked guitar, VCS-3, ARP synthesizer*
WATERS *VCS-3*
WRIGHT *Hammond organ, Farfisa organ, tack piano*
MASON *percussion*
RECORDED *23-29 February, 22-27 March 1972 at Chateau d'Herouville, France*

Dark Side Of The Moon

1972

The most accomplished and complete concept album in rock, the album that Pink Floyd had been working up to since *A Saucerful Of Secrets*, opens and closes with the sound of a beating heart. In between was the most ambitious, yet commercial, song suite Pink Floyd had yet dared to record.

An album where both Roger Waters and Dave Gilmour blossomed as talents, it marks the only occasion when a perfect balance was achieved between Waters's lyrical concepts and Gilmour's musical genius. The Lennon and McCartney of progressive rock had made their epoch-defining breakthrough album - the career equivalent of The Beatles' groundbreaking *Revolver*. Their music, and that of adult-oriented rock, would never be the same again.

The album's premise is that modern life is a recipe for insanity, and that a human has to fight hard to escape madness. Clearly a notion that struck a universal chord, because the album has sold steadily, indeed dramatically, for over 23 years. Over 27 million copies have been sold worldwide, and it has spent a staggering 760 weeks on the American chart (*Sergeant Pepper* managed 200 weeks). It's estimated that one in every 14 people in the USA under the age of 50 owns a copy. One pundit has suggested that the album "so outdistanced the competition that most thinking people believe it may never be equalled". Much of its success was surely due to its integration on all levels; melodies, lyrics, the imagery of contradiction (us and them, light and dark

RECORDED *June 1972, and between October 1972 and January 1973, Abbey Road Studios 2 and 3*
ENGINEER *ALAN PARSONS*
MIXED BY *CHRIS THOMAS*
PRODUCED BY *PINK FLOYD*
SLEEVE DESIGN & PHOTOGRAPHY BY *HIPGNOSIS*
RELEASED *24 March, 1973*
CHART PLACING *Number 2 in the UK; Number 1 in the US*

Dark Side live performance.

The pyramids: symbols of man's vain but spectacular ambition and folly.

and the constant tug of opposing impulses), the clean sounds and simple visuals are all tightly gathered together into one highly accessible, though demanding and sophisticated package.

Released worldwide on 24 March, 1973, *Dark Side Of The Moon* had been in preparation since December 1971, when the Floyd began rehearsing a suite of songs for a British tour in the new year. Booking a rehearsal studio in Broadhurst Gardens, North London, they'd convene daily to sort through ideas and jam together. One afternoon, sitting in Nick Mason's kitchen pondering the music they had prepared, Roger Waters announced that he had a theme for the set. "We thought we could do a whole thing about the pressures we personally feel that drive one over the top . . . the pressure of earning a lot of money; the time thing, time flying by very fast; organised power structures like the church or politics; violence, aggression. It's a musical version of that kind of truism, 'Today is the first day of the rest of your life'. It talks about the illusion of working towards ends which might turn out to be fool's gold."

For once, Waters's ideas were expressed perfectly in simple, direct lyrics. This was a profound change in approach for the band who'd always clouded the meaning of their songs with murky, equivocal words. "I had something definite I wanted to say. People were always misinterpreting the lyrics, so I thought it was time to make it as direct and specific as I could."

Within six weeks, the basic outline was complete and the lyrics written. Taking the working title of *Eclipse (A Piece For Assorted Lunatics)*, the suite made its debut on the first date of the world tour beginning on 17 February, 1972, at the Rainbow Theatre in London. Recording of *Eclipse* began on 1 June, the day after the tour finished, by which time the music was finely honed. Part of the album's success is its precision and the fact that it achieves the perfect balance between Waters's lyrical ideas and Gilmour's musicianship - this would never quite be achieved again, as Waters's concepts outgrew the band.

Most of the basic recording was done in Studio 2 at Abbey Road with innovative engineer Alan Parsons, interrupted only by group breaks to watch *Monty Python's Flying Circus* or the occasional football match on TV - and a US tour halfway through! Drums and bass were recorded onto 16 track, then reduction mixes were made which were transferred onto another master tape for further overdubs. The Floyd had the album sequenced (i.e. the running order of the songs planned) very early on, the form broadly following the *Eclipse* show. The crossfades and segues between tracks were all mapped out at this early stage with the aid of a huge track sheet that ran the entire length of the studio.

"They'd spend days getting sounds and working all the timings out," recalls Alan Parsons. "I actually feel that they spent less time getting sounds on *Dark Side* than on previous albums, so that gives you some idea of what a Floyd session was like. They were perfectionists. But we recorded everything very simply. The album sounds more complex than it actually is." The sessions were relatively smooth, and it was only when it came time to prepare the final mix that tempers frayed. Gilmour wanted an expansive, heavily reverbed sound while Waters wanted a 'no frills' sound that would leap out of the speakers. This unresolvable dispute threatened to hold up the release of the album, so manager Steve O'Rourke called in his friend, Chris Thomas (formerly an engineer on The Beatles' *White Album* and the future producer of Roxy Music, Sex Pistols, The Pretenders, INXS and Pulp) to do a mix independently of both factions. His fresh pair of ears reinstated some solos that the band had tired of over the months, and brought the album a new sonic perspective that was a satisfactory compromise between Waters's and Gilmour's ideas.

Seven mock-ups of potential sleeves were presented to the Floyd. They unanimously decided on the designs of long time associates Storm Thorgerson and Aubrey 'Po' Powell, who visually matched the Floyd's musical economy and restraint on *Dark Side*. The prism, pyramids and ECG heartbeat trace were simple, timelessly striking and provided ample room for tie-in graphics and merchandise, which would make the Floyd's pyramids as instantly recognizable as the logo of a giant corporation. For Roger, the pressures of touring, madness, ambition, fear of death and the desire to give it all up and quit the insanity of the rat race were summed up by the Hipgnosis artwork. The triangle became the symbol of ambition; the prism showed how purity becomes split into its component parts - corrupted; the pyramids a larger symbol of man's ambition and human folly.

The album's press premiere was set for Tuesday, 27 February, 1973, at The London Planetarium. The original plan had been to play a quadraphonic mix of the album through a specially designed four-way speaker system. When the big day dawned the quad mix had still not been completed and the PA that EMI had hired for the occasion comprised, according to Mason, "the most terrible speakers imaginable". The Floyd did not attend. Their places were taken by cardboard cut outs. One journalist quipped that he couldn't tell the difference.

Despite mixed reviews, the album quickly hit the number 2 spot on the UK album chart (in over 350 weeks on the chart it would never reach number 1), and in the US became an FM radio favourite overnight. The band themselves still have little idea as to why *Dark Side Of The Moon* was the Big One. To them it was just another Pink Floyd album, a mere continuation of the ideas and methods they'd been exploring since 1968. "Why it goes on and on selling, I don't know," says a bemused Rick Wright. "It touched a nerve. It seemed like everyone was waiting for this album, for someone to make it."

Speak To Me

(MASON)

With the concept album becoming the standard form for adult-oriented rock bands, Nick Mason was keen to ensure that the new Floyd suite was tightly focused. While Gilmour and Waters provided most of the musical and lyrical direction, it was Mason who

SPEAK TO ME

MASON *tape effects and editing*
WRIGHT *keyboards, vocals, VCS-3, Synthi-A*
CHRIS ADAMSON/GERRY DRISCOLL *spoken words and laughter*
CLARE TORRY *vocals*

RECORDED *and assembled at Abbey Road Studio 3*

Pink Floyd playing **Dark Side Of The Moon** *live as the second half of their Eclipse tour of 1974. As the album sales increased large amounts of money were spent on making the stage show a multimedia tour de force. Back projections, film sequences and a state of the art lighting desk made the live show the most sophisticated yet for any rock band.*

'The old faithfuls: the Binson Echorec (atop Roger Waters's amplifier), Rick Wright's Farfisa, Hammond and Fender Rhodes piano and to the right of the picture the updated 'suitcase' version of the VCS 3 Putney synthesiser-the Synthi-A- which played such a crucial part in the creation of the album.

provided much of its conceptual unity, effectively becoming the album's project manager. Assembled and recorded late in the sessions, once the sequencing of the other tracks was complete, this brief montage was Mason's idea for an overture, encapsulating all the album's themes by blending snatches of music and sound effects from throughout the record. The voices were all responses to a questionnaire that the Floyd compiled to elicit responses to the various themes: death, violence and insanity. Nick Mason had the idea of a spontaneous word association, like a psychological test for various friends and acquaintances to answer. Studio 3 was dimly lit, and set up with a single desk and a chair above which hung a solitary microphone. On the desk was a series of cards. Each interviewee was asked to sit down and, once the red light came on, turn the first card over, read the question and give the first answer that came into their head. The questions included, "Do you fear death?", "When was the last time you hit anyone?", "Are you mad?" and "Is there a dark side of the moon?". Paul and Linda McCartney, recording with Wings in Studio 2, were among those interviewed but the two were so used to dealing with the media that their replies were guarded. Those whose responses were used included Irishman Jerry Driscoll, the staff cleaner and sometime doorman at Abbey Road, Henry McCulloch of Wings and his wife, and the Floyd roadies Liverpool Bobby, Chris Adamson, Puddy Watts and, the most infamous voice of them all, Roger The Hat. Initially 'Speak To Me' was going to be part of 'Breathe' but Mason wanted a publishing credit. While most of the tracks on the album had titles dating from the *Eclipse* show, the newly conceived tracks were only christened the day before the sleeve art was due at the printers. The working title on the giant track sheet had been 'Nick's section'. Its new title originated from the phrase repeatedly used by Alan Parsons when getting levels during the questionnaire recordings.

BREATHE

GILMOUR *vocals, guitars*
MASON *drums*
WRIGHT *Hammond organ*
WATERS *Fender bass*

RECORDED *Abbey Road, Studios 2 and 3*

Breathe

(WATERS, GILMOUR, WRIGHT)

Roger Waters was 27 when he began work on the *Eclipse* suite, and he was already plagued by the idea that life was passing him by. His biggest fear was that his principles and his quality of life were being compromised and eroded by money, fame and the pressure to produce hit albums. Waters, a life-long socialist, was finding it harder and harder to reconcile his life as a successful rock star with his political beliefs.

'Breathe' concerned his frustration over the pursuit of "pointless goals" while never having time to appreciate the richer meaning of life. Many of these ideas were prompted by the work Waters did with experimental composer Ron Geesin, in 1969 on the soundtrack to a film called *The Body*. Directed and photographed by film maker Tony Garnett, it was a humanist's attempt to look at the body as a giant metaphor for human existence, fusing internal micro-cinematography with scenes such as a powerful speech by Peter Kerrigan, about the importance of fighting for the dignity of others who are less fortunate, to produce an extremely life-affirming piece. The opening lyrics to this track, "Breathe, breathe in the air", were the first words heard on the soundtrack of *The Body*.

On The Run

(GILMOUR, WATERS)

Originally known as 'The Travel Sequence', this sound collage, painstakingly assembled over the course of a week in Studio 3, is a masterpiece of sweaty death-inspired paranoia.

By late 1972 Pink Floyd were in possession of the latest advance in synthesiser technology - the Synthi-A. The updated version of the VCS-3 Putney synth that they'd been using since 1969, the Synthi-A had a huge advantage over its predecessor in that it included a sequencer, allowing the programming of patterns of notes. "We found a very mobile, repetitious, travelling type of sound," recalls Gilmour of his piece. "One can look back on it now with a certain dismissiveness, but it was a very serious attempt to achieve a certain effect at the time, a feeling of movement." It's often assumed that the percussive hi-hat came courtesy of Nick Mason, but this too was produced using the Synthi-A. Over the synth riff, an announcer lists flight departures, taken from material recorded for a comedy album cut at Abbey Road three years earlier. 'On The Run' builds as a breathless traveller races to catch the plane, and Gilmour's grotesque arcing guitar distortions create an intense crescendo. The overheated jet engine noise was performed on Gilmour's guitar and the final plane crash was created on the VCS-3 and the Synthi-A.

The voice saying "live for today, gone tomorrow, that's me", and the stoned laughter just before the explosion, belongs to Floyd roadie Roger The Hat, the star of the Floyd questionnaire sessions. This was his response to the question, "Do you fear death?" It fitted perfectly with both the theme of the piece - Floyd's collective fear of flying - and Waters's overall concept of how pursuit of pointless goals will drive you insane. The footsteps and the extraordinary puffing and panting you can hear

ON THE RUN

GILMOUR *guitar effects, Synthi-A, Leslie cabinet*
WATERS *bass drone*
ROGER THE HAT *voice*

RECORDED *Abbey Road, Studios 2 and 3*

Rick Wright, on a **DSOM** *live show.*

TIME

GILMOUR *vocals, guitars, Synthi-A*
MASON *drums, Roto-toms*
WRIGHT *Rhodes piano, Hammond organ, Synthi-A*
WATERS *bass guitar*
DORIS TROY, LESLEY DUNCAN, LIZA STRIKE, BARRY ST JOHN *backing vocals*

RECORDED *Abbey Road, Studios 2 and 3*

THE GREAT GIG IN THE SKY
GILMOUR *Stratocaster guitars*
MASON *drums*
WRIGHT *Steinway piano, Hammond organ*
WATERS *bass guitar*
CLARE TORRY *vocal improvisation*
DORIS TROY, LESLEY DUNCAN, LIZA STRIKE, BARRY ST JOHN, JERRY DRISCOLL, ROGER THE HAT, *backing vocals*
UNKNOWN FEMALE *spoken sections*

The 'clock section' was a highlight of the Dark Side live shows.

throughout were recorded in Studio 2, and involved assistant engineer Peter James running around in heavy shoes until, finally, out of breath, he collapsed on the floor.

Time

(MASON, WATERS, WRIGHT, GILMOUR)

Waters became obsessed with the idea that we waste much of our time on habitual behaviour without questioning it, leaving us open to madness once we come to understand that we have in fact achieved nothing for our pains. "I spent an awful lot of my life - until I was about 28 - waiting for my life to start," he recalled in 1982. "I thought that, at some point, I'd turn from a chrysalis into a butterfly, that my real life would begin. If I had that part of my life to live again, I would rather live the years between 18 and 28 knowing that that was it, that nothing was suddenly going to happen - that time passes, and you are what you are, you do what you do."

'Time' was meticulously designed to mirror these sentiments, from Waters's damped, oscillating picked bass, reminiscent of a ticking clock, to the chiming cacophony of clocks that opens the track, to the way Nick Mason drums slightly ahead of the beat, to leave the listener with a feeling that they're trying to keep up. The clocks were recorded by Alan Parsons, before work on the album began, for a quadraphonic sound effects record. He took a small Uher portable tape recorder to a St Johns Wood antiques shop, close to Abbey Road, and recorded each clock separately. Once back at the studio he transferred the sound of each clock onto separate tracks on the sixteen track tape machine, and the chimes were cunningly timed to coincide. Originally the section included the sound of a cuckoo clock, but it destroyed the ambience of the piece and was removed. The 'clock section', spilling out of the speakers of the Floyd's quadraphonic sound system, became one of the highlights of the live shows on the *Dark Side Of The Moon* tour.

The Great Gig In The Sky

(WRIGHT)

One of the most extraordinary vocal performances ever captured on record, the improvized vocals of Clare Torry provide the perfect counterpoint to Rick's beautiful piano paean to the ever-present spectre of death. Initially the band felt the track didn't fit, though Wright's piano had a mournful grace that fitted the album's dynamic flow. Wright was also anxious to get a composing credit on the album. "It was to make sure that everyone got a little bit of the publishing," confirms Gilmour.

Originally written for the *Eclipse* show, this keyboard passage accompanied parodied readings from Ecclesiastes, included to illustrate the way in which religion might induce insanity, a theme that was dropped for fear of causing offence. The track was subsequently refocused to towards Wright's fear of dying in a plane crash. Wright was note perfect by the time the track was recorded, in one session at Abbey Road. "We decided we wanted that big classical piano sound, so we set up the Steinway in Studio 2 and went for it. He only needed a few takes and the sound you hear is exactly as it went to tape," says Parsons. "He was so good at playing it, we once played back the take he'd just done (in his headphones) instead of what he was actually playing, and he didn't notice the difference!"

Listening to playbacks, after the band had overdubbed powerful bass, drums, guitar and swirling Hammond organ, Roger decided something was missing - a wailing

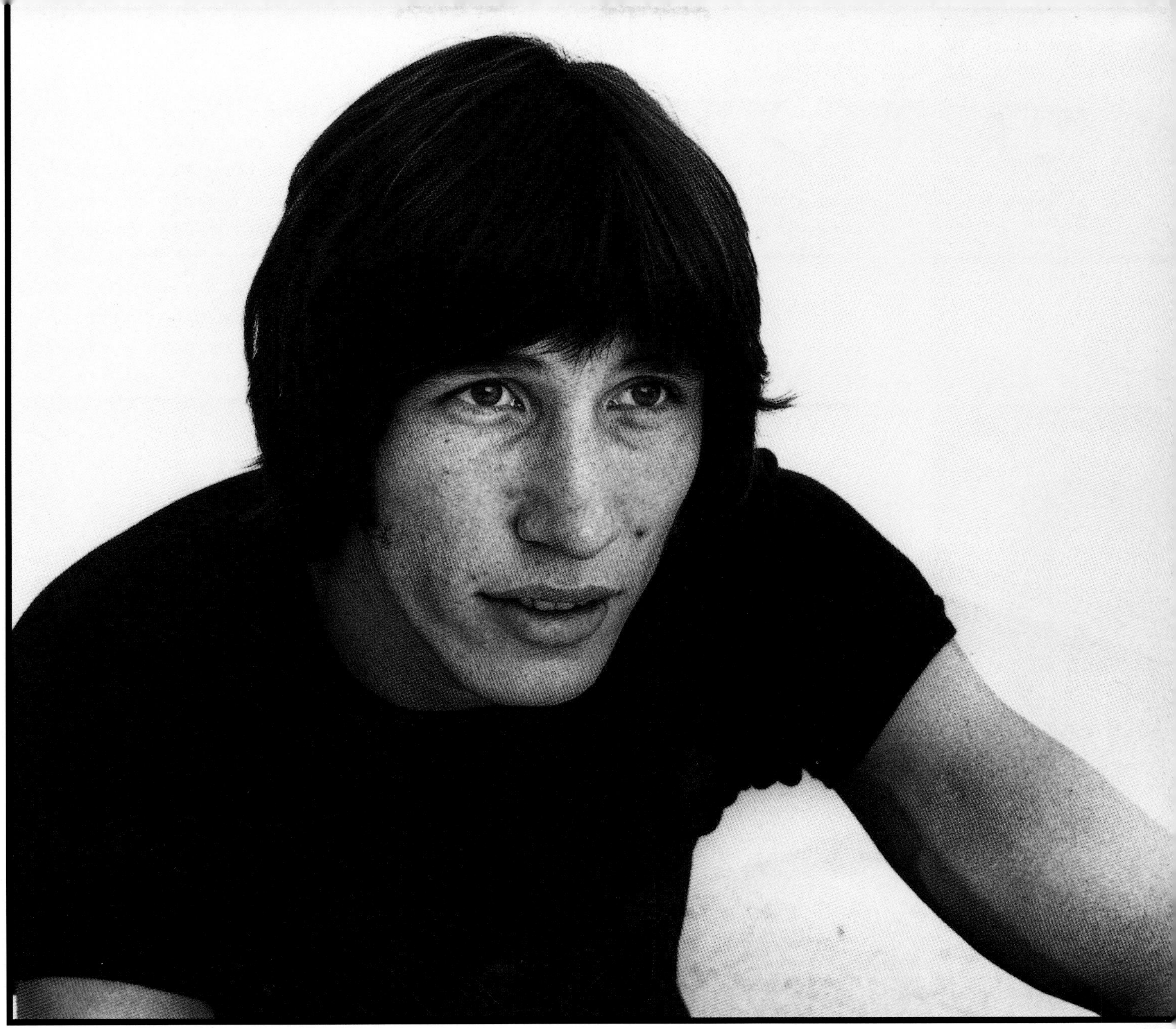

Waters, 28, "waiting for the start".

voice to express the anguish and ecstasy of life and death. Parsons had worked with Clare Torry, a modest session singer, on an album for the budget MFP label featuring MOR versions of rock favourites, and had been impressed with her vocals on a cover of The Doors' 'Light My Fire'. He suggested that she be brought in, to improvize in a similar way on Rick's track. "She had very vague direction from Roger, who flapped his hands up and down and brought her rising to a crescendo, or down to a soft pianissimo," remembers Parsons. "I think she found the whole thing quite intimidating actually. Here were these long-haired hippie types asking her to sing a song with no words, about death." After three takes, Parsons put a composite performance from the best sections onto one master track, and called the band in for a playback. "We were stunned," says Gilmour. "It was very different for Pink Floyd, quite jazzy in a way, but breathtaking."

Money

(WATERS)

When he began work on *Eclipse*, Waters knew there had to be a song dealing with money, and the way it can corrupt one's personal ideals. Once again his socialist principles come to the fore in this wry and ironic dismissal of wealth and its deleterious effects. It proved a great source of anguish to Waters, when they eventually took *Dark Side Of The Moon* on tour, that he was constantly confronted by people, Americans in particular, who believed that he'd been extolling the benefits of money to buy football teams, stay four-star and eat caviar.

These days, sounds are looped using samplers and computers. In the early 70s, it had to be done by recording the sound onto tape and physically making a loop to play on a standard tape machine. Depending on

MONEY

GILMOUR *lead vocals, guitars, tape effects*
MASON *drums, tape effects*
WRIGHT *wah wah Rhodes piano, vocals*
WATERS *Fender bass, tape effects*
DICK PARRY *saxophone*

the length of the 'sample', tape loops would vary in size and, in order to run at the correct speed would often have to be threaded around other objects between spools on the machine to create the correct tape tension. The opening cash register sequence of 'Money', assembled in the tricky 7/4 time signature, is a masterpiece of editing. "It was hilarious, a control room with tape machines and mike stands all over the place, with great huge loops of tape wandering all over the place, breaking . . . people treading on them," recalls Gilmour. "They were always going somewhere you didn't want them to."

The opening is compiled from the sound of tearing paper, looped cash registers, taken from a sound effects album, and the Floyd's recording of a bag of 50p coins being dropped. These were edited together to create the basic 'Money Loop' which the band then played along to in the absence of a metronome that could reproduce the unusual time signiature. Dick Parry, one of Dave Gilmour's friends from his pre-Floyd band, Jokers Wild, plays the sax break. A Top 10 hit in the US when it was released as a single, the effect 'Money' had on the Floyd audience was dramatic. "People were quiet when we played," said Gilmour during the US tour that followed the album's release. "You could hear a pin drop. But suddenly we were an arena act, the lyrics had become universally accepted, and people were shouting, singing along, demanding to hear 'Money'. Our music would never be the same, never as experimental. It's a shame in a way but you gain a lot and lose a little."

ANY COLOUR YOU LIKE

(INSTRUMENTAL)

GILMOUR *guitars, vocal noises*
WATERS *Fender bass*
MASON *drums*
WRIGHT *EMS Synthi-A, Hammond organ*

Us And Them

(WATERS, WRIGHT)

US AND THEM

GILMOUR *lead vocals, guitars*
WATERS *Fender bass, backing vocals*
MASON *drums*
WRIGHT *Hammond organ, Steinway piano, backing vocals*
DICK PARRY *saxophone*
DORIS TROY, LESLEY DUNCAN, LIZA STRIKE, BARRY ST JOHN *backing chorus*
ROGER THE HAT *spoken words*

Us And Them' dates from the *Zabriskie Point* sessions of 1969. Originally titled 'The Violent Sequence' it was intended as accompaniment to a scene in the film where baton-wielding police lay into a UCLA crowd. Michelangelo Antonioni rejected it as "too sad", and it remained shelved until the 'Eclipse' rehearsals in 1972. Roger drew on his Cambridge childhood to address the gulf between the haves and have-nots, specifically how 'developed' nations waste food and resources while people go hungry in other parts of the world. Waters's mother, Mary, was heavily involved in social issues, and the family home was often used as campaign HQ for various pressure groups. Roger would later acknowledge that his own problems with the vast wealth he'd amassed resulted from the discrepancy between the strong humanitarian values instilled in him by his mother and the ruthless motives of a big business like the music industry. "I was brought up on Friends Meeting Houses and British China Friendship Association and all that stuff, the people's struggle . . . ('Us And Them') is also about being in London at that time - there were already people living on the street. Are they on the streets because they're worthless, shifty, no good, useless, anti social ingrates? No, they're on the street because they can't cope. They're displaced and need looking after."

The extraordinarily long echoing repeats on 'Us And Them' were another pioneering Floyd effect. Using a one-inch 3M 8 track tape machine, the outputs of each head were fed back on themselves and across each individual track to create a very long repeat.

Any Colour You Like

(GILMOUR, MASON, WRIGHT)

Realising that *Dark Side Of The Moon* would be the band's most structured, song-oriented album yet, the Floyd decided that at least one track should hark back to their free-form instrumental past. Gilmour calls it, "Our excuse for a good old fashioned jam session. We used to do a lot of very long extended jamming on stage - interminably, some people thought, and probably truly - but we liked those jams." Originally labelled 'Dave's scat section' the final title came from long-time Floyd roadie Chris Adams. The phrase "you can have it in any colour you like" was his response to being asked to do something that was not entirely feasible or desirable. It was his way of saying, "You can make do with what you're given," and originates from Henry Ford's famous boast of the 20s that Ford cars were available in any colour you like, as long as it was black.

An early Ford: any colour you like as long as it's black.

Brain Damage

(WATERS)

The song that would become 'Brain Damage' was originally titled 'The Dark Side Of The Moon' and formed the original finale to the *Eclipse* suite. Written during the *Meddle* sessions, it's a thinly veiled reference to departed frontman Syd Barrett. One of Waters's first attempts to reflect on the events surrounding Syd's departure from the group, it was prompted by EMI's decision to release an album of oddments from the Floyd's early days, including 'Arnold Layne' and 'Paintbox', the budget-priced *Relics* compilation. The band, busy working on *Meddle*, had to review all their early material during the sessions, including unreleased Barrett gems such as 'Scream Thy Last Scream' and 'Vegetable Man'. Listening to the latter one evening, the band were unable to contain themselves and, in a rare display of communal amusement, ended up rolling on the studio floor in hysterics.

Although Syd was the trigger for the song, providing inspiration for the line "And if the band you're in starts playing different tunes, I'll see you on the dark side of the moon", Waters later gave the song a broader perspective. "It would be easy to say this song was influenced by what happened to Syd, but I guess it's more particularly about the real human living inside the outer being that the rest of the world sees. In other words, the lunatic is really us, here, that we're trying to keep in this box. An awful lot of us stop being able to respond to the child in us, because the adult takes over and holds sway of the controls, and we obey those instructions."

Eclipse

(WATERS)

The glorious climax to the album is based around the simple image of the tiny, dead, barren moon blocking out the huge life-force of the sun. Throughout the album, the images for good and evil, success and failure, sanity and insanity, are represented by the twin images of the sun and the moon. Through these images, Waters united the songs in the suite - hence the original title of 'Eclipse'. "There was no riddle. It's saying that all the good things in life are there for us to grasp, but that the influence of the dark forces in our natures prevents us from seizing them." Waters claims that the line "I'll see you on the dark side of the moon" acknowledges that all humans share these feelings but can conquer them by coming together, closing the album on a powerful, optimistic note. "When Doris Troy did her wailing on 'Eclipse', we knew it was the climactic ending we wanted. She did two passes and it was incredible. We knew we had the album in the bag." The album closes with the heart beat fading away and the voice of Jerry Driscoll musing, "There is no dark side of the moon, really. Matter of fact, it's all dark."

Eclipse: negativity winning out.

BRAIN DAMAGE

WATERS *lead and double tracked vocals, bass guitar*
GILMOUR *treated guitar, lap steel (slide) guitar*
MASON *percussion*
WRIGHT *Hammond organ, VCS-3*
DORIS TROY, LESLEY DUNCAN, LIZA STRIKE, BARRY ST JOHN *backing chorus*
ROGER THE HAT *spoken words*

ECLIPSE

WATERS *lead vocals, bass guitar*
GILMOUR *guitars, backing vocals*
MASON *drums, tape effects, backing vocals*
WRIGHT *Hammond organ, backing vocal*
DORIS TROY, LESLEY DUNCAN, LIZA STRIKE, BARRY ST JOHN *backing vocals*

Star of* DSOM*'s finale, Doris Troy.

RECORDED *6-9 January, 3-6 February, 3-12, 24-27 March 5-9 May, 2-3, 5 June 7-11, 14-19 July, 1975 at Abbey Road Studios*
PRODUCED BY *PINK FLOYD*
SLEEVE DESIGN AND PHOTOGRAPHY BY *HIPGNOSIS*
UK RELEASE *15 September, 1975*
CHART PLACING *Number 1 in the UK and the US*

Dark Side Of The Moon was undoubtedly the critical and commercial watershed in the Floyd's career. They would never make the same kind of music again, or play to the same kind of audiences. They had become a super-group, and audiences would no longer sit in rapt and silent attention as they listened to the band play. This rapid change of circumstances wasn't without its problems. The period immediately after the release of *Dark Side* is remembered by all concerned as the most arduous, exhausting and artistically vexatious in the group's history. The band themselves readily admit that they were all "mentally ill", by the end of 1974, exhausted and shell-shocked by their unexpected elevation to the status of rock deities. *Dark Side Of The Moon* was well on the way to selling its ten millionth copy (the album has, to date, sold nearly 27 million), and the Floyd's internal and personal relationships were in turmoil as a result. "It was fucking insane! All at once, every one of our ambitions was realised," recalls Waters. "When you're 15 you dream of a hip bachelor

Wish You Were Here

A tired and not altogether happy Pink Floyd in December 1974, still reeling from the incredible changes that the success of Dark Side Of The Moon *had brought to their lives. Both the physical and emotional exhaustion had left them artistically bankrupt. ' We were all mentally ill.' said Mason.*

pad, a pretty girlfriend, not getting up until the afternoon, being in a band and having a big hit. Suddenly you have the big hit and your ambitions just evaporate. We were millionaires, and whatever they say, money changes everything. It put us in a very curious and unpleasant limbo."

In an attempt to come to terms with the profound changes they had undergone, the band fragmented, early in 1974, and tried to rest. Rick Wright bought a yacht, Nick Mason invested in a country mansion and a fleet of vintage Ferraris, Gilmour went on extended vacation, while Roger Waters hid himself away in his North London house and attempted to overcome the profound feelings of emptiness and ennui that had taken hold during the *Dark Side* tour. Not only were his treasured socialist principles being sorely tested as the royalties mounted up, but his marriage to fellow socialist Judy Trim was on the rocks, partly due to their difficulty in producing offspring, and partly due to Waters's re-evaluation of exactly what it was he actually believed, when push came to shove. Mason's marriage to his beloved Lindy was also coming to an end. There was an air of general despondency around and, not for the first or last time, the band were on the verge of taking a prolonged sabbatical from the world of rock.

There had been an attempt to start work on another album. The ill fated *Household Objects* album was mooted in the autumn of 1973, and got as far as three tracks being recorded. Inspired by Waters's work with Ron Geesin back in 1968, when they had used the sounds of the body to make music on the soundtrack to Tony Garnett's film *The Body*, Waters had suggested doing an album that was made up entirely from the sounds of household objects. After three weeks of messing about with half filled milk bottles, scissors and cardboard boxes, the group abandoned the project.

It wasn't until the summer of the following year that they managed to raise enough enthusiasm to reconvene at a Kingsway rehearsal studio (it was dingy, but it was close to the station so all concerned could retire to their country seats without too much trouble). The original plan, cooked up during these rehearsals, was to make 'Shine On You Crazy Diamond' the first side of the album, 'Raving And Drooling' and 'You Gotta Be Crazy' the other.

EMI, meanwhile, and Capitol records in the US, were growing impatient, pressurising the band for a conceptual follow up and eagerly telephoning the band's manager Steve O'Rourke for some indication as to when the band would be returning to the studio. "The whole vibe around the band changed when the cash started to roll in," says Wright now. "Suddenly one was aware that Pink Floyd was becoming a product, and that most of our time from then on would be devoted to the business side of the group rather than playing."

It was a very different Pink Floyd who entered Abbey Road Studios during the first week of January, 1975. Curiously, the band sought sanctuary in the recording studio, because a recording project was at least preferable to dealing with their shattered lives on the outside of the Floyd bubble. Waters claims it was boredom that finally drove the band back into the studio to record. Having achieved all their goals, the band eventually reached the point where "there's still a need to go on, because you realise that where you've got to isn't where you thought it was. There was that feeling that somebody would eventually come up with something, an idea. The interesting thing is that when we finally did do an album, the album is actually about not coming up with anything, because it's about none of us really being there. At the beginning of the *Wish You Were Here* recording sessions, most of us didn't wish we were there at all, we wished we were somewhere else." This led to a now infamous soundbite from Waters who claimed that the album should have been called *Wish* We *Were Here* . . .

The sessions were a miserable affair, and, Pink Floyd being what they were, they went on for nine months, interspersed with gruelling US tours. Mason, in particular, seemed incapable of functioning as a drummer by this point. "(My) alarming despondency manifested itself in a complete, well, rigor mortis . . . I didn't quite have to be carried about, but I wasn't interested. I couldn't get myself to sort out the drumming, and . . . that, of course, drove everyone else even crazier."

There was a lot of sitting around with long faces and stoned eyelids at Abbey Road during the spring of 1975. Since the French tour of summer 1974, the plan for the next album had always been to simply put 'Shine On' on one side of the album, and the other new songs ('Raving And Drooling' and 'You Gotta Be Crazy') on the other. The band pressed on through the general ennui of the recording process, before things came to an inevitable impasse. Waters decided to take control of the album, and in a brilliant piece of lateral thinking, suggested dropping 'Raving And Drooling' and 'You Gotta Be Crazy' in favour of new songs that would echo the state of mind the band were in at the time. He convened a meeting, at which the band unburdened themselves about their state of mind and the reasons why the album was going so disastrously wrong. By the end of the meeting Wright and Mason understood that this was the perfect encapsulation of the experience the band were living through. Waters eventually suggested that these ideas should form the concept behind the album - absence. Only Gilmour dissented, adamant that they should record 'Raving And Drooling' and 'You Gotta Be Crazy', simply because they had rehearsed to the point where recording would be easy. In Waters's view, Gilmour never quite understood the concept behind *Wish You Were Here* - perhaps because he simply couldn't identify with the problems to the same extent as the others. He had found a new love, with the straight talking American, Ginger, and was happy with his lot in life. But Pink Floyd were a partnership, and when it came to voting on Waters's idea it was three against one. This change of course resulted in three new songs: 'Welcome To The Machine', 'Wish You Were Here' and 'Have A Cigar'.

However, the sessions became more tortured, as the band additionally subjected themselves to the gruelling hardship of two American tours. This made completing and mixing tracks extremely difficult. Waters admitted that by the time the second American tour was over he hadn't got an ounce of creative energy left for recording. "Those last couple of weeks were a real fucking struggle."

Despite the enormous hardship that surrounded the making of *Wish You Were Here*, the album proved to be an enduring Floyd classic. From the comfort of the 90s, even the remaining members of the band will grudgingly admit that it has become one of their favourites. "I particularly like that record," says Rick Wright. "In fact I think it's my favourite album we ever did. I like the feel of it - and in it. I feel the best material from the Floyd was definitely when two or three of us co-wrote something together. Afterwards we lost that. There wasn't that interplay of ideas between the band members."

The sleeve design was the most complex and symbolic artwork Hipgnosis would ever create for Pink Floyd. Storm Thorgerson spent weeks, while the band were on a gruelling US tour in April, scrutinising the lyrics and discussing the album's themes with Roger Waters, before coming up with his cover concept. This intensely researched overview gave the album an extremely powerful visual identity, characteristically surreal, but one which reinforced the ideas of absence and loss. Thorgerson says the most formative influence was the track 'Shine On You Crazy Diamond', in particular Gilmour's haunting four note guitar refrain, which seemed to encapsulate Syd's decline, and the more general themes of emptiness, deception and absence, so succinctly. The other tracks suggested the idea of the various psychological barriers and deceptions that people employ to escape showing real feeling.

The postcard included in the original vinyl packing was intended to be a 'Wish You Were Here'. Thorgerson designed a 'handshake' on the sticker, as much an empty gesture as a genuine greeting. The idea that the album should come wrapped inside a black plastic shrink wrap also tied in to the general theme of absence, the thinking being that the artwork itself should be absent. This idea came to Thorgerson in America when he noticed that Roxy Music's album *Country Life* came wrapped in green plastic, because the sleeve was deemed sexually suggestive. Despite the protestations of the US record company, who felt the band were being deliberately diffident, the black wrap sleeve won the unanimous approval of the band. The only indication that this was the new Pink Floyd album was the sticker on the front, of two robotic hands shaking. In the background of the sticker can be seen visual representations of the four elements of earth, air, fire, and water, which corresponded respectively to the astrological signs of the four artists. Waters the Virgo, Wright the Aquarius, Mason the Leo, and Gilmour the Piscean.

With the man diving into Lake Mono in California, Thorgerson wanted to create the impression of man diving without leaving a splash. The man concerned was a yoga expert, who performed a handstand in a metal bucket frame and had to hold his breath for minutes at a time so the ripples would die away. This process was undertaken sixty times before the right shot was taken. 'Have A Cigar' and 'Welcome To The Machine' eventually gave the album its cover concept of two figures shaking hands. Waters and Thorgerson agreed that the handshake itself was the ultimate empty gesture. It was a symbol of the record company executives, the kind of unctuous sharks who exploit the more vulnerable artiste. The man in flames was meant to be indicative both of the fear of exposing one's real feelings and of being 'burned'. In Waters's case the feeling was that the record industry itself had 'burned' both the band and Syd, in particular. Unfortunately when it came time to photograph the two men shaking hands, the wind caught the flames coming from the man's asbestos suit and blew them back into his face, severely burning his moustache. "We had, in fact, to get him to turn the other way and shake hands with his left hand, and then reverse the photo in the final print, which does give it a slightly strange quality. Art by misadventure," said Thorgerson. Perhaps the most striking image of all is what appears to be, at first glance, a red veil adrift in an avenue of larches. Look closely and you can just see the outline of a nude woman - another absentee.

The references on the back cover are more oblique. The besuited Pink Floyd 'salesman' laden with a suitcase covered in the stickers from *Dark Side Of The Moon*, who is "selling his soul in the desert", refers to a lyric in an unreleased Roger Waters song, 'Bitter Love'. The band had agreed to have their 1974 tour sponsored by Gini, the French soft drink company. The lyrics dealt with the idea of selling one's soul in the desert, the setting for the Gini adverts. To Waters, at least, sponsorship was akin to selling Pink Floyd and their music to 'The Man'.

Shine On You Crazy Diamond Part I

(WRIGHT, WATERS, GILMOUR)

SHINE ON YOU CRAZY DIAMOND PART I

WATERS *lead vocal, bass*
GILMOUR *guitars, bass, VCS-3*
WRIGHT *quadruple tracked VCS-3, EMS Synthi-A ARP synthesizer, Hammond organ, bass footpedals*
MASON *drums, tape effects*
DICK PARRY *saxophone*
VENETTA FIELDS
CARLENA WILLIAMS
backing vocals

This twenty six minute epic track forms the centrepiece of the *Wish You Were Here* album, and was arguably the Floyd's finest single achievement since founder member Syd Barrett's departure into schizophrenic exile nearly seven years earlier. Following the success of *Dark Side Of The Moon*, it became increasingly obvious to all concerned that Roger Waters had become the main architect of the Floyd's sound, and consequently the Pink Floyd bassist bore much of the pressure to produce a hit follow up album. It was he who came up with the album concepts, the lyrics and many of the basic melodies. Despite his writer's block, Waters was working around the general themes of alienation, fragmentation and insanity, with specific reference to the errant Syd Barrett.

The last any member of the Floyd heard, Syd was seen dressing in women's clothing and living in Chelsea Cloisters, a London apartment block which he had equipped with seven huge bubble TVs that he watched simultaneously, two large fridge freezers, several stringless guitars and no natural daylight. His own recording career had come to an ignominious halt with an aborted Abbey Road session at which Syd reputedly turned up with a manic stare in his eyes, clutching a guitar with no strings on it, which he later insisted on 'playing', despite the fact that it made no sound whatsoever! However, the royalties he was receiving from the repackaging of the early Floyd albums, released in the wake of the success of *Dark Side*, along with David Bowie's *Pinups* cover version of 'Arnold Layne', allowed him to lead a life of relative luxury. Increasingly eccentric, the one time Adonis-like star was refusing to wash, and left his flat rarely, except to drink Guinness at his local pub.

Waters drew on Syd's experience, as well as his own guilt over the way he and the rest of the band had treated Syd during the fragmentation of the original line up in 1968. The result was a mournful paean to the errant star. As Waters now acknowledged, "The Floyd couldn't have happened without Syd, yet it could never have progressed with Syd. I had to get as close to what I personally felt as I could. *Dark Side Of The Moon* was an album about the universal condition of insanity. *Wish You Were Here* was a personal album about me, about us, about Syd. I had a lot of difficult emotions to deal with over Syd, and 'Shine On' was the way I expressed them at the time."

The track itself was sketched out during summer of 1974, during rehearsals. The opening riff to 'Shine On' came from one of the interminable sessions when the band were looking for ideas, after Waters heard Dave Gilmour playing the track's signature - what became known by the band as 'Syd's Theme' - a mournful four note guitar refrain, on his Stratocaster. "I played it a few times, and I put some digital delay lines and other effects on it, and started playing again and it sort of pinged out and sounded nice and I said, 'Oh, that's really great.' Roger really got off on it, he got exactly the same from it as I was getting from it. I don't know quite how it happened, but those sort of things happen. That was like the start of . . . gave us the start for making the whole record." Gilmour's playing, as so often, provides an emotional anchor to a band in constant danger of becoming detached, cold and removed from their audience. On later albums this delicate balance would be lost.

The track was then fleshed out during a twenty date French tour. The infamous synth drones added in by Rick Wright, the sax break and finally the lyrics coalesced into the final version in June 1975. The characteristic synth wash that introduces the track was another great Floyd studio innovation. This was created using some very sophisticated studio trickery. Rick Wright's synths were layered, one on another on another, then assigned faders on the desk so each one controlled a cluster of tracks. The faders were controlled to give the impression of a synth orchestra, swirling underneath the track. These days, a sampler or a digital synth could easily deal with it, but in those days the only way was to repeatedly and laboriously double track until the sound was big enough.

Even the recording itself was beset by problems. Having spent four days laying down a drum and bass track, Waters decided it was listless and that it had to be redone over the next few days. Unfortunately nobody understood the desk properly and when the new track was eventually played back, the band found that the echo returns from the headphone mix had been routed on to on the main recording, and that the tracks were swamped in reverb. There was no way of saving it, so the band had to cut it a third time. None of this helped the atmosphere. Waters was dictating the direction, the pace and the mood. Inevitably, perhaps, this led to frustrations within the rest of the band, and the sessions for 'Shine On', sections of which were recorded separately over the first month at Abbey Road, and later segued by Waters and producer Alan Parsons, became very laboured. Wright, whose synthesizer washes form the moody droning backdrop to the track, sought refuge in cocaine, while Dave Gilmour directed his anger at Mason, who, he maintained, was simply not pulling his weight.

Mason was going through a personal crisis precipitated by a messy divorce and fuelled by his own cocaine habit. These failings, he now admits, manifested themselves in "a complete and utter rigor mortis. I was dead at the drum kit and it drove everyone crazy. Nothing got done. We'd go through endless takes and still it wasn't right. I have no fond memories of any of those sessions at all, especially 'Shine On'. It was so labour-intensive, and Roger was starting to demand that things be done his way in the studio. I was just sick of hearing his voice telling me to do it again, so I just withdrew." Waters himself claims that the band came very close to simply calling it a day during the recording of this twenty six minute epic. "We were there in body but our spirits were elsewhere. Ultimately I just submitted and decided that the album and particularly 'Shine On' should reflect precisely that feeling of listlessness and angst. It seemed that our own individual alienation and fragmentation was neatly dovetailing with the theme of Syd's breakdown."

The lyrics to 'Shine On' simultaneously celebrate Syd's insanity, while mourning his loss: "You reached for the secret too young/Black, black holes in the sun/Shine on you crazy diamond". This line, according Waters, was a direct reference to Syd's destructive LSD use, the experiments that, Waters feels, sent him spiralling into a mental limbo from which he will never emerge. "It was very strange. I don't know why I started writing those lyrics about Syd . . . I think because that phrase of Dave's was an extremely mournful kind of sound and it just . . . I haven't a clue

Gilmour's schoolfriend Dick Parry, who plays sax on **Shine On.**

. . . that sort of indefinable, inevitable melancholy."

Waters wanted the lyrics to get as close as possible to the feelings he was now having about Syd. Having dismissed Syd's condition back in 1968, Waters was beginning to understand at least some of the pain associated with Syd's descent into madness. "Syd's state could be seen as being symbolic of the general state of the group, i.e. very fragmented." Bound up in all of this was an inevitable sense of guilt at the way Syd's condition had been dealt with. It was Waters who had eventually plucked up enough courage back in 1968 to oust Syd from the band. Waters was an intensely ambitious man, who was determined to become successful. When that success eventually came, he began to realize at what cost. "I'm very sad about Syd; I wasn't for years," said Gilmour in an interview with Tommy Vance, "For years I suppose he was a threat because of all that bollocks written about him and us. Of course he was very important and the band would never have fucking started without him because he was writing all the material. It couldn't have happened without him, but on the other hand it couldn't have gone on with him . . . but he was merely a symbol for all the extremes of absence some people have to indulge in, because it's the only way they can cope with how fucking sad it is - modern life - to withdraw completely."

A final bizarre irony occurred at the final mixdown session for 'Shine On You Crazy Diamond' on 5 June, 1975. David Gilmour was celebrating his wedding to his American girlfriend, Ginger, at the studio, because the band were due to begin a US tour the next day. The couple decided to invite everyone down for a small party, after a few vocal overdubs had been performed by Waters in Studio 3. There was a frantic atmosphere in the studio as the tape shuttled backwards and forwards and the takes were perfected. Waters was behind the glass in the vocal booth, doing patch ups, dropping in for the odd line here and there that he felt needed redoing. John Leckie was in the control room, working the desk. "Roger was singing, checking the takes, behind the glass, and this fat bald-headed guy came in with a carrier bag, in an old white vinyl trenchcoat, with a toothbrush in his pocket. The tape stopped and Roger started pointing through the glass, at me? I thought maybe he didn't know that I was on the desk so I said, 'It's John Leckie, the engineer. I've taken over for a while.' And he said, 'No, who's the other bloke next to you?' I looked over and I couldn't believe it, there was Syd. I'd last seen him on the sessions for *Barrett* which I'd engineered, and here he was, this strange grinning person. I said, 'Hey Syd, how you doing?' and he just smiled. We didn't talk."

At first all present, including Nick Mason and original Floyd manager Peter Jenner, assumed this strangely attired visitor was an EMI 'whitecoat' employee or a press officer. As Jenner recalls, "I wandered into the control room, looked over at this slightly weird looking person and sat down next to Roger, who leaned over and said, 'Do you know who that guy is?' 'No,' I said. 'Isn't he a friend of yours?' 'Think,' said Roger. 'Think!' I looked, and suddenly it dawned on me. It was Syd! I looked round, and Roger had tears in his eyes. It was terribly sad. There was this great fat, bald, mad person who we used to know and who this song was all about sitting there yet quite obviously in another world."

Later, at the Gilmours' wedding reception down in the EMI canteen, Syd chatted with shocked ex-colleagues including Peter Jenner. "It was very weird, 'cause he kept brushing his teeth with this little toothbrush. I asked him what had happened, you know, what he'd been doing, and he just smiled. He was what I'd call barking mad . . . it was terribly distressing." Syd later explained his appearance to Jenner, by saying, "I've got a very large fridge and it has a lot of pork chops in it," before simply disappearing off into the night. The next day the Floyd flew to Cleveland for the start of their US tour. Although his presence still hovers like a spectre over the Floyd, none of the band have seen him again, to this day.

WELCOME TO THE MACHINE

WATERS *lead vocal, bass*
GILMOUR *lead vocal, guitars, bass, EMS Synthi-A*
WRIGHT *ARP synthesizer Hammond organ*
MASON *drums, timpani*
VENETTA FIELDS
CARLENA WILLIAM
backing vocals

Welcome To The Machine

(WATERS)

Once Roger Waters had decided that the album should be based on the themes of absence, and the band's own sorry predicament, the Floyd had to work on music and lyrics to fit the theme. The working title for this piece was 'The Machine Song', and the lyrics sought to express the way in which the music business chews up and spits out the vulnerable artists. The Floyd had always held the media and the record industry at arm's length, believing that the business was rather grubby, and run by crass sharks. It is also a comment on the media's way of elevating and destroying people seemingly at will. This led many journalists, especially the young turks at the NME, to accuse Waters of biting the hand that fed him.

When it came time to sing those lyrics, Waters found that he couldn't reach one of the high notes, so the tape was slowed to drop everything down a semitone and enable him to hit the right note when dropping in the problem line. The track ends with the sound of a

A world weary Floyd in 1975.

crowd, which, Waters felt, symbolised the kind of empty celebration that people routinely engage in: "To me that epitomises the lack of contact and real feelings between people."

Have A Cigar

(WATERS)

Many people accuse Roger Waters of having no sense of humour. 'Have A Cigar' is proof that, while extraordinarily dry, he was, at one time, in possession of a tidy line in laughs. This a semi-comical, but indubitably cynical, look at the world of rock 'n' roll clichés, as preached by A&R men, PRs and record company executives. The song was written after the final US tour of 1975. Taking 'Shine On' as a starting point, Waters decided to write a song that was to do with a person succumbing to the pressures of life in general and rock 'n' roll in particular. "We'd just come off an American tour when I wrote that, and I'd been exposed to all the boogaloo . . ." Unbelievably, the line "by the way, which one is Pink?" was a question the band were constantly being asked by interviewers who thought Pink Floyd was a real person.

Waters had written most of the words and the actual tune some months before it was recorded. Gilmour then added the prelude and coda to the vocal in the studio. The vocal on the track is taken, for the first and only time, by someone outside the Floyd. Waters's struggles to get to grips with the vocal on 'Shine On You Crazy Diamond' (which he had to sing line by line) had left his voice severely stressed and overworked. Gilmour didn't feel he could do the song justice, although his real reason for not singing it was the fact that he wholeheartedly disapproved of Waters's "whinging and whining" about the business. Gilmour shared none of the angst about the business that Waters did, and found his partner's obsession with loneliness, isolation and madness hard to fathom. Roy Harper, the Floyd's Harvest

HAVE A CIGAR

ROY HARPER *lead vocal*
WATERS *bass*
GILMOUR *guitars, bass, VCS-3*
WRIGHT *Fender Rhodes piano, ARP synthesizer, Hammond organ*
MASON *drums*
VENETTA FIELDS
CARLENA WILLIAMS
backing vocals

labelmate, was in Studio 3, recording his acclaimed *HQ* album at the time, and Waters decided that the uncompromising singer - who had inspired the Floyd to produce 'Echoes' - would be perfect for a song about the evils of the music business. Despite the end result being one of the best vocals on the album, Waters now feels that he should have done it himself, if only to ensure continuity.

Wish You Were Here

(WATERS, GILMOUR)

The busker's favourite, 'Wish You Were Here' was the first Waters song for which the lyrics were written long before the music. Post-Barrett Pink Floyd, and Waters in particular, had always left lyrics until the last possible minute, preferring the music itself to influence the mood and, often, the subject matter, too. Because of this, many of the lyrics were simple impressionistic words of little specific meaning. Waters was anxious to ensure his post-*Dark Side Of The Moon* songs were rooted in more specific issues. Beginning life as a series of scribbled couplets and assorted word doodles on a note pad, this track was one of those early attempts at lyrical realism.

Waters has suggested that the lyric was a Jekyll and Hyde affair, addressing the 'other half' of his own schizoid personality. On the one hand he felt he was a humanist, concerned with the welfare of others - the socialist in him, no doubt. On the other, he felt he was selfish, ambitious and self-congratulatory. He described this aspect of his personality to journalist Karl Dallas as the "grasping, avaricious, selfish little kid, who wants to get his hands on the sweets and have them all". The song oscillates between these two personae, Waters calling to the positive side of his character, saying, "How I wish you were here." It is also a mournful paean to Syd Barrett, who was most definitely not there. More especially, it was addressed to the band themselves, who, Waters observed, were not really there in spirit during the making of the album. The lyric was discarded while the band recorded 'Have A Cigar', then dusted down towards the end of the sessions. Gilmour added the guitar and gave the whole piece a wonderful elegiac mood.

Violin virtuoso Stephane Grappelli makes an

Roy Harper, a key Floyd influence.

Grappelli: Floyd session man at 67.

WISH YOU WERE HERE

WATERS *bass*
GILMOUR *lead vocal, guitars*
WRIGHT *Yamaha piano, Hammond organ*
MASON *drums*
DICK PARRY *saxophone*
VENETTA FIELDS, CARLENA WILLIAMS *backing vocals*
STEPHANE GRAPPELLI *violin*

uncredited appearance on the track, though you wouldn't necessarily know it. Grappelli and fellow violinist Yehudi Menhuin were downstairs in Studio 1 at Abbey Road, working on a Wagner album. Gilmour suggested "a bit of country fiddle playing" would provide the perfect elegiac counterpoint for the end of the track. The Floyd had met Grappelli's agent in the US and managed to score an introduction.

Originally, Grappelli and Menuhin contributed flourishes to the track, but Menuhin found improvizing beyond his classically schooled abilities. Grappelli, who had worked with gypsy guitar king Django Reinhardt in the 40s, was a natural. After negotiating a £300 fee, the violinist did three passes in the track's outro. Readers with access to ultra-sensitive acoustic listening devices can catch that violin solo as the wind effects enter the mix at the end of the track. The band decided not to credit Grappelli, because they thought he might become offended that his 'contribution' had been put so low in the mix. "We thought he might think we were taking the piss," said Gilmour.

The track starts with the sound of a transistor radio being retuned, before the opening strains of Gilmour's acoustic guitar are 'found' on the airwaves, segueing into the track proper. 'The Radio Section' was actually recorded on a car radio, with a microphone pointed at the speaker in the dashboard. In their combing of the frequency bands, the band caught a snatch of Tchaikovsky's *Fourth Symphony* in the opening radio sequence. At live gigs, the band would often use a real radio, and, for the segue, EQ Gilmour's guitar to sound like it was coming from a cheap transistor radio. At one memorable London show, Capital Radio broadcast the opening moments of the track from its studios in Euston to the venue, Earl's Court, where it was picked up and rebroadcast over the PA.

Shine On You Crazy Diamond Part 2

(WRIGHT, WATERS, GILMOUR)

The roaring wind outro of 'Wish You Were Here' segues into the final instrumental reprise of 'Shine On'. Dave's lap steel guitar delivers two choruses of portamento slide over the new 12/8 shuffle feel, moving into the refrain of 'Syd's Theme' and a funky jam in G minor. The final section is a consciously optimistic major chord progression, written by Rick Wright, his last solo Floyd composition. It was created using the Moog synth pedals, and eventually fades into the album's opening theme, bringing proceedings full circle.

SHINE ON YOU CRAZY DIAMOND PART 2

(INSTRUMENTAL)

WATERS *bass*
GILMOUR *guitars, lap steel guitar, bass, VCS-3*
WRIGHT *EMS Synthi-A, ARP synthesizer, Hammond organ, Moog bass footpedals*
MASON *drums*

Animals

1977

RECORDED *March-December 1976 at Britannia Row Studios Islington, London*
RELEASED *23 January, 1977*
PRODUCED BY *PINK FLOYD*
SLEEVE DESIGN BY *ROGER WATERS, ORGANIZED BY STORM THORGERSON AND AUBREY POWELL*
GRAPHICS BY *NICK MASON*
CHART PLACING *Number 2 in the UK; Number 3 in the US*

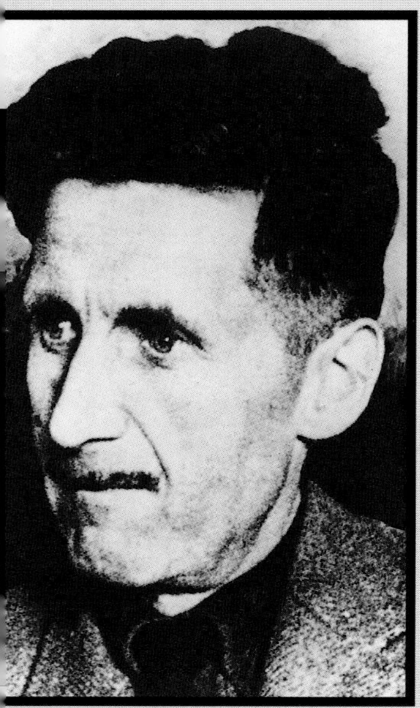

George Orwell.

Battersea Power station, Gilbert Scott's overpowering brick edifice on the south side of the River Thames provided Waters with the perfect symbol of power and the quest for success. 'It has four very phallic towers.' he said. It is the most iconic of all the Floyd's covers.

At a time when the pop world, in the UK at least, was in the first pensive throes of a full scale musical revolution - Punk - Pink Floyd entered their most introspective and, some would argue, least creative period. By 1977, Johnny Rotten had already scrawled the manifesto of the new movement on a Pink Floyd T-shirt, when he wrote the words 'I hate' over the Floyd logo. While most music-buying members of the public still enjoyed the music of the Floyd, to the music press they were no longer hip, and some considered them the very enemy of rock 'n' roll; anachronistic, flabby and indulgent.

The Floyd themselves were in no condition to fight back. They spent most of 1976 out of the spotlight, recovering from the previous four years of stadium overkill, at work in Britannia Row studios in Islington, North London. They had ploughed nearly half a million pounds into equipping a state of the art 48 track studio with the latest equipment, and were anxious to road test it - if only because it was a tax loophole for the millions that were accruing from the release of the multi-million selling *Dark Side Of The Moon* and *Wish You Were Here*. The sessions were surprisingly cordial, and although Waters was dominating the group, Gilmour was tired, and happy to let Waters take control, despite being frustrated by the situation.

As the band moved further and further from *Dark Side Of The Moon*, so Waters's dominance over the group grew. Such was the success of his lyrical concept that, without anyone else in the band who could turn their hand to decent lyrics, they came to rely on him for ideas and inspiration. In Waters himself, a profound shift was taking place that would set the agenda for the rest of his career, and *Animals* chronicles the switch from vague lyrics to those that address specific themes. "I was trying to push the band into more specific areas of subject matter, always trying to be more direct. Visually, I was trying to get away from the blobs . . . there isn't much left for you to interpret."

When recording began there was no concept, and just three sections of music - all of them discarded oddments from the previous five years. It was only half way through the recording process that Waters conceived that the whole lot could be knitted together using pigs, dogs and sheep as allegorical parallels for the people he observed in society.

"All animals are equal, but some are more equal than others," a line from George Orwell's allegorical parody of socialism *Animal Farm*, quoted in the songbook of the album, provides the thematic frame of reference for the lyrics. In Waters's anthropomorphic socio-political redrawing of the world, you are either a dog, a pig or a sheep. Dogs are the astute 'corporate compromisers', the cunning and aggressive predators who run in packs, and who are hell bent on survival even if it means devouring others to do it. The pigs are the clever, tyrannical moralists, born leaders

motivated by greed for power, who, despite their fear of the unknown, often ascend to positions of high office in order to impose their world view on others - the sheep. They often shield a personality that is neurotic, and seek refuge in the darker side of life. The sheep are the passive followers, the docile innocents - representing, in short, the common man, there to be exploited by the dogs and pigs. They remain exploited until they get together and eventually rise up against their oppressors, only to be pacified and exploited all over again. It's a savage humanism, made all the more powerful by being represented in a series of crude animal caricatures.

The album's lack of focus, the difficulties in recording it and, some would argue, its obvious lyrical concept masked a more general malaise within the band, who felt they no longer had any reason to keep going. For Rick Wright, *Animals* marked the beginning of a slow but perhaps inevitable decline in the unity of the band, and of the move towards Pink Floyd as a vehicle for Waters's aspirations. "That's when it was beginning, where Roger wanted to do everything. There are certain bits of music that I quite like, but it's not my favourite album of the Floyd." Wright himself had hit a creative block that was to last almost a decade, with his marriage and his confidence in tatters.

Waters, on the other hand, talking with journalist Miles on the album's release, claimed the reverse. "I think we've been pretty close to breaking up for years. I'm glad we didn't, because I like the album, and look forward to going out and playing it."

This is the first album where the music clearly plays a secondary role to Waters's lyrics, and is almost reduced to the status of a vehicle for his ideas. However, despite the lack of musical focus, the album did prove to be something of a landmark in the Floyd's career, if only for its superb Hipgnosis cover. The most iconic of all the Floyd album covers, *Animals* transformed Battersea Power Station, Gilbert Scott's vast chimney-dominated edifice, into one of the most recognizable landmarks on Earth. Then, the power station was still in use, though at the end of its working life, and it was still surrounded by train tracks, coal heaps and wreaths of smoke from the furnaces. In true Floyd fashion, there is little obvious link between the power station and the themes on the album. Waters chose it, he claimed, because it was dark and Orwellian (this time, *1984*) and had four extremely phallic towers, "And the idea of power I find rather appealing in a strange way."

Waters had the idea of the inflatable pig over the power station, as a symbol of greed and power, but he wanted the sleeve to be done without photo-trickery. An inflatable pig was commissioned from a firm in Germany, and delivered in time for the photo shoot. When the day dawned, it was perfect. The sky was bruised and dramatic, reminding Storm Thorgerson of "Turner and Constable". The pig was inflated, but it took so long that attempts to launch it were dropped that day. Forty photographers from the world's music media remained idle, as did the marksman, with his rifle, hired to shoot down the pig if it escaped its mooring ropes and sailed off into the skies. On the second day, he was dismissed on grounds of cost, and the inflated pig was launched into the air, secured by guy-ropes in between the towers. As the assembled representatives of the world's music press snapped away, a violent gust of wind broke the ropes, and it lurched off into the sky. There was no time to get the longed-for photo for use on the cover. With no marksman there to shoot it down, the pig sailed away unimpeded across South London.

The episode then took on comedic proportions as the pig ascended into the flight paths of incoming jets landing at London's Heathrow Airport, causing one Qantas pilot to report to air traffic control at West Drayton that he had just been buzzed by a giant inflatable pink pig. Legend has it that he was breathalysed upon landing. The Civil Aviation Authority finally lost radar contact with the pig over Kent, where it was flying at a height of 18,000 feet and heading east towards Germany, where it was made. However, the pig finally lost power and came to earth in a field. Floyd roadies rescued it that night, returned it to London, mended the punctures and got it ready for the photo shoot the next day. Ironically, despite all the efforts to revive the pig, the shots that Thorgerson and co. took were not considered striking enough, and the pig was stripped into the final artwork from a shot which had been taken on the first day.

Pigs On The Wing (Part One)

(WATERS)

PIGS ON THE WING (PART ONE)

WATERS *acoustic guitar, double tracked vocals*
RECORDED *November 1976, Britannia Row Studios, Islington*

The album begins and ends with this fragile acoustic love song written by Waters to his new wife, Carolyne Christie (niece of the Marquis of Zetland and former secretary to producer Bob Ezrin). In between the first verse, which opens the album, and the last verse, which closes it, Pink Floyd sandwiched a concept album. Waters is quoted as saying that without this track to provide an optimistic prelude and coda, the

Replica pigs were used to promote the* In The Flesh *tour.

album would have been one long "scream of rage".

Starkly beautiful, this is perhaps the closest thing to a conventional love song Pink Floyd ever recorded. Carolyne seemed to understand the thirtysomething Waters's persistent existential angst better than anyone, and appeared able to deal with the pressures of being the partner of one of Rock's richest but most anxiety-prone men by providing him with a humorous foil. Peter Jenner claims that Carolyne provided Waters with an agile mind to argue with and against. "Roger was very good with words, and you had to be skilled in semantics to beat him in an argument. Poor Syd didn't have that skill, and neither did any of the others for that matter. I think he was looking for someone to stand up to him all along."

The track was written towards the end of the sessions, based on an idea that Waters had demoed at home some three months earlier. The theme deals with Waters's feeling that he has found someone able to prevent him from being consumed by the machinations of the dogs, the pigs and the bleatings of the sheep. Certainly, after the problems surrounding the making of *Wish You Were Here* and the fall-out from the enormous success of *Dark Side Of The Moon*, Carolyne made Waters happier both about himself and about his deeply held socialist principles, which he felt he had betrayed once the band had hit the big time. It was Carolyne who, in Waters's view, had prevented him from becoming one of the pigs himself! According to his fellow band members, he became a lot easier to work with.

The third line of the song came from the song 'Raving And Drooling', itself the forerunner of the track 'Sheep'. Waters took the title from the stock British phrase for an event that is impossible, preposterous or destined never to take place, "and pigs might fly".

Dogs

(GILMOUR, WATERS)

'Dogs' has its origins in the track 'You Got To Be Crazy' performed by Pink Floyd live during July and August of 1974, as part of the first half of the *Dark Side Of The Moon* show. The lyrics and structure of this 18 minute epic are almost identical to the ones that eventually ended up on 'Dogs', the third variety of animal in Water's anthropomorphic triptych of beasts. Lyrically, 'Dogs' is a vitriolic depiction of the kind of people who are cutthroat mercenary, and to whom everyone is a potential victim; they are out to get whatever they want, anthropomorphic yuppies-in-the-making. Eventually, having clawed their way to the top, they end up dying of cancer or dragged down by the weight they used to need to throw around.

The words "dragged down by the stone" are captured on a tape loop and repeated until they decay and become just a dog-like howl. The stone is used by Waters to help him make the point that this kind of mercenary behaviour serves no end, because ultimately you die, and all you have to show for life is the knowledge of having shafted people to get what you have got. The stone is an image that has occurred many times in Waters's writings, a symbol of the negativity that ultimately gets

DOGS

WATERS *bass, lead vocals (verses 5,6,7), Vocoder, tape effects*
GILMOUR *Ovation acoustic guitar, electric guitar, double-tracked lead vocals (verses 1,2,3,4)*
WRIGHT *Hammond organ Fender-Rhodes piano Yamaha piano, ARP String Machine synthesizer, backing vocals*
MASON *drums, percussion, tape effects*
RECORDED *March-December 1976 Britannia Row Studios, Islington*

Gilmour, Waters and Wright, greatly changed by the enormity of their early 70s successes, pictured during the* In The Flesh *tour.

in the way of our enjoyment of life and our spiritual fulfilment. It's possible that the last section of the lyric was inspired by Allen Ginsberg's *Howl*, in which each line begins with the word 'who'.

The music itself originated from a demoed chord sequence that Dave Gilmour had recorded, at home in Essex on his 8 track set up, and then brought into the rehearsal studio during pre-production for *Wish You Were Here*. This was discarded by Waters, who could not fit a lyric to it at the time. Now, with the band at a loss for new material, these old ideas were dusted down. Once ensconced in their own studio, Britannia Row, where they were not under the usual time constraints, the band worked on the song. Despite the fact that they were still getting to grips with the new studio when the original parts were recorded, Gilmour delivers some of his most accomplished solo guitar, and, to this day, he rates it as one of his greatest, most evocative lead guitar parts.

The solo is doubled, and was the result of two passes Gilmour did on the track. Unfortunately, Waters, unfamiliar with the exact configuration of the new studio, left the tape machine in 'record' mode when Gilmour came to do his second pass at the solo, and the original take was accidentally wiped. Gilmour maintains that the version on the final album, though good, never quite managed to eclipse the transcendent original. The solo was Gilmour's attempt to recreate the snapping and gnashing of a dog, and was a combination of the two remaining passes he did.

The strange sounds of the dog barking, in the middle section, were achieved using a Vocoder, a device that creates synthesised chords from a single sound source such as a voice. A tape recording of a barking dog was processed through the Vocoder, then amplified through a Leslie rotating speaker.

PIGS (THREE DIFFERENT ONES)

WATERS *bass, double-tracked lead vocal*
GILMOUR *guitar*
WRIGHT *Hammond organ, ARP synthesizer*
MASON *drums*

RECORDED *April-May 1976, at Britannia Row Studios, Islington*

Pigs (Three Different Ones)

(WATERS)

Waters saw the pigs as the people in society who seek to persuade us all that they have the answers, and know what is best for those of us who do not. The lyric makes it plain that these people are frightened 'charades', whose feelings of moral superiority belie their own deep-seated fear of life.

Each verse describes a different 'Pig'. The first is the well heeled 'Business Pig', who lies, cheats and deceives his way to the top. In the second verse we meet the 'Bus Stop Ratbag', based on observation of a sour faced

Mary Whitehouse, a strident campaigner for smut-free TV and a media free of sex, violence and bad language.

'Sheep' parodies the 23rd Psalm.

woman Waters had seen at the bus stop on Islington High Street, near Britannia Row, though some claim that this is an early reference to Margaret Thatcher, who was then making her way towards high office in the Conservative Party. Waters would later confess that the lyric had taken precisely that meaning during the Thatcher years, when he sang the song live on the *Radio KAOS* tour in 1987.

Only in the third verse does Waters become explicit. With genuine bile, he sings of the houseproud town mouse called Whitehouse. This refers to the censorious Mary Whitehouse, the then head of the National Viewers and Listeners Association, and one of the most ardent campaigners for censorship of radio and television in Britain. Waters characterizes her as a frustrated busybody spinster, accusing her of "trying to keep our feelings off the street" and of being "all tight lips and cold feet". Waters had worked on the song lyric for some six months, continually discarding the verse that mentioned Mary Whitehouse, for fear that it was too specific even for his new, less equivocal approach to lyric writing. Whitehouse had denounced the Floyd, back in 1967, along with a great number of others, as demonic advocates of LSD, free sex and hedonism of the worst kind. Eventually, Waters was driven to include her, by her continued appearance in the newspapers and on television during 1976, in particular, when she made vociferous objections to Ken Russell's *Lisztomania* film. "She doesn't really merit the attention but . . . she is really a terribly frightened woman, isn't she?" said Waters at the time. "Why does she make such a fuss about everything if she isn't motivated by fear? She's frightened that we're all being perverted."

The middle instrumental section includes the sound of Gilmour using a voice box to give his guitar the disturbing sound of a whining pig. This device (made famous by Peter Frampton, on his *Comes Alive* album of 1975) involved the player feeding a plastic tube into the mouth, which could then be used to shape the equalisation of the sound, allowing the guitar to 'speak'.

Sheep

(WATERS)

During the French tour of July and August 1974, and the British winter tour later that same year, the Floyd played a song set that consisted of three new songs in the first half, followed by *Dark Side Of The Moon* in the second half, and an encore of 'Echoes'. The new songs were 'Shine On You Crazy Diamond' (which, of course, appeared on *Wish You Were*

SHEEP

WATERS *bass, vocal*
GILMOUR *guitar*
WRIGHT *Fender-Rhodes piano Hammond organ*
MASON *drums*
RECORDED *April, May and July 1976 at Britannia Row Studios Islington, London*

Here), 'Raving And Drooling', and 'You Gotta Be Crazy'. Waters had written 'Raving And Drooling' at home, specifically for the tour, on which, he felt, the band needed to play some new material.

At performances of 'Raving And Drooling' on the 1974 British winter tour, a tape was used, cut into sections and randomly reassembled, of BBC Radio 2 disc jockey Jimmy Young, to represent Waters's idea of a man who was clearly raving and drooling (i.e. insane). For a while, thanks to the intro tape, the track was renamed yet again as 'I Fell On His Neck With a Scream', a line from the second verse.

In its final form, with lyrics re-written, 'Sheep' can almost be seen as a mini-*Animal Farm*, in which the exploited masses, grazing peacefully away on their way to the slaughterhouse, gather together, achieve consciousness and then rebel.

This idea is echoed in the bizarre parody of the 23rd Psalm from the instrumental middle section of 'Sheep'. This of course had its precedent in the section of the *Eclipse* show which parodied Ecclesiastes in the same way. That had been left out for fear of upsetting rabid right wing fundamentalists in the US. This time, the band had no such fears. In fact they were some of the very people the album sought to parody! Originally this bastardized Biblical staple was performed by Nick Mason, though on the album it was performed by an anonymous Floyd roadie and is rendered almost indecipherable by the trusty Vocoder. It begins benignly enough:

> The Lord is my shepherd, I shall not want
> He makes me down to lie
> Through pastures green he leadeth me the
> silent waters by
> With bright knives he releaseth my soul
> He maketh me to hang on hooks in high places
> He converteth me to lamb cutlets
> For lo, he hath great power, and great hunger.
> When cometh the day we lowly ones
> Through quiet reflection, and great dedication
> Master the art of karate
> Lo, we shall rise up
> And then we'll make the bugger's eyes water

On Waters's distopian 'Animal Farm' the sheep eventually revolt, killing the dogs. Waters based his observations of the "revolting sheep" on the Notting Hill riots of the early 60s, when inhabitants of the West London neighbourhood, mainly West Indians, rioted over race policy in Britain. A life-long socialist and an acute observer of social trends and undercurrents, Waters had been thrown into a questioning of his own political beliefs during the two years since *Dark Side* had wrought such an extraordinary change in his own life. 'Sheep' was in effect a comment on what might happen socially, and was based on the growing sense that people would revolt against the conditions, both social and physical, in which they found themselves. By the late 80s, Waters claimed that the lyrics were almost a prophesy of the civil unrest that would upset Britain during the mid-80s.

"Sheep was my sense of what was to come down in England, and it did last summer with the riots in England, in Brixton and Toxteth, . . . and it will happen again. It will always happen. There are too many of us in the world and we treat each other badly. We get obsessed with things, and there aren't enough of things, products, to go round. If we're persuaded it's important to have them, that we're nothing without them, and there aren't enough of them to go round, the people without them are going to get angry. Content and discontent follow very closely the rise and fall on the graph of world recession and expansion."

Gilmour nearly revived 'Sheep' for the 1987 comeback tour, but felt he couldn't recapture the venom which Waters had infused into the vocals. He has been threatening to revive it ever since,

Pigs On The Wing (Part Two)

(WATERS)

The second verse of the love song that opens the album, Waters intended this to be the upbeat coda to what had, by his own admission, been a very downbeat album. He was acutely aware that the length of the pieces and the dense, relentless cynicism of the album as a whole might lead to accusations that the Floyd had become unduly maudlin. The lyric was simple and direct, founded in Waters's love for his new wife Carolyne. If you find someone who cares for you, and you care for in return, then the pigs, the sheep and the dogs can't drag you down, or overwhelm you. Throughout the album, Waters evokes the image of the heavy stone as a symbol of the negativity, bitterness, deceit and corruption that will "drag you down" if you let it. In an

PIGS ON THE WING (PART TWO)

WATERS *Ovation acoustic guitar, double tracked vocals*

Flying pig : a live show highlight.

interview with journalist Karl Dallas, Waters explained that the first verse poses the simple question, "Where would I be without you?" and the second verse says, "In the face of all this other shit - confusion, sidetracks, difficulties - you care, and that makes it possible to survive."

Animals was also issued on 8-track cartridge tape format in 1977. 8-tracks, when they ended, automatically started over again. Waters decided that a special bridging section of guitar motifs from the album should be recorded for the cartridge version, creating a continuous version of the album that could, in theory, go on forever! Guitarist Snowy White, who worked with the band as a second guitarist on the 1977 *In The Flesh* tour, recorded a short solo that linked the two verses of 'Pigs On The Wing', providing an additional 48 seconds of music.

The Wall

1979

RECORDED *April-November 1979, at Britannia Row, Super Bear, Miravel, France, CBS, New York (orchestral sections), Producer's Workshop, Los Angeles*
PRODUCED BY *BOB EZRIN DAVID GILMOUR AND ROGER WATERS*
CO-PRODUCED AND ENGINEERED BY *JAMES GUTHRIE*
SLEEVE DESIGN BY *GERALD SCARFE AND ROGER WATERS*
BACKING VOCALS BY *BRUCE JOHNSTON, TONI TENILLE, JOE CHEMAY, JOHN JOYCE, STAN FARBER, JIM HAAS AND (ON 'ANOTHER BRICK IN THE WALL, PART 2') ISLINGTON GREEN SCHOOL FOURTH FORM MUSIC CLASS*
ORCHESTRA ARRANGED BY *MICHAEL KAMEN AND BOB EZRIN*
RELEASED *30 November, 1979*
CHART PLACING *Number 3 in the UK; Number 1 in the US*

Following the eventful 1977 *In The Flesh* tour, the band fragmented. Gilmour and Wright began work on solo albums (for tax reasons more than artistic necessity), while Roger Waters retired to his Islington townhouse to begin work on two related song cycles. The first went under the title of *Bricks In The Wall*, the second a related clutch of songs based on a dream, called *The Pros And Cons Of Hitch Hiking*. After completing ninety-minute demo tapes for both concepts - projected double albums - Waters summoned the other band members together for a pre-production meeting in July 1978, played them both tapes and asked them which was to be the next Pink Floyd album. Gilmour took the tape away, and two days later returned with his verdict: *Bricks In The Wall* won it. "I couldn't listen to it. It was too depressing, and too boring in lots of places. But I liked the basic idea." Though Gilmour felt the piece was "musically weak", he conceded that it was conceptually and lyrically interesting, and had a "universality" that *The Pros And Cons Of Hitch Hiking*, a very personal exploration of Waters's psyche, did not.

Conceptually, *The Wall* has its origins in the extraordinary 1977 Pink Floyd world tour, *In The Flesh*. Despite the enormous success of *Dark Side of The Moon* and *Wish You Were Here*, this was the first time Pink Floyd played a full blown 'stadium tour', performing at the largest venues on Earth, often to more than 100,000 fans at a time. Though financially rewarding (it boosted the Floyd into the top five grossing acts of that year), it was a disastrous period for the band. Waters, in particular, was beginning to feel isolated and dislocated by the stadium experience, his fractured mental state giving rise to feelings of hatred for his audience. Those travelling with the Floyd entourage noticed a marked change in his behaviour, as the strain of the gruelling tour took its toll. They had, after all, seen it before with Syd Barrett who, though his isolation

Inset: ***Rick Wright***

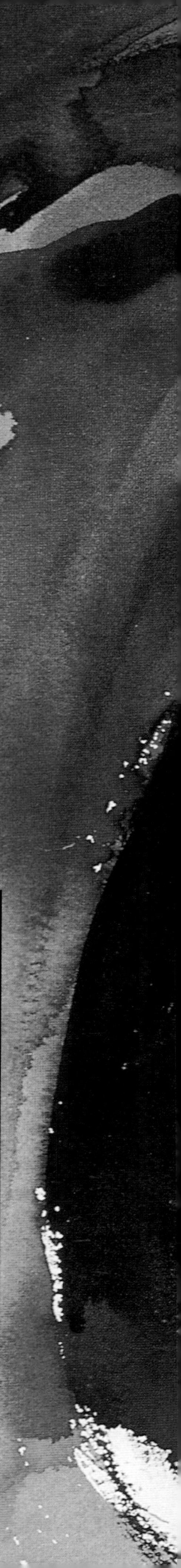

The Wall: ***Scarfe's original artwork.***

AN ALAN PARKER FILM
PINK FLOYD
THE WALL

Syd Barrett in 1978.

came primarily from drugs, was not helped by the incredible pressures the audience placed on the band. In a renactment of the events that had surrounded Barrett's slide into schizophrenic exile, Waters was having difficulty communicating with his fellow band members, and it got to the point where he would fly to the venues in a chartered helicopter while the rest of the band travelled together in a humble stretch limousine.

By the end of the sixty date tour, Waters had begun to see his audience as sheep: dumb, stupid people, ripe for exploitation at the hands of a touring leviathan like the Floyd. He increasingly saw himself as a dictator, a despot, and the band as fascistic. The denouement came one night in Montreal, in front of 90,000 fans, when a cracked and exhausted Waters picked on a member of the audience who he believed was trying to provoke the band, beckoned him to the front of the stage and spat in his eye. Waters, horrified by his own behaviour, began, from that moment, to conceive of a physical barrier between himself and the audience, an audience who misunderstod him and his music. Initially he envisaged a black polystyrene wall, but as he worked at home in London, the piece gained a wider remit.

Waters had been contemplating various ideas for a film as early as 1974, and *The Wall* was simultaneously conceived as a stage show, an album and a film. The metaphor of the wall grew in sophistication, and expanded naturally to include the personal barriers that people erect around themselves as protection from all kinds of hurt, and the walls society erects against freedom of expression. But as he worked on the narrative, the story became much more personal, as Waters developed the story of alienation into an autobiographical composite picture of Syd Barrett and his own recent experience, binding it all up in a narrative about a rock star called Pink, who is teetering on the brink of a breakdown. Many expressions of his own pain and angst went into it, such as the loss of his father in World War Two, his experiences in the oppressive school regime, and an unfaithful wife - each painful experience becoming another 'brick' in Pink's wall. The result, after six months' intensive work, was Roger Waters's, and Pink Floyd's, most conceptually complex work to date.

Unlike earlier albums where many of the ideas were the result of studio experiments and jams, everything on *The Wall* is scripted precisely. The architecture student had finally constructed an edifice of epic proportions. "I always maintain that if he hadn't made it in the rock world, Roger would have beeen a famous architect by now," maintains Peter Jenner.

Work began on editing the lyrics and music during October 1978, though recording didn't start until April 1979. Gilmour immediately saw the need for the album to be fleshed out, to add a certain degree of musicality to it. Waters was especially insistent that his lyrical ideas didn't get subsumed by the music, as they had been on *Wish You Were Here* and, to a lesser extent, on *Animals*. This naturally led him into conflict with Gilmour, who was keen to ensure that the album was at least as much his as Waters's. To help mediate between the two, producer Bob Ezrin was called in. His presence proved vital in ensuring that the right creative balance was achieved between the two estranged band members. Ezrin, forceful, and able to stand up to Waters, proved to be the perfect foil for him, capable of demanding that changes be made to the lyrics. He also served as a very effective mediator between Gilmour and Waters, who by this time found it difficult being in the same room together.

Ezrin and Gilmour took the demo tape and immediately sorted the strong material from all the weak chaff, Gilmour working on the music while Ezrin honed the storyline. In one all-night session he rewrote the record, taking Waters's songs and rearranging their order until he had a forty page book that represented the entire album. One of the most important changes he made was to excise all the date and place references that Waters had included, autobiographically, including the age of the main character Pink who, coincidentally, was the same age as Waters himself! "Kids don't want to know about old rock stars," said Ezrin at the time. "I insisted we make the record more accessible, more universal." Waters was then sent away to do rewrites, and the project began to take off.

Ezrin's contribution also strayed into the writing of the music. With Rick Wright in creative limbo, and only sporadically present at the sessions, Ezrin stepped in on keyboards and also helped Nick Mason to get to grips with the drum scores. Mason was feeling less than enthusiastic about the project and found it increasingly difficult to meet the rigorous technical standards demanded by Waters during the recording. He played to a drum machine click track on most tracks, and the final drum track was usually a compilation of all the best parts of the numerous takes he would have to do in an effort to get it right.

After recording at Britannia Row Studios for some months, operations were moved, for tax reasons, to Miravel, France. The Floyd's investment company Norton Warburg had suffered a total collapse, taking the band's investments down with them.

Effectively broke, and facing crippling tax bills from the Inland Revenue, Gilmour and Waters decamped, with Ezrin, leaving engineer Nick Griffiths at Britannia Row to supervise the recording of sound effects.

In The Flesh?

(WATERS)

The title and the inspiration for the opening track on *The Wall* came from the Floyd's 1977 *In The Flesh* tour. An uncharacteristically heavy piece of rock, Waters intended the track as a self-parody of what he believed the Floyd had become.

In particular, Waters had grown acutely aware that the Floyd themselves had forsaken subtlety in favour of rock theatrics and powerchord bombast, particularly on their last world tour, when they had played their hardest music ever to their biggest audiences ever. Disillusioned with touring and the stadium experience, Waters came to the conclusion that rock concerts were more like a war than entertainment. Indeed, in the original film script he had conceived the concert scenes to include shots of the audience being blown to pieces, applauding as they exploded!

In terms of the album's narrative, the track establishes 'Pink Floyd' as a rock artist about to play a stadium show in America.

The song also establishes that we are going to "find out what's behind these cold eyes": the eyes of Pink, the rock star who appears to be teetering on the brink of insanity.

In the live show of *The Wall*, this first song was played by a 'surrogate band' consisting of Andy Bown, Snowy White, Willie Wilson, and Peter Wood. Pink Floyd themselves were backstage, though from a distance, with the surrogate band wearing masks of the band members, they looked convincing.

Waters memorably described the band as a kind of 'Nazi apparition' and they were there to signify what Waters believed Pink Floyd had become in recent years.

Pink himself was the insane gestalt figure leading the show. Astute listeners will notice that the words ". . . we came in?", accompanied by some plaintive Yiddish violin playing, are the first thing heard on the album.

This makes no sense until you hear the last words on the album, "Isn't this where . . .", implying that the whole thing is a cycle, and that once the wall is broken down, you start building a new one. Just as he had done on *Animals*, Waters had made the entire album an eternal cycle.

The Wall ***in Berlin: return of the pig.***

IN THE FLESH?

WATERS, GILMOUR, MASON, WRIGHT.
FREDDIE MANDELL *organ*
LEE RITENOUR *rhythm guitar*
PETER WOOD AND BOB EZRIN *keyboards*
JEFF PORCARO *drums*

The Thin Ice

(WATERS)

THE THIN ICE

WATERS, GILMOUR, MASON, WRIGHT
FREDDIE MANDELL *Hammond organ*

For Waters and Syd Barrett, the first brick in their respective walls was the death of their respective fathers. Waters's father was killed in Anzio in 1944, when the young Roger was less than one year old. Barrett's father died of inoperable cancer when Syd was just 12. Indeed, when Waters and Barrett lived together in London during the earliest days of The Pink Floyd it proved to be an unspoken bond between the two of them, according to friends - perhaps the only thing they truly had in common. The song narrative parallels that of 'Embryo' a decade earlier, in which Waters examined the way the trust and perfect innocence of a baby is destined to be eroded by the pressures of the real world.

The spectre of Syd Barrett was uppermost in Waters's mind when he wrote the piece, as one who had slipped through "the crack in the thin ice". In the narrative, Waters uses the song as a device to suggest that the newborn Pink is destined to suffer horribly, as one of life's sensitive but damaged people. In the film, this is the scene where we see the very beginning of Pink's story, his childhood home, shot in East Molesey, Surrey, not far from Waters's own birthplace of Bookham. Some have suggested that the "thin ice of modern life" was inspired by Jethro Tull's 'Skating Away On The Thin Ice Of A New Day', from their *Minstrel In The Gallery* (1974).

Another Brick In The Wall Part 1

(WATERS)

The loss of his father during World War Two provides the first brick in Pink's wall. In a parallel with both Waters's and Barrett's experience, the song deals with Pink's awareness of the painful gap in his young life left by the absence of a loving "daddy", who remains only as "a snapshot in the family album". This image is painfully poignant, drawn from Waters's own memories of childhood and the father he never knew. It pained Waters in particular that, according to his mother, Eric Fletcher Waters was very musical. Having never met his father or really known who he was, Waters could only ever ask what his "daddy was like". He has, however, specified that the song is not just about children whose parents were killed, but about being left and forsaken more generally, and about how that sense of being somehow incomplete causes the emotional defences to be raised - another brick in the wall.

Nigel Gordon, who knew Syd Barrett both in Cambridge and in London, claims that LSD caused Syd more pain than most, because it brought to the surface the sense that he was essentially alone in life: "It was almost as if he was trying to blast the hurt out of his psyche."

The film version continues with scenes from Pink's early childhood, and the song accompanies a scene in which Pink and his mother attend the memorial to those who lost their lives at Anzio (the place where Roger Waters's father was killed).

The Happiest Days Of Our Lives

(WATERS)

Opening with the screams of the Scottish schoolmaster (who turns out to be a World War Two flying ace in *The Final Cut*), Pink's schooldays form the second brick in his wall. Subjected to ridicule and sarcasm at the hands of the schoolmaster, his wall grows higher. Though he did enjoy at least some of his time at school, Waters was targetted by certain schoolmasters at Cambridge High School for Boys who were determined to humiliate their charges. Cambridge High was a grammar school that prided itself on its standards of academic excellence, but often employed draconian methods to achieve them. Waters was encouraged in the sciences, but his attempts to write creatively were ridiculed.

"My school life was very like that," said a reflective Waters when the album was released. "Oh, it was awful . . . really terrible . . . it was a very difficult time for me at school because, as I didn't have a father, I tended to look, I suppose, to these schoolteachers for support and encouragement, which I got from some of them, but from a lot of them I got schmuck. I was considered without question to be a complete twat at almost everything, particularly English . . . I want to make it plain that some of the men who taught there were very nice guys. It's not meant to be a blanket condemnation of teachers everywhere, but the bad ones can really do people in . . . just putting them down, putting them down all the time. Never encouraging them, just trying to keep them quiet and still, and crush them into the right shape, so that they would go to university and 'do well'." In the film, Pink is abused by a bitter schoolmaster, who ridicules his poems in front of the class by reading them out in a sarcastic tone. The lines

"We don't need no . . ."

of poetry used just happen to be the opening verse to 'Money' from *Dark Side Of The Moon*. Though Waters did not write 'Money' at school, his creativity was ridiculed by one teacher in particular, and the memory of that humiliation stayed with him.

Another Brick In The Wall Part 2

(WATERS)

Consistently misinterpreted, much to Waters's chagrin, this is not an anti-education rap. Instead, it seeks to convey the message that vindictive and bitter teachers, and factory schooling, can break a child for life. The effect on such children is one of demoralising them to the point where they repress their innate creativity.

After completing a miserable stint at Cambridge High School, Waters chose to continue his education by studying architecture in London. Here, he caused a minor furore among the lecturers by consistently questioning their teaching methods, which relied heavily on learning things by rote. This is what Waters meant by "thought control". His belief was that such teaching methods discourage independent thought and imagination, and churn out individuals who think similarly. The song is thus an ironic comment on the way schools can actually do more to destroy a child's prospects than to enhance them.

Gilmour performed the now famous guitar break on his 1959 Gibson gold-top, and it was then effortlessly double-tracked. The song's main hook, however, is that kiddy chorus singing "We don't need no ed-jew-kay-shun". The song was originally recorded with the voices of Waters and Gilmour. The idea of overdubbing the kiddy chorus, to add a touch of irony, came while the band were in LA. They rang engineer Nick Griffiths at Britannia Row, and asked him to do what he could. Griffiths simply went to the local primary school in Islington and asked the music teacher, Alan Redshaw, if the whole class of kids would like to come to the studio and do some singing. He readily agreed, envisaging that he could eventually record his own 'Requiem For A Sinking Block Of Flats'.

Griffiths got the kids into a screaming frenzy by jumping up and down a lot in the studio, attempting to get them to put all their frustrations about school into this performance - which they did. He got them to do several passes at the song, then added all the vocal tracks together to give one huge chorus of disaffection.

The tapes were flown out to the band in LA, where they met with an ecstatic reception, and it was decided to mix the kids' voices to the forefront instead of using them as a backing chorus.

The released version is a composite of two different mixes. The original tapes were copied and mixed, one with Gilmour and Waters performing the vocals, the other with the kiddy chorus. The two were then edited together, the join coming in the second verse.

Released with a truncated solo from Gilmour, two weeks before the album, 'Another Brick In The Wall Part

ANOTHER BRICK IN THE WALL (PART 2)

WATERS, GILMOUR
MASON WRIGHT.
FREDDIE MANDELL *organ*
THE CHILDREN OF ISLINGTON GREEN PRIMARY SCHOOL FOURTH FORM *chorus*

The Wall*'s very Freudian mother.*

2' became a instant number one hit, and it stayed in the charts over Christmas 1979. Most who bought the single knew little of Pink Floyd, but because of the song's (gasp!) danceable Chic-style disco production and beat, and the controversial theme, which became a playground rallying cry, it became a universal anthem. In South Africa, the song was taken up by school boycotters, causing a national ban on its sale or broadcast. Waters was naturally thrilled that his song had such an unforeseen political impact.

Then came the backlash. The track precipitated a tabloid scandal when it was revealed that the multi-millionaires, Pink Floyd, had not paid the pupils from Islington Green School, and, worse still, hadn't even given the kids a copy of the finished album! The school were eventually allowed to use Britannia Row to record in, and given a lot of money for new musical equipment. Waters also personally ensured that each student received a copy of *The Wall*.

Mother

(WATERS)

MOTHER

WATERS, GILMOUR
MASON, WRIGHT.
FREDDIE MANDELL *organ*

Brick number three in Pink's wall is his mother, who tries to compensate for the absence of Pink's father by smothering her child with love, in a protective embrace. This, as Waters was anxious to point out, was not an autobiographical Freudian portrait of his own mother, but a rather more general observation on the way some mothers seek to cocoon their children from the perils of life, resulting in emotionally vulnerable adults. Some of the minor observations, he did admit, came from his own mother, Mary (a socialist, a member of CND and an activist for human rights, whose beliefs helped form Waters's early political and social understanding). The image of the mother is a composite that Waters 'cobbled together' from conversations and the experiences of friends. The way in which the mother figure obstructs Pink's relationship with women in general is crucial to the narrative.

It's interesting to note that, on his withdrawal from the pop world, Syd Barrett returned to live with his mother Winifred in her house Cambridge, until her death in 1991.

The track was re-recorded for the film in a much simpler, sparser form with the sound of a mother's heartbeat, and quiet bells were used instead of the acoustic gutar. The scenes shown with this song are those of Pink's relations with the women in his life, drawing Freudian parallels between Pink's attitude towards his mother and the way he relates to other women.

Goodbye Blue Sky

(WATERS)

GOODBYE BLUE SKY

WATERS, GILMOUR
MASON, WRIGHT.
FREDDIE MANDELL *organ*

As Pink stands on the verge of adulthood, he reflects on the world he is leaving behind - the world of childhood innocence. Saying goodbye to the blue skies of innocent childhood, he welcomes in the real world, a brave new world, unfurling beneath them. Waters described this song as an evocation of "remembering one's childhood and then getting ready to set off into the rest of one's life". This was one of Pink Floyd's most oft-visited themes, and the track takes its title from a phrase that became popular during World War Two as a frivolous way of acknowledging that there were big problems (i.e. war) ahead. It is significant that the track opens with a child looking into the sky and pointing out an aeroplane as it flies past - a possible acknowledgement of impending war.

In the film, the track accompanies a visual flashback to Pink's childhood, followed by one of Geralde Scarfe's incredible animation sequences, depicting imagery of war, fear, and death. This striking scene relates the themes of *The Wall* to their larger context.

Empty Spaces

(WATERS)

Originally a track called 'What Shall We Do Now?' was sequenced at this point in the album but, due to the time constraints of vinyl, this was dropped. This happened at such a late stage that the lyrics and track listing entry on the album's sleeve, already at the printers, still included it. The song was meant to represent Pink's attempts to find a job, and a purpose, as he sets off into the world. 'Empty Spaces' was intended simply as a reprise of 'What Shall We Do Now?' at the end of the second side, and it echoes the first four lines of the original song. Waters later admitted that it made less sense than the original track, but the latter had to be cut.

Before the track starts, there appears to be some garbled backwards speech. Those of you still in possession of a record player will be able to hear the album's hidden message, if you play the section backwards. For those of you with CDs, the message says, "Congratulations, you have just discovered the secret message. Please send your answer to Old Pink, care of the Funny Farm, Chalfont."

. . . Roger, Carolyne's on the phone.

EMPTY SPACES

WATERS, GILMOUR
MASON, WRIGHT.
FREDDIE MANDELL *organ*

Young Lust

(GILMOUR, WATERS)

Unsurprisingly, Pink decides to be a pop star. This fits with both Waters's and Syd Barrett's lives - both enjoyed the idea of being adored from a distance, and would often discuss the nature of being famous when they lived together during the early days of The Pink Floyd. "They wanted cars and girls and everything else," recalls Peter Jenner. "They certainly weren't averse to the trappings of fame. At least, not at that point, but then none of them had really experienced what it was really like. When it did hit, and it hit hard, Syd couldn't cope."

Pink, while waiting to do his show, is overwhelmed by feelings of 'young lust' as he is surrounded by eager, nubile groupies. Groupiedom was a phenomenon that Waters had experienced first hand, most notably on the band's tours of the US, where anonymous girls would parade themselves around hotel lobbies, and backstage, in the hope of being bedded by one of the band. However, this only became the focus of the lyric during one of the rewrite sessions instigated by Bob Ezrin. Originally the song told of young Pink's obsession with the kind of anonymous sex personified in porno films and books. "(It was about) being very interested in sex, but never actually being able to get involved because of being too frightened actually," says Waters. "It's meant to be a pastiche of any young rock 'n' roll band out on the road." 'Young Lust' drew at least some of its lyrical inspiration from the 'The Nile Song', a similar pastiche of a youthful sexual encounter.

The most important part of the song in terms of the narrative, however, is the spoken dialogue at the end. His wife's unfaithfulness is the final brick in Pink's wall. Pink, on tour, tries to call his wife at home in England, only to hear another man answering when the operator tries to connect him. This was a real MCI operator, who was unaware that she was being set up for the purposes of the recording. It is thought that this episode is based on a similar event that occurred during the breakdown of Waters's marriage to his first wife, Judy Trim.

In the film action, we see the groupies using their feminine charms to get backstage. Pink allows one of them back to his trailer, and then on to his hotel room.

YOUNG LUST

WATERS, GILMOUR
MASON, WRIGHT.
FREDDIE MANDELL *organ*

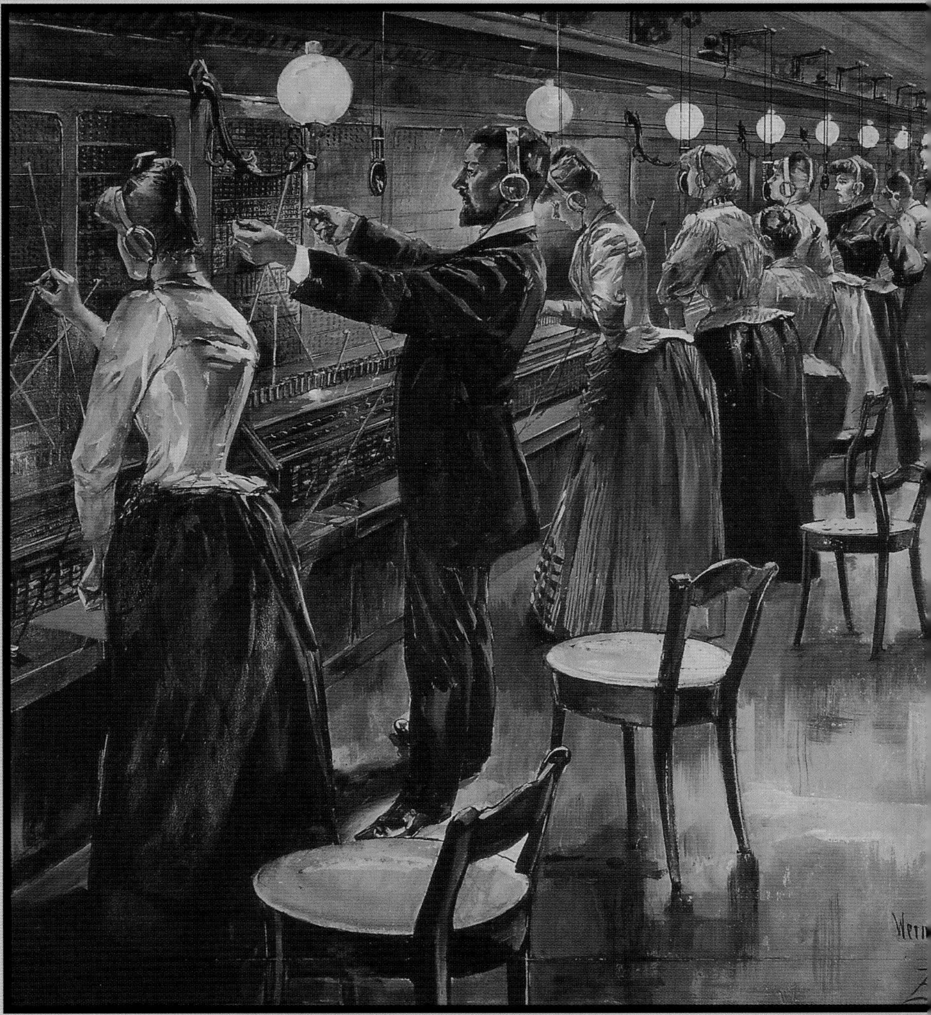

An old-fashioned telephone exchange.

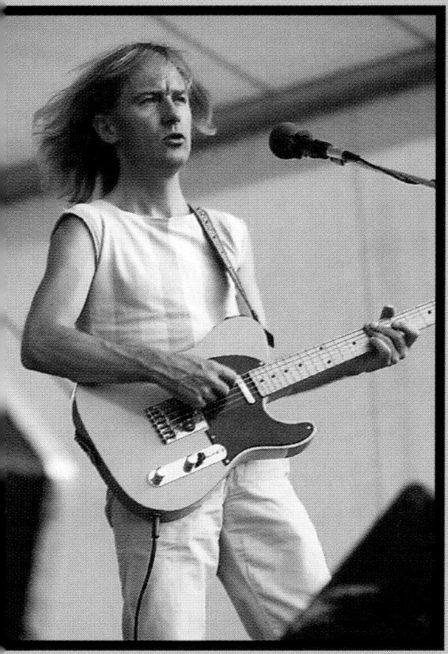

Roy Harper: "just one of my turns".

ONE OF MY TURNS

WATERS, GILMOUR
MASON, WRIGHT.
FREDDIE MANDELL *organ*

DON'T LEAVE ME NOW

WATERS, GILMOUR
MASON, WRIGHT.
FREDDIE MANDELL *organ*

ANOTHER BRICK IN THE WALL PART 3

WATERS, GILMOUR
MASON, WRIGHT.
FREDDIE MANDELL *organ*

GOODBYE CRUEL WORLD

WATERS, GILMOUR
MASON, WRIGHT.
FREDDIE MANDELL *organ*

One Of My Turns

(WATERS)

This track, in which Pink goes berserk and smashes up his hotel room, was based on a real-life incident involving English folk rock singer Roy Harper. At the Knebworth concert premiere of 'Wish You Were Here', on 5 July, 1975, Harper discovered his stage costume had disappeared within minutes of the band taking to the stage. He flew into a destructive rage in the Floyd's trailer, smashing the interior and cutting his hand badly.

Waters came to see this kind of temporary insanity as a symptom of an inevitable breakdown - it is certainly the first hint of Pink's. In conversation with BBC Radio 1's Tommy Vance, Waters described his thinking, "He's had it now, he's definitely a bit 'yippee' now, and 'One Of My Turns' is just, you know, him coming in and he can't relate to this girl either, that's why he just turns on the TV: they come into the room and she starts going on about all the things he's got and all that he does is just turn on the TV and sit there, and he won't talk to her." In the film version, Pink flips on the TV and ignores the groupie, caught up in his own thoughts. As a tear rolls down his cheek, he is suddenly consumed with rage, destroying his hotel room. During Pink's rage, Bob Geldof, who played the character, cuts himself quite badly, as Harper did.

Don't Leave Me Now

(WATERS)

Pink, confused and isolated, can't understand why his wife is with another man, and the song becomes an agonized plea for the return of the woman he thinks he loves. Pink's angry outburst has done nothing to alleviate the pain, and, as he thinks through events, the song becomes a catalogue of the many abysmal ways he has mistreated his wife and others who have loved him. Whether or not any of this was pertinent to Waters's own marriage breakup with Judy Trim is not known. Waters later claimed that the song was not just to Pink's wife but to anybody, from any man to any woman.

Beneath the obvious narrative lies a bitterly ironic commentary on contemporary relationships Waters had observed. To Tommy Vance, Waters outlined the thinking behind the sentiment, "A lot of men and women do get involved with each other for lots of wrong reasons, and they do get very aggressive towards each other, and do each other a lot of damage. I, of course, have never struck a woman, as far as I can recall . . . and I hope I never do, but a lot of people have, and a lot of women have struck men as well. There is a lot of violence in relationships often that aren't working. I mean this is obviously an extremely cynical song, I don't feel like that about marriage now."

At the end of the song can be heard a variety of TVs being turned on, combining to make a jumble of audio babble. Each TV is systematically smashed by Pink, providing a bizarre but dramatic segue into to the next song. When Syd Barrett briefly moved back to London, during the mid-70s, and was living in Chelsea Cloisters, a ritzy apartment block, he was, at one point, in possession of five colour TVs, often watching two or three at a time.

Another Brick In The Wall Part 3

(WATERS)

From this moment onwards, Pink's wall really starts to build. Isolation is the only solution. Rejected and hurt, Pink decides he doesn't need the world, his wife or any other crutch, and he retires, alone behind his wall. It is easy to see this as a reference to Syd Barrett, and indeed friends of Barrett often remark about how rapidly his retreat into catatonia occurred. "It was Syd in there behind that wall, the drugs or the illness, whatever you want to call it," says Andrew King. "You'd occasionally see brief flashes of that wonderful imagination, echoes of that extremely pleasant lad who had written 'Emily' and 'Arnold Layne'. But you got the sense that he was trying to battle his way through the most enormous barrier just to be able to say two coherent words. Eventually I think he just stopped trying. It was too difficult and painful for him. It was terribly sad to see, and none of us will ever forget what happened. He was isolated beyond anyone's help. Utterly alone."

Goodbye Cruel World

(WATERS)

The wall around Pink is impenetrable, and the star is now living in an isolated cocoon. These lyrics are not those of a suicidal man but rather of a man who is turning his back on the world and sealing himself firmly into his capsule. "That's him going catatonic, if you like . . . and he's going back and he's just curling up and he's not going to move. That's it, he's had enough, that's the end."

In the live shows, Waters would perform the song looking out through the last remaining hole in the wall. As the song ends, the last brick is inserted, making Pink's wall complete. From this moment on, the action all takes place in Pink's troubled mind. The band were now playing from behind the wall and all the audience saw was a mass of white bricks.

The action has shifted in flashback to the beginning of the film: sitting catatonic in his hotel room, an untouched cigarette between his fingers, Pink says goodbye to the world.

Geldof's Pink in the movie **The Wall.**

Hey You
(WATERS)

One of the most crucial songs on the album, the lyrics do not directly relate to the character at all, but seem to be a passionate plea for real human contact between people, for the courage necessary for them to reach out to someone through their defensive walls and make a connection with them. It is a wish for harmony and brotherhood - "Would you help me to carry the stone? Open your heart" - and one of the most beautiful songs Roger has composed. The image of the 'stone' was first mentioned in the lyrics to the album *More* in a somewhat different context, and explored further in *Animals* in a context that relates more directly to *The Wall*, the stone being a symbol of the negativity you carry with you: the burden of life that will drag you down if you let it. "'Hey You' is a cry to the rest of the world, you know, saying, 'Hey, this isn't right'," said Waters, cryptically.

Locked in his hotel room, this is Pink's plea to past loves and friends not to foresake him. The song also mentions the worms for the first time in the piece. Originally, they were a major feature of *The Wall*, symbols of decay that eat into you once you have isolated yourself and allowed them to feed on your psyche.

Waters's message was simple, and one that he knew only too well to be true. He felt that if you isolate yourself you decay. Pink has been bricked in and is susceptible to the worms - the emissaries of his own negativity and self-loathing. At the end of the track, Pink makes a cry for help, but realizes that it's too late. "All of us, I'm sure, from time to time have formed sentences in our minds that we would like to say to someone else, but we don't say it, you know? Well, that's no use, that doesn't help anybody, that's just a game that you're playing with yourself," added a cryptic Waters in a radio interview.

'Hey You' was moved from its original situation at the end of side three to a far better location at the beginning. Bob Ezrin had listened to side three of the album and told Waters that he didn't think it worked. Waters himself had been feeling uncomfortable: "I

HEY YOU

WATERS, GILMOUR
MASON, WRIGHT.
FREDDIE MANDELL *organ*

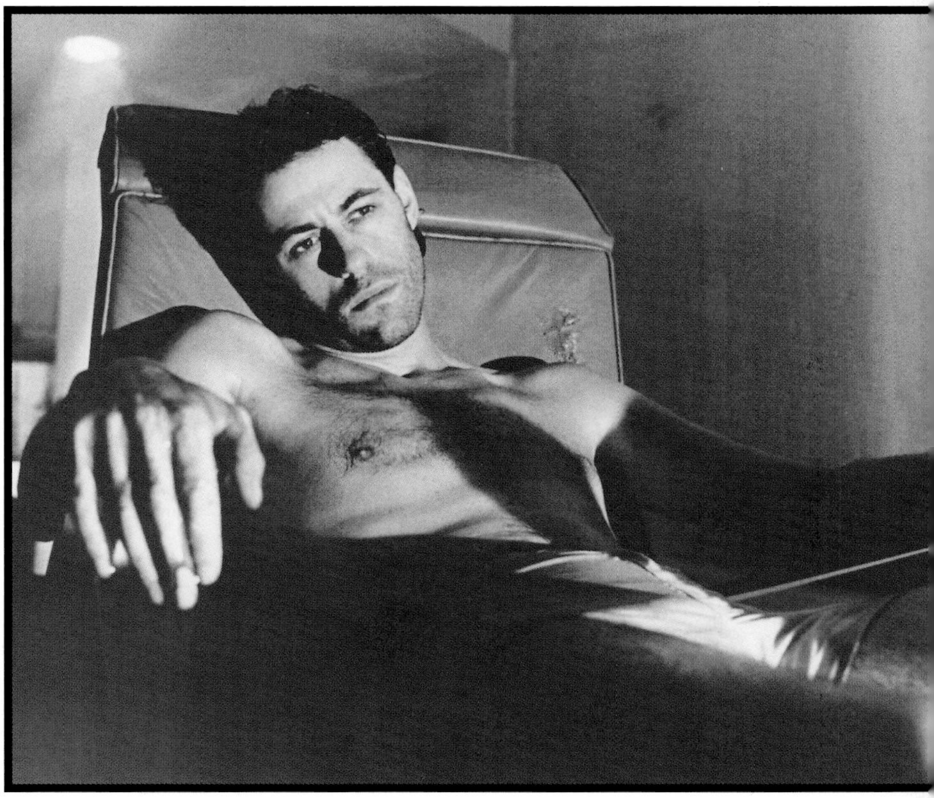

Geldof performed unscripted acts of Barrett-like insanity.

thought about it, and in a couple of minutes I realised that 'Hey You' could conceptually go anywhere, and it would make a much better side if we put it at the front of the side, and sandwiched the middle theatrical scene, with the guy in the hotel room, between an attempt to re-establish contact with the outside world, which is what 'Hey You' is, and the end of the side . . . so that's why those lyrics are printed in the wrong place, because that decision was made very late. I should explain at this point, the reason that all these decisions were made so late was because we'd promised lots of people a long time ago that we would finish this record by the beginning of November, and we wanted to keep that promise" (Vance interview).

For the live performances, this song was played at the end of the interval, while the house lights were still up and people were filing back from the hot dog and ice cream stands. It was another of Waters's attempts to disorientate the audence.

Is There Anybody Out There?

(WATERS, EZRIN)

IS THERE ANYBODY OUT THERE?

WATERS, GILMOUR MASON, WRIGHT. FREDDIE MANDELL *organ*

Pink realizes that his predicament - his isolation - is serious: having received no response to his plea in 'Hey You' he is moved to ask, "Is there anybody out there?"

Gilmour originally played the mournful guitar paean on this piece on a nylon string guitar with a leather pick, but he was unable to play it properly when it came time to finger pick the part. A session player was used instead.

The dialogue at the beginning playing on the TV in Pink's hotel room is from US TV western show *Gunsmoke*.

This track forms the basis of one of the most important and powerful scenes in the film. As a portrait of growing psychosis, it is masterful. The music lapses, and Pink enters the washroom to shave. His now distorted mind takes the concept to ridiculous lengths, and he ends up shaving his chest and eyebrows as well, in a bloody scene that is one of the most difficult in the film to watch. Geldof wasn't scripted to perform this, but he felt himself seized by the role and did it spontaneously. To those who knew Syd, this was an uncanny echo of the founder Floyd's erratic and disturbing behaviour as he slipped into catatonia. Barrett had once shaved his eyebrows off, and had taken to wearing a dress around the King's Road. On one legendary occasion he left a packed dinner party, cut off his long hair with blunt scissors and returned to the dinner table without saying a word, as if it was the most normal thing in the world to do. June Bolan was close to Syd during the *Piper* era and on seeing the film she was moved to tears by this scene. "I was absolutely shell-shocked: it was so close to Syd I couldn't bear it."

Gunsmoke, ***an old US TV western: on in Pink's hotel room.***

Nobody Home

(WATERS)

Pink now submits himself to a degrading and pathetic self-scrutiny, in which he examines every last sorry detail of his appearance and state of mind, arriving at the conclusion that he is bereft of emotion: that there is "nobody home".

The influence for this catalogue of pathos came directly from Waters's observations of those who, he felt, had slipped down behind similar walls themselves. The first and most notable reference is, of course, to Syd Barrett. Indeed the song itself harks back to Syd Barrett's 'Vegetable Man', a track that he had written towards the end of his tenure with the Floyd but which Waters had vetoed as a track for inclusion on *A Saucerful Of Secrets*, feeling it was too dark, and too telling of Barrett's condition. Written in Peter Jenner's kitchen, Syd had apparently sat down and ironically described the clothes he was wearing, from paisley shirt to smelly velvet trousers, adding, "But oh oh my haircut looks so baaaad." Waters was particularly disturbed by the track, which was a chronicle of a man in the throes of a mental

The Floyd with Barrett (seen here with his 'obligatory Hendrix perm) who was heavily influenced by Dylan and Lennon and posessed a powerful ego, believing that he too was their equal.

breakdown. The line "I've got elastic bands keeping my shoes on" is a direct reference to Barrett, one of the dandiest of the King's Road psychedelic set, who took to wearing scruffy Gohills boots, held together with elastic bands, towards the end of his tenure with the band. The mention of the "obligatory Hendrix perm" relates to the £20 Hendrix corkscrew perm that Syd had had done at a fashionable Knightsbridge hair salon. "Syd was obsessed with his hair," recalls Andrew King. "It was never quite right, and he could never get it to stay the way he wanted it, and he decided because Hendrix had one, and Clapton and a few others had one, that he was going to have a perm too. Well, he had it done, and and, my god, he looked incredible. He and Lyndsey [Korner] were the most beautiful couple in town."

Waters then shifts the focus of this picture of decrepitude to someone closer to home. The line about the grand piano propping up "my mortal remains" is apparently a reference to Rick Wright, who, according to Waters, was too "burnt out" to appear on the album. The line about silver spoons is thought to be a reference to Wright's liking for cocaine at the time.

Vera

(WATERS)

Vera Lynn was the 'Forces' Sweetheart', a female singer who was very popular during World War Two and helped to boost the morale of the men fighting in Europe and Africa. The lyrics to this piece echo the refrain of one of her best known wartime songs, 'We'll Meet Again', which, to many servicemen and women, who knew they might never see each other again, became a poignant song of reflection. This sudden reverie in Pink is triggered by the fact that a war film - *The Battle Of Britain* - is showing on TV in his room.

Bring The Boys Back Home

(WATERS)

Waters claims that this, at least as far as he is concerned, is the central song of The Wall. This is probably because it evokes the sense of loss that he felt at his father's failure to return home after the war. "It's partly about not letting people go off and be killed in wars," admitted Waters, "but it's also partly about not allowing rock 'n' roll, or making cars or selling soap or getting involved in biological research or anything that anybody might do, not letting that become such an important and 'jolly boys' game' that it becomes more important than friends, wives, children, other people."

This song was newly recorded for the film, featuring the Pontardulais Male Voice Choir, which Roger travelled to Wales to record, as well as additional brass and orchestral instrumentation. It was released as the B-side of the 'When The Tigers Broke Free' single. It accompanies the emotional scenes in the film when the soldiers and their families are reunited, breaking into a passionate song for reconciliation and peace. In a neat example of serendipity, *Pink Floyd The Wall* premiered at the Empire Theatre, Leicester Square, exactly 30 days after the end of the Falklands conflict, just as the troops were returning home.

NOBODY HOME

WATERS, GILMOUR
MASON, WRIGHT.
FREDDIE MANDELL *organ*

VERA

WATERS, GILMOUR
MASON, WRIGHT.
FREDDIE MANDELL *organ*

BRING THE BOYS HOME

WATERS, GILMOUR
MASON, WRIGHT.
FREDDIE MANDELL *organ*

'Forces' Sweetheart' Vera Lynn.

Comfortably Numb

(GILMOUR, WATERS)

COMFORTABLY NUMB

WATERS, GILMOUR MASON, WRIGHT.
FREDDIE MANDELL *organ*

'Come on Big Bum', as the track has become known over the years to the band, on account of it being Dave Gilmour's big moment, is the track that many consider to be the greatest the Floyd have ever committed to tape. It is certainly true that 'Comfortably Numb' is one of the most emotive and transcendentally powerful pieces of guitar soloing Gilmour has ever recorded. More than that, however, it strikes the perfect balance between Gilmour's musical lyricism and Waters's wonderfully observed and written narrative.

At this point in the narrative, the time has come when Pink is supposed to go on stage to perform. Voices echo through his mind, on a tape loop that begins this track to signify that Pink is overwhelmed, trapped and dislocated utterly from reality. A roadie enters the room, telling Pink it's showtime, but getting no response he calls the doctor, who administers a shot to keep the star "going for the show". 'Doctor Feelgoods', as they were known, were common on huge tours where hundreds of thousands of dollars were at stake at every gig. An exhausted performer could mean a cancelled show, and refunds! Waters had read of Elvis's Doctor Feelgood, who was paid to administer drugs to the imploding star, in order to keep him recording and performing. "They're not interested in any of these problems, all they're interested in is how many people there are and tickets have been sold and the show must go on, at any cost to anybody. I mean, I, personally, have done gigs when I've been very depressed, but I've also done gigs when I've been extremely ill, where you wouldn't do any ordinary kind of work," recalled Waters on the album's release.

The scenario that follows, however, is straight from the recollection of Syd Barrett's final days with the band. The Pink Floyd were billed to play the *International Love-In* concert event, midsummer 1967, and with 'See Emily Play' riding high in the charts, the band were expected to be the highight of the show.

The late June Bolan recalled that, when the time came for the show, Barrett was nowhere to be found. She wandered the corridors and finally found him in a dressing room, "absolutely gaga, just totally switched off, sitting rigid like a stone." Syd did not recognise Bolan, and continued to stare blankly into space. The audience, who had paid their money and wanted a show, grew restless waiting for the Floyd and the stage manager, as Bolan recalls, was knocking at the door shouting, "Time to go! Time to go!". Barrett had to be helped onto the stage by Waters and Bolan, who simply slung his white Stratocaster guitar around his neck and pointed him towards the mike. Syd stood quite motionless for the whole concert, with his hands hanging limply by his side.

The track oscillates between the reality and the fantasy world of Pink's psyche. The first and third verses are delivered by Roger, playing the role of the evil Doctor Feelgood, who is medicating Pink for the purpose of getting him to play. The second and fourth verses, sung by Gilmour, are the internal reverie of Pink as he recalls the past, and significant moments in his development. It's a powerful self-diagnosis as Pink realises that the drugs the doctor has administered have made him comfortably numb - a reference to heroin perhaps? The beautiful and poignant lyrics in the fourth verse hint at the idea that there was a moment, buried in his past, when Pink was happy. Waters had often stated, both in his songs and in interviews, that there is a simple

***Pink as marionette, no longer in control, in* Comfortably Numb.**

understanding that comes with childhood. After such recollection, the harsh reality of going on stage for yet another stadium show is almost too much for Pink to bear, and the mental anguish gives way to an emotive guitar solo from Gilmour.

During the stage show, this solo was performed on a hydraulic lift, which raised Gilmour to the top of the wall, where the backlit image created a giant shadow over the audience.

Most of the music for 'Comfortably Numb' was written by Dave at the conclusion of the sessions for his 1978 eponymous solo album, at Super Bear Studios in France. Written too late for inclusion on the album, the melody was later revived for *The Wall* and rewritten with Waters, who wrote all the lyrics. Gilmour recorded two solos, and compiled one blistering track that took the best from both.

The Show Must Go On

(WATERS)

Pink is en route to the show and has made it back to the real world. Waters uses the song as a vehicle to express his own thoughts on the way the music business demands that you perform - the show must go on at any cost, regardless of the state of the star's body or mind. Once again this a reference to both Waters's experiences and Barrett's. Waters had on a number of occasions performed when his doctor had claimed he was dangerously ill, while Syd was being asked to perform rock concerts when he should have been on a psychiatric ward!

Orginally, Waters had wanted to offset the heaviness of the song with some light Beach Boys-style harmonies, and actually booked The Beach Boys. Mike Love decided that Waters's themes didn't fit with their wholesome (ahem) image, and declined. Beach Boy Bruce Johnston however, did agree, and, along with session singers, managed to recreate the Beach Boys sound.

THE SHOW MUST GO ON

WATERS, GILMOUR
MASON, WRIGHT.
FREDDIE MANDELL *organ*
BRUCE JOHNSTON, TONI TENILLE, JOHN JOYCE, JOE CHEMAY, STAN FARBER, JIM HAAS
backing vocals

In The Flesh

(WATERS)

This song provides a 'flash-forward' from the beginning of the album. Pink is escorted to the stage, just as Syd was, and he begins his twisted performance. Through the lyric "Pink isn't well, he stayed back at the hotel", Pink indicates that he has left behind his normal persona in favour of his darker side, bitter and angry. The decay that ensued on completion of the wall has reached an extreme point, and Pink creates a caricature of his own self-loathing, imagining himself as a fascist leader at his own rock 'n' roll Nuremburg.

Roger first developed the idea that walls between people lead to the blossoming of feelings of hatred and intolerance at the final fateful show of the *In The Flesh* tour, at Montreal Stadium. Ravaged from the constant stress of touring, Waters found himself directing his performance at one hapless fan who had caught his eyes, a few rows back. Waters beckoned the kid forward throughout the show, bringing him through the security cordon of police until he was right beneath the lip of the stage. When he was in range, Waters spat in his face. Horrified, Waters returned home to England consumed with guilt, and with the feeling that his whole career was a fraudulent play for power.

In such dehumanising venues, completely lacking in intimacy, it seemed impossible to get in touch with the audience at a heart level, or indeed any level. He had come to believe that they were not understanding, or were misinterpreting, the feelings and ideas he was trying to convey. It was on this tour that he realized that the wall between himself and his audience was creating these feelings inside him, and it was at this show that they reached a climax. In short, Waters began to feel the madness himself. Epiphany came.

Roger: "What he wanted was a good riot, and what I wanted was to do a good rock 'n' roll show and I got so upset in the end that I spat at him, which is a very nasty thing to do to anybody. Anyway, the idea is that these kinds of fascist feelings develop from isolation."

'In The Flesh' tells of how Pink, pumped on drugs, decides to antagonise and intimidate the audience who have come to see him. This is drawn from Waters's own feelings of hatred for the audience that accompanied the *In The Flesh* tour. In his diatribe, Pink attacks every minority in the audience from Jews to homosexuals and 'niggers'. Waters knew that the end product of all the isolation and decay was this self-loathing, transferred onto one's audience. It was, Waters recalled, "an attack on parts of myself I disapprove of".

For this song, the film intercuts, extremely rapidly, a number of scenes from the movie, depicting things in the past, things yet to come, and scenes that didn't make the movie's final cut, except in their brief appearance here. These scenes of hate, betrayal, marriage, school, mother, rejection, loss, women and violence add up to the sum total of the bricks in Pink's

IN THE FLESH

WATERS, GILMOUR
MASON, WRIGHT.
FREDDIE MANDELL *organ*

wall. The wall is almost complete, and in terms of the film, this is a recap of all that has gone to make it so.

The riot scenes glimpsed here and there during parts of the song were shot at the gasworks at Beckton, and included 150 rioters and police. Among the rioters were the Hammer Guard skinheads, who feature later in the film, but who found it difficult to separate truth from filmic fiction. Things eventually got out of hand and a mini-riot ensued.

The scenes for 'In The Flesh' were filmed at London's New Horticultural Hall. Assistant director Ray Corbett had to organise nearly 400 skinheads, 24 of which formed Pink's crack Hammer Guard. The toughest section of the skinhead crowd were a group called the Tilbury Skins, from East London.

Run Like Hell

(GILMOUR, WATERS)

RUN LIKE HELL

WATERS, GILMOUR
MASON, WRIGHT.
FREDDIE MANDELL *organ*

Beginning with Gilmour's idiosyncratic, repetitive, staccato muted guitar, this track was routinely introduced by Waters at concerts as "'Run Like Fuck', a number for all you paranoids out there". It raises one of Waters's perennial themes, a paranoia about fascism and a totalitarian police state, to a frightening pitch. Waters's interest in fascism, and the way in which fascist leaders gain power and political muscle, came through his general interest in the war, in turn prompted by the need to know about how and why his father had died. Interest in the rise of Hitler, Mussolini and their ilk translated itself into a more general appreciation of the way in which power is exercised over crowds. One book in particular proved crucial to this understanding - Elias Cannetti's *Crowds And Power*, an almost philosophical treatise on the way in which fascist leaders gain psychological power over their people. For some time, Waters had been musing on the strong parallels between fascist dictators of old and the kind of stadium experience that rock bands generate, the implication being that it was a sense of mass hysteria, of being part of the crowd vociferously chanting the manifesto or the lyrics to the songs, that allowed the fascist dictator, the charismatic leader who could whip up the crowd, to succeed in his purposes. Pink is personified as just such a character.

'Run Like Hell' is supposed to be a song from Pink's set, in which he mulls over the paranoia of a fascist police state and rails against those elements of society that attempt to pull us towards intolerance and abandonment of individual rights and freedoms.

Though substantially reworked, the original chord

Behind the scenes with Gerald Scarfe

A Mosley 'Blackshirt' rally.

sequence dates from 1978, and Gilmour's demos for his *About Face* solo album. Waters and Gilmour worked hard to create a teutonic feel, the feel of a Nazi march or a fascists' rally. Mason's 2/4 beats were mixed high to evoke the menacing presence of a massed band and the sound was achieved by combining conventional close miking of the drum kit with miking from a distance of thirty feet.

Waiting For The Worms

(WATERS)

Waters had long been an observer of fascism in all its forms. From Elias Cannetti's account of the rise of charismatic leaders, *Crowds And Power*, to the films of Leni Riefenstahl, he was all too aware of how easy it is to stir the masses up and fill them with simple ideas. He had to some extent already explored this theme on 'Sheep', but in the context of Pink's story, the emphasis was on the figurehead, the leader, the man who holds the power.

The track opens with shouts of "Pink Floyd!", which slowly mutate into screams of "Hammer!", the former through the left channel of the stereo, the latter through the right. The parallel was obvious - Waters saw being in a stadium rock band as something akin to being part of a group of fascists in control of a crowd of malleable proles, and he has explicitly stated that the idea came from those concerts where the audience would chant the name of Pink Floyd. "This is the Pink Floyd audience, if you like, turning into a rally," he once commented. "The idea is that we've been changed from the lovable old Pink Floyd that we all know and love [into] our evil alter egos."

In Pink's mind the rock show he is about to perform has taken on the appearance of a fascist rally where he is the leader, the supreme ruler, the man with the power - the power to weed out the unhealthy and the undesirable. The Nazi connotations are obvious. As we retreat further into Pink's mind, and his fascist fantasy grows more and more extreme, he imagines himself leading rallies, and touring the streets with a loud-hailer, gathering support against minorities such as the 'Jewboys', 'queers' and 'coons'.

The marching was triggered by film Waters had seen of the marches by Mosleyites or 'Blackshirts' during the late 30s in London, when the baronet Sir Oswald Mosley, sympathetic to Hitler, gathered his group of men and women together. It was also influenced by the growing tide of racial unrest in both Germany and Britain during the late 70s, in particular a rally by the National Front, a white supremacist neo fascist political outfit, in Hyde Park in the summer of 1978.

WAITING FOR THE WORMS

WATERS, GILMOUR
MASON, WRIGHT.
FREDDIE MANDELL *organ*
BRUCE JOHNSTON, TONI TENILLE, JOHN JOYCE, JOE CHEMAY, STAN FARBER, JIM HAAS
backing vocals

STOP
WATERS, GILMOUR
MASON, WRIGHT.
FREDDIE MANDELL *organ*

THE TRIAL
WATERS, GILMOUR
MASON, WRIGHT.
FREDDIE MANDELL *organ*

During Pink's self-imposed trial he brings forward all the characters from his past. Their character assasination forces Pink to break through the wall to the real world.

Pink calls his sect The Hammers and nicknames them The Worms. The crossed hammers, red and black, present on Scarfe's illustrations inidcate that this is designed to be seen as a Nazi style outfit, though strictly they owed more to Mosely's 'Blackshirts'. Waters was also influenced by the appearance of the film of pioneering German cinamatographer Leni Riefenstahl, whose *Triumph Of The Will*, with its choreographed sequences of Aryan youths with blond, cropped hair, provided him with a visual context for the scene in the film version.

During this song, Pink begins to flip back and forth between his more normal persona (at the beginning and end of the song) and his evil alter ego (the middle section). In the studio, Waters achieved the dramatic effect of the fascist leader addressing his people by shouting the lyrics through an old fashioned brass megaphone.

'Waiting For The Worms' features the top harmonies of Bruce Johnston (The Beach Boys) and Toni Tenille (Captain and Tenille). Bruce Johnston, to this day, remains justly proud of his contribution to the album, though he still claims not to know what it is about. "Even with Roger there to tell me what was going down, I couldn't get it. It was a pretty neat sounding album though, and I think our voices added just the right amount of sweetness to a very bitter track."

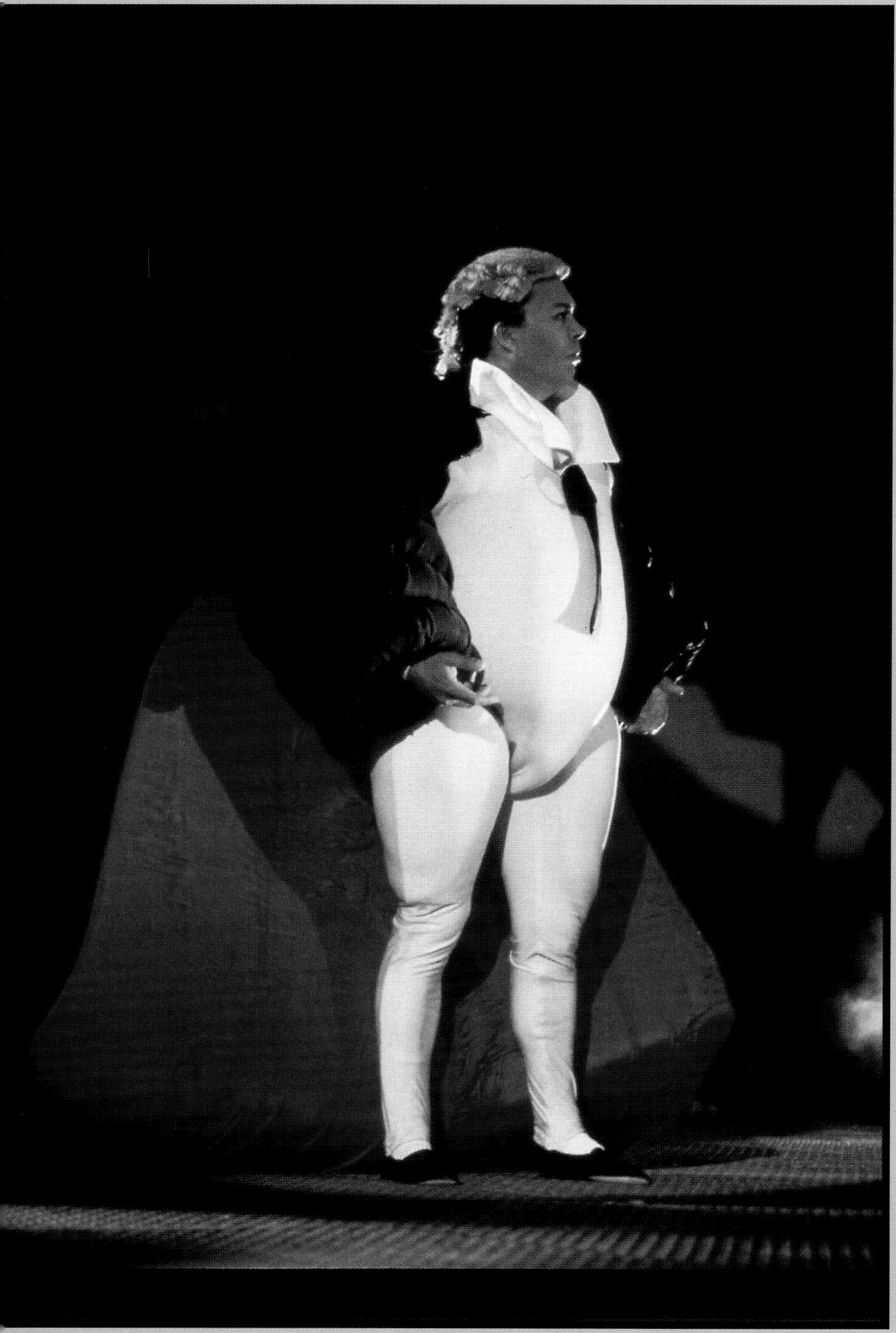

Stop

(WATERS)

Waters described this as Pink's "moment of clarity". The drug injection wears off, and Pink starts to flip uncontrollably backwards and forwards between his real life persona and his paranoid, sickly, cracked and wasted persona. Just as it looks as if The Worms will devour Pink, he shouts, "Stop! I wanna go home, take off this uniform and leave the show." Having decided to fight The Worms, the shattered Pink must now face himself in a trial to find out whether he has been guilty all along, or if he will be set free from his past and his mental enslavement.

The Trial

(WATERS, EZRIN)

In his confused, paranoid state, Pink believes that the only way to exorcise his inner demons and break through the wall is to put himself on trial, with himself as judge, jury and prosecutor. All the major characters in the story make a reappearance in Pink's trial, from his mother and the schoolteacher to his overbearing wife, delivering their savage attacks on his damaged psyche.

Waters felt, through coming to terms with his own attitudes to both his enormous wealth and to his mixed feelings towards his audience, that the only way to break through the wall is to acknowledge who you are, face up to your position and responsibilities and start interacting with society again. To be "exposed before your peers" is painful, but ultimately a moment of profound liberation. The scream that accompanies the final breakdown of the wall indicates that this is a

painful and profound moment, a piece of primal therapy. Originally, Waters intended to end the album and the film with the wall in place, but he decided this was "too tough . . . too 'Fuck you'." With help from Bob Ezrin, a humanistic note of optimism was struck, to send the punters home happy . . .

Outside The Wall

(WATERS)

In the aftermath of the wall's destruction, strains of a poignant Yiddish violin tune waft from the debris. This is the coda to the album, there to serve as a reminder to the listener that the whole thing was only theatre and not to be taken too seriously. It has the feeling of an author's afterword, in which Waters addresses the listener directly, appealing to one and all to come out from behind their own walls, to where "the ones who really love you" are walking up and down waiting to embrace you. Waters was acutely aware, as he had been on *Animals*, that without such a postscript to to the piece, it might be taken literally, rather than as a poignant and powerful theatrical metaphor. His other big worry was that people would accuse him of being unnecessarily depressive!

At the very end, the words "Isn't this . . ." are heard. The remaining words, forming the rest of the sentence, "where we came in?", are the first words heard at the very beginning of the album, bringing everything full circle. The implication is that once the wall has been destroyed, the process of building it up begins all over again.

The very last sounds heard on the album are those of a dive-bombing Stuka - a German fighter plane - which kills Pink's father. At Anzio, Waters's father was killed by a Stuka.

OUTSIDE THE WALL

WATERS, GILMOUR, MASON, WRIGHT FREDDIE MANDELL
Hammond organ

The finale of the live shows was the destruction of the wall, signifying that Pink has escaped his past and the demons that had forced him to erect his wall in the foirst place. This shot was taken at Roger Waters Berlin concert in the Potsdammerplatz

The Final Cut

1983

A Roger Waters solo album in all but name, *The Final Cut* delivers a musical diatribe on the futility and stupidity of war.

The working title for the LP, *Spare Bricks*, gives some indication of the album's content. Made up from music recorded and discarded from the album *The Wall* and the film, *Pink Floyd The Wall*, the album was originally intended to be a separate soundtrack to the film. Before long, it had become a full-blown concept album in its own right, with new songs and a new lyrical perspective. The advent of The Falklands War between Britain and Argentina (famously described by J. L. Borges as "two bald men fighting over a comb"), which began on 2 April and ended on 14 June, 1982 (30 days before the release of the movie *The Wall*) was the creative catalyst, spurring Roger to develop new material for the forthcoming album. Its name was changed to *The Final Cut*, a reference to the last production stage of a movie when the final cut and print are readied for copying. It makes for the most lyrically unequivocal of all Pink Floyd albums.

THE FINAL CUT (A REQUIEM FOR THE POST-WAR DREAM BY ROGER WATERS, PERFORMED BY PINK FLOYD)
RECORDED *July-December 1982 at Mayfair, Olympic, Abbey Road, Eel Pie, Audio International, Rak, Hook End, and the Billiard Room Studios (a room in Roger Waters's London home).*
DAVID GILMOUR, NICK MASON AND ROGER WATERS.
ALL LEAD VOCALS BY WATERS *(except on 'Not Now John', by Waters and Gilmour).*

ADDITIONAL INSTRUMENTATION

MICHAEL KAMEN *piano, harmonium*
ANDY BOWN *Hammond organ*
RAY COOPER *percussion*
RAPHAEL RAVENSCROFT tenor sax
THE NATIONAL PHILHARMONIC ORCHESTRA *CONDUCTED AND ARRANGED BY MICHAEL KAMEN*
PRODUCED BY *ROGER WATERS, JAMES GUTHRIE, MICHAEL KAMEN*
RELEASED *21 March, 1983*
CHART PLACING *Number 1 in the UK; Number 6 in the US*

The Final Cut, though heavily influenced lyrically by the events surrounding the Falkands conflict was also an album that dealt with Waters' personal feelings of loss, guilt and shame at his fathers death in Anzio in 1944.

The Final Cut: virtually Waters solo.

The cover, which was designed by Roger Waters and photographed by his wife Carolyne's brother, Willie Christie, is an extreme close-up of a World War Two officer's uniform and medals. The medals include the DFC (Distinguished Flying Cross, awarded for acts of extreme courage or devotion to duty while flying), the DM (Defence Medal, for three years' wartime service), the Africa Star (for participation in the North African campaign) and the 1939-45 Star (a plain medal that denotes wartime service).

Sessions began almost as soon as the film *Pink Floyd The Wall* was put on cinematic release in July of 1982, and ran through until December. For a Floyd album, this was a relatively short recording period, reflecting the fact that most of the material had already been recorded in some form for *The Wall*. "I got on a roll, and started writing this piece about my father," recalled Waters in a rare interview with a fanzine. "The fact of the matter was that I was making this record. And Dave didn't like it. And he said so."

Gilmour, not a man prone to extended bouts of self-examination, believed that the album was indulgent and pessimistic and that it had nothing at all to do with his own beliefs.

In his view, the more specific Waters became in his references, the more the Floyd enigma was being sacrificed to Roger's therapeutic benefit. He also took the view that the songs had not been thought good enough for *The Wall*, and asked why bringing them back for *The Final Cut* made them any better.

The rest of the group's dismay at Waters's domination of the project culminated in a mighty row, which resulted in Gilmour withdrawing as co-producer of the album, leaving Waters to produce, with Michael Kamen and engineer James Guthrie. To be fair, Waters did ask Mason and Gilmour if they wanted it to be issued as a Waters solo album. They declined, but their presence is minimal, a fact underlined by the album's subtitle. As for Rick Wright, a founder member of Pink Floyd, he was out of the picture altogether and makes no appearance on the album sleeve at all.

For Mason, it was the most testing time in the band's recent turbulent career. The cohesion that had created the classic Floyd albums had been irreconcilably undermined. "I saw that album as the beginning of the end," he said. "I just thought, 'I can't really see how we can make the next record, or if we can it's a long time in the future, and it'll probably be more because of feeling some obligation that we ought to do it, rather than from enthusiasm'."

This dilemma was avoided by Waters's decision, made during the early stages of work on *The Final Cut*, that he would never work with Gilmour or Mason again.

Despite reaching number 1 in the UK and a respectable number 6 in the US, the album was not a lasting seller and only notched up 3 million sales, which in Floydian terms is a failure.

The Post-War Dream

(WATERS)

THE POST-WAR DREAM

WATERS, GILMOUR, MASON.
MICHAEL KAMEN *harmonium*
ANDY BOWN *Hammond organ*
NATIONAL PHILHARMONIC ORCHESTRA *brass and strings.*

The broadcast with which the album begins includes an item on the decision by the British

Mrs Thatcher, jingoistic British PM.

government to have the replacement ship for *The Atlantic Conveyor* (a requisitioned container vessel that sank in the Falklands following a rocket attack, with the loss of 24 crew) built in Japan rather than in the Clydeside shipyards where the contract was desperately needed to keep men in work.

It had long been Waters's abiding belief that we are all guilty of perpetuating war, seeing it as a grim necessity. The song suggests that, in war, the lives of people like Waters's father are sacrificed to an economic principle that has its basis in trade and political machinations.

"Economic cycles still override everything, with the best intentions, the cycle of economic recession, followed by resurgence, still governs our actions," said Waters in an interview with journalist Karl Dallas. "We'll get into a great big down and somebody somewhere, by some mistake, or just because they think it seems like a good idea, will press the button and that'll be the end."

The song was widely criticised at the time. There were those who saw Waters's cynical sideswipes at 'Maggie' (the former British prime minister Margaret Thatcher who swept to victory for a second term after the Falklands conflict, on a tide of post-war jingoistic euphoria) as hypocritical in the light of Waters's extraordinary wealth. The term 'champagne socialist' was bandied about.

But the song also got Waters into trouble for his use of the British slang pejorative 'Nips', to refer to the Japanese, and for suggesting that the young are all hell-bent on committing suicide! Waters defended himself. "Just because something's going to be a lyric in a song that lots of people may listen to, doesn't mean that one should temper one's personal feelings any more than one would talking to somebody in a pub."

Waters evokes powerful memories of the holocaust using holophnic sound effects of clanking railway cars of the kind that transported Jews, homosexuals and undesirables to their deaths at Dacchau, Belsen and Auschwitz.

Your Possible Pasts

(WATERS)

YOUR POSSIBLE PASTS

WATERS, GILMOUR, MASON.
MICHAEL KAMEN *piano*
RAY COOPER *tambourine*
ANDY BOWN *Hammond organ*

Over a backing track originally written for *The Wall* and using lyrics from the version of 'Stop' from the *Pink Floyd The Wall* movie, 'Your Possible Pasts' begins with a 'Holophonic' recording of the ominous sound of the clanking of railway wagons, evoking the long freight trains that transported Jews, gypsies, homosexuals and opponents of the Nazi regime to their doom in concentration camps.

Waters makes the point that the past is mutable and that it is easy to forget. Long a fan of Orwell, one of the first writers to address the nature of war, propaganda and the economic reality behind international conflict, Waters felt deeply that war crimes of biblical proportions, that had occurred so recently in our collective past, had apparently taught us nothing about the nature of those conflicts and why they arose.

Having been recorded some time earlier, the track features a very saturated guitar solo from Dave Gilmour which adds some traditional Floydian interest to Waters's bleak emotional landscape.

One Of The Few

(WATERS)

ONE OF THE FEW

WATERS *bass, lead vocal*
GILMOUR *acoustic guitar*

This short bridging piece is used to establish that 'the teacher' - a character familiar to us from *The Wall* - had once been a bomber pilot in the war and, having survived it (unlike Eric Fletcher Waters), had turned to teaching as a career. Having fought himself, and seen so many die, the schoolteacher is now preparing his pupils for the same eventuality, educating them for death.

The title is taken from Winston Churchill's legendary address to the nation which stated, "Never in the field of human conflict was so much owed by so many to so few,"

Rupert Brooke, World War One poet.

about the RAF pilots who fought and won The Battle Of Britain. Eric Fletcher Waters served in Bomber command.

The Hero's Return

(WATERS)

THE HERO'S RETURN

WATERS *vocals*
GILMOUR *lead and rhythm guitar*
MASON *drums,*
ANDY BOWN *Yamaha electric piano*

'The Hero' is tormented by images and dreams of the dead that he's unable to discuss with his stentorian wife. In the lyric the schoolteacher tells his pupils of how, at their age, he was facing death on a daily basis, while they are ingrates who show no sign of appreciation. And while he was cheered and the banners were unfurled on his return from war, no one ever addressed the memories. At the end, we hear what must be "the gunner's dying words on the intercom", as the plane goes down: 'the gunner' is Eric F. Waters.

Journalist Miles recalls how Roger was overwhelmed by the reaction to this piece of a lady, standing behind him in a checkout queue at a London store, who asked him, out of the blue, where his father was killed. He was taken aback, until the woman revealed that her father, too, had been killed in the war, and that *The Final Cut* had brought back very moving memories, reducing her to tears. This apparently justified everything to Waters, who was still not entirely sure why he'd allowed his obsession with the war and his father's death to dominate his life and the music of Pink Floyd for so long.

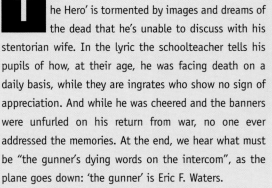

RAF bomber crew, World War Two.

The Gunner's Dream

(WATERS)

THE GUNNER'S DREAM

WATERS *bass, lead vocal*
GILMOUR *acoustic guitar* **MASON** *drums,* **RAPH RAVENSCROFT** *sax*
ANDY BOWN *Steinway piano*
NPO *strings*

'The Gunner's Dream' concerns every ex-serviceman's and woman's desire to see an end to war and atrocity, and the hope that we should in some way strive for a more humanistic, egalitarian and utopian society, free of violence. Unfortunately, as veterans from many twentieth century conflicts, from World War One to Vietnam, can attest, this idealism is almost always betrayed by governments and a society anxious to forget war, or a population unable to imagine the reality of front-line combat, finding it hard to assimilate returning veterans.

In the last verse, Waters lifts a line from one of the most powerful pieces of war poetry ever written, Rupert Brooke's World War One sonnet *The Soldier*. Brooke, a Cantabrigian who lived for many years in the Grantchester area, was an enduring influence on Waters, from his very earliest compositions with The Pink Floyd. The sonnet contains the famous lines "If I should die, think only this of me/That there's some corner of a foreign field/That is forever England". Running as an undercurrent through the song and the album is a deep paranoia and suspicion of governments who play people to suit their own political and economic ends. "'The Gunner's Dream' is about powerlessness," commented Waters. "The door opens suddenly and you find you're face to face with blokes in jackboots in a country like South America or Algeria or France during The Occupation . . . you cry, 'No you can't do that to me - I'll call the police!' and they reply, 'We are the police'."

In the video that accompanied the album we hear 'The Hero/Teacher' (played by Alex McAvoy who was also 'The Teacher' in *The Wall*) talking about losing his son in the Falklands conflict.

Musically, the track is one of the best on the album, featuring a powerful, dynamic sax break from Raph Ravenscroft, the man who made Gerry Rafferty's 'Baker Street' an international hit back in the late 70s.

Paranoid Eyes

(WATERS)

PARANOID EYES

WATERS, GILMOUR, MASON.
ANDY BOWN *organ, piano*
RAY COOPER *percussion*
NPO *strings* **ZUCCERELLI LABS** *Holophonic effects*

'Paranoid Eyes' is a moving portrait of the rapidly disillusioned and ageing schoolmaster and others like him, who have sacrificed their dreams for people who neither understand nor care what they went through to provide them with their continued liberty.

When *The Final Cut* first hit the stores there was a major media buzz about the use of the 3D 'Holophonics' system. This complex recording process, patented by Zuccerelli Labs, is a computer-enhanced system that creates the illusion of 3D sound effects in a two-dimensional recording. The opening section is almost entirely orchestral, infused with a variety of holophonic effects, including the teacher weaving his way to the pub to blot out the memories and the misery, a whispered approach from a prostitute and then the sounds of drinking and gambling. The song then explores the way in which people are expected to maintain a 'stiff upper lip' over the pain they've suffered in war. This was influenced by Waters's reading of the life story of World War Two air ace Douglas Bader who, despite enormous setbacks in his life, such as having two tin legs (his own having both been amputated after a plane crash) and having seen so many young men fly to their deaths, continued to fly, but led a crippled emotional life because he could never free himself of the guilt and sadness of what he had seen.

Get Your Filthy Hands Off My Desert

(WATERS)

GET YOUR FILTHY HANDS OFF MY DESERT

WATERS *vocals*
NATIONAL PHILHARMONIC ORCHESTRA *strings*

Side two opens with one of the most spectacular uses of sound effects on any Pink Floyd album. In this case, the treated sound of a missile, which launches in front of the listener, passes overhead and then explodes to the rear (try it on headphones!).

Over a simple string quartet arrangement, a croaky Waters takes a typically cynical look at the politics that began the Falklands conflict. Leonid Brezhnev was Premier of the former Soviet Union (which was engaged in a Vietnam-like war in Afghanistan), Menachem Begin was Prime Minister of Israel and Leopoldo Galtieri was the President of Argentina and instigator of the Falklands conflict through his attempted occupation of the Falkland Islands, a British crown colony. Margaret Thatcher announced to the world that she was sending a task force to claim the islands back from the Argentineans (who believed the islands were rightfully theirs, being somewhat closer to Argentina than Britain). Waters satirises the apparent ease with which politicians dispatch men to their deaths, by referring to the moment when Thatcher decided, at a Cabinet luncheon, that Britain was at war with Argentina. His wordplay on desert and dessert sets up a neat conceptual parallel between bloated politicians fighting over their desserts at some great political banquet, and the way they fight over land and peoples, like children over an ice cream.

Sir Galahad, sunk in the Falklands.

Left: Paranoid eyes.

THE FLETCHER MEMORIAL HOME

WATERS *vocals*
GILMOUR *guitar* **BOWN** *piano*
MASON *drums*
NPO *strings*

The Fletcher Memorial Home

(WATERS)

In the album's moment of dark humour, Waters imagines a fictitious rest-home for ageing dictators, The Fletcher Memorial Home, clearly named after Roger's father. In this bitter lyric, which Waters practically spits at the listener, he expresses his feelings about the tyrants - including everyone from Thatcher and Reagan to Ian Paisley, Senator McCarthy and Richard Nixon - who have toyed with human life with the kind of abandon that a child might demonstrate in playing with plastic soldiers. Roger's 'final solution' for these uncaring demagogues is the same as that which one of their number dreamed up at Wannsee, Germany on 20 January, 1942: extermination in some similarly vile, inhuman fashion.

SOUTHAMPTON DOCK

WATERS *acoustic guitar, bass, vocals*
ANDY BOWN *piano*
NPO *strings*
ZUCCERELLI LABS *holophonics*

Southampton Dock

(WATERS)

When the task force set sail for the Falkland Islands, Southampton Dock was the embarkation point. Requisitioned cruise liners had been fitted out with helicopter decks and guns. As the fleet set sail, the dockside teemed with wives and loved ones saying goodbye to men and women on their way to the unknown. It was an occasion that was appropriated for a display of patriotism, covered on all the news media, who relished the heart-rending stories of newly married couples being parted and parents being separated from their children. What struck Waters, as he watched the curiously upbeat and optimistic footage, was that the troops were going off to fight in a real conflict from which some of them would never return. In the second verse it's likely that the woman standing upon Southampton Dock is Margaret Thatcher, and the 'slippery reins' that she grips are the reins of state.

Part of the song's imagery, as well as that of 'Your Possible Pasts' is the poppy, an important symbol of war in Europe, with red paper poppies worn in tribute to war veterans, living and dead, each Remembrance Sunday in the UK. The seeds of poppies can lie in the ground for years without germinating, and grow once the ground has been disturbed; consequently, after the battles of World War One violently churned the soil, the ground where many men had died became a blaze of blood-red flowers: nature's memorial to the fallen.

THE FINAL CUT

WATERS, GILMOUR, MASON
BOWN *piano, keyboards*
RAY COOPER *tambourine*
NPO *strings*

The Final Cut

(WATERS)

In film terminology the 'final cut' is the finished article, the edited version from which the negative and all future prints will be made. It's also an expression for a Brutus-like stab in the back, which was what Waters felt he had suffered as a result of his frustrating experiences with *The Wall* director Alan Parker. On the album sleeve, Waters, dressed in a military jacket, with a meat cleaver between his shoulder blades, can be seen holding film cans. For performances of the material during his solo live shows, Waters had a jacket made which had a knife protruding from the back that oozed fake blood when he squeezed a bulb in the pocket.

NOT NOW JOHN

WATERS *vocals, tapes, synth*
GILMOUR *vocals, bass, guitar*
MASON *drums*
THE BLACKBERRIES *b.vocals*

Not Now John

(WATERS)

This song has Gilmour and Waters, surprisingly, sharing the vocal duties, although this was only because Waters needed another voice to portray the character of the man who, despite what he sees going on around him, avoids confronting it and simply ignores injustice because he has to get on with being a rock star. Roger Waters: "It's a very schizophrenic song, because there's this one character, singing the verses, who's irritated by all this moaning about how desperate things are, and doesn't want to hear any of it anymore. There's part of me in that. Then there's this other voice which keeps harping back to earlier songs, saying 'make them laugh, make them cry, make them dance in the aisles', which is from 'One Of The Few'. So it's a strange song."

The song also parodies the English football hooligan or lager lout, narrow-minded xenophobes who demand that foreigners speak in English, specialise in racial abuse and aggressive taunting of rivals and have a tendency to bellow patriotic songs such as 'Rule Britannia' when they've had a few drinks. It is Waters's comment on the blind nationalism that seems to drive so many people.

For the single release, the line "Fuck all that" was replaced by "Stuff all that". Gilmour had to go back into the studio with some backing singers, especially to re-sing the word "stuff". Twenty years and 130 million album sales later, the Floyd were still at the mercy of the BBC censors.

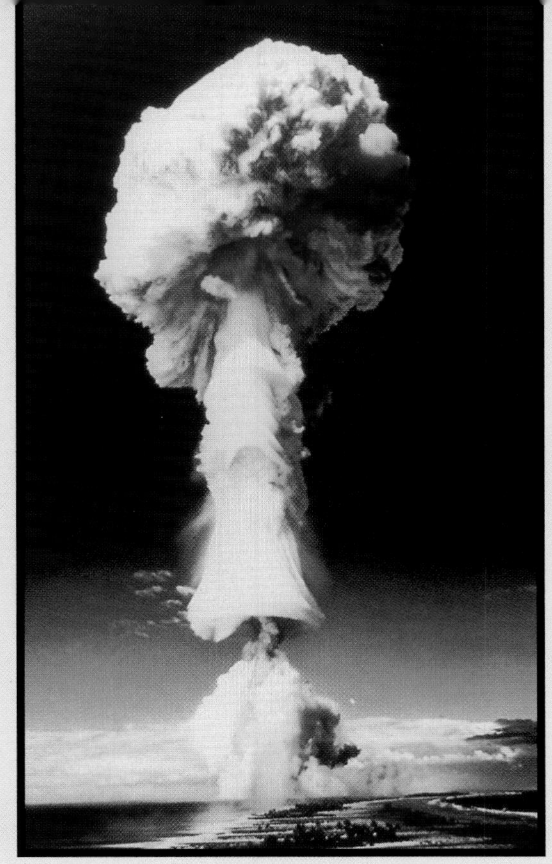

Far left: Once estranged from the other members of Pink Floyd Roger Waters found public interest in his records and live shows dwindled.'

Left: A classic atomic mushroom cloud, a powerful symbol of the cold war years which Waters evokes in* Two Suns In the Sunset. *Waters was inspired by such films as* The War Game. *This was the last tack recorded by the Waters led Pink Floyd.

Two Suns In The Sunset

(WATERS)

As the album began with a radio broadcast, so it ends with one, as 'The Hero' drives off into the sunset and is dazzled by a second sun in his rear-view mirror. The inspiration for the image of the two suns came while Waters was driving home from the studio and began thinking about the notorious film *The War Game*, which he'd seen on TV the week before. Made for BBC TV in 1961, the film wasn't screened at the time because it was, in the words of the censors, too realistic. *The War Game* depicts a nuclear bomb dropping on London, and the possible aftermath. A government embargo was slapped onto the documentary-styled drama amid claims that the film-makers were scaremongering. More likely was that the government were concerned that the film's shocking and terrifying scenes would undoubtedly cause the public to question the nuclear arms policies of the time.

"We all sit around and talk about the possibility of accidents, or as I put it in the song, people just getting so bloody angry that finally somebody pushes a button. Well, the song's all about that moment when suddenly it happens, you know it's happened and you know, it's the end, you're dead, and it's the end of the world, and that you'll never see your kids again or your wife or anybody that you love, and it's over." To make this point, Waters uses the voices of his two children, Harry and India. Whereas previous songs on the album seem, mostly, to be about betrayal of past generations, the finale concerns itself with loyalty to future generations, underlining one the album's central themes, that it is our current duty not to let war happen, that it can be avoided, and that our belief that we cannot do anything to prevent it is our failing.

"It's very easy to go, 'Oh yes, well, there may be an accident and the holocaust may happen,' without having the feeling of what it might be like," commented Waters. "And that's why it says in the song, 'Finally I understand the feelings of The Few' which is supposed to be a reference to the bomber and the gunner and all those people, my dad, and all the other war casualties. That song, I suppose, in a way, is going back to the second song where there's a line, 'a warning to anyone still in command of their possible futures to take care'."

The drums on the track were eventually played by Andy Newmark, famed for his work for everyone from Sly Stone to Roxy Music. Mason attempted to play the part for about a week, but couldn't get the feel that Waters wanted. "Finally I thought, 'Let's not get too precious about this, let Andy Newmark do it the way you want it done,' rather than me spend weeks trying to get it absolutely stylistically right," says Mason. "It still doesn't seem that important to me."

'Two Suns' was the last track recorded by the original

TWO SUNS IN THE SUNSET

WATERS *acoustic guitar, vocals, bass*
GILMOUR *rhythm guitar*
ANDY NEWMARK *drums*
ANDY BOWN *organ*
RAPH RAVENSCROFT *sax*

A Momentary Lapse Of Reason

1994

RECORDED *June 1986-Summer 1987 at* Astoria *(Gilmour's houseboat studio on the Thames at Hampton), Britannia Row Studios, Islington, A&M Studios, Los Angeles, Can Am Studios, Los Angeles, Village Recorder, Los Angeles, Mayfair, London, Le Mobile, Los Angeles, Audio International, London*
DAVID GILMOUR *guitars, all lead vocals, keyboards, sequencers*
NICK MASON *electric and acoustic drums, sound effects*

ADDITIONAL INSTRUMENTATION

RICHARD WRIGHT *piano, vocals Kurzweil, Hammond organ*
BOB EZRIN *keyboards, percussion sequencers*
TONY LEVIN *bass guitar, Chapman stick*
JIM KELTNER *drums*
STEVE FORMAN *percussion*
JON CARIN *keyboards*
TOM SCOTT *alto and soprano saxophones*
SCOTT PAGE *tenor saxophone*
CARMINE APPICE *drums*
PAT LEONARD *synthesizers*
BILL PAYNE *Hammond organ*
MICHAEL LANDAU *guitar*
JOHN HALLIWELL *saxophone*
DARLENE KOLDENHAVEN, CARMEN TWILLIE, PHYLLIS ST JAMES, DONNIE GERRARD *backing vocals*
RELEASED *7 September, 1987*
CHART PLACING *Number 3 in the UK; Number 6 in the US*
PRODUCED BY *BOB EZRIN AND DAVID GILMOUR*
COVER BY *STORM THORGERSON AND NEXUS*

As early as 1985, spurred by the realisation his solo career wasn't going to take off, Dave Gilmour had decided it was the Pink Floyd name that was important to the fans, not the individual band members. Waters's solo outings had been poorly received too, his tours sometimes playing to less than 2000 paying fans, a clear indication that if the band were to achieve any level of success they had to revive the Pink Floyd brand name. Waters had made it plain that he was not intending to record with Pink Floyd again, and had given the band freedom to use the name, believing that they could not function without his input. It was an act of hubris that Waters would live to regret.

Just as Jenner and King had felt that the Pink Floyd were simply not a viable proposition without Syd, so Waters had believed that Gilmour, Mason and an errant Wright would simply not have the creative wherewithal to structure the kind of album that the public expected from an act such as Pink Floyd. Even EMI, the Floyd's label, had its reservations, and refused to put up the substantial advance necessary to record a Floyd album, wary that a Waters-less Floyd would not be accepted by the public.

Gilmour was determined to make the album a Pink Floyd project. Resolve was strengthened when Roger Waters issued a statement to the effect that he would not be recording again with Pink Floyd, describing the remaining members and the Pink Floyd name as "a creatively spent force". It was assumed that this was the end for one of the most popular groups in rock history.

At a meeting of Pink Floyd Music Ltd, the clearing house for all Floyd-related projects, where he learned that a new bank account had been set up to receive money from a new and untitled Pink Floyd project, Waters, convinced that the Floyd could not go on without him, had agreed to let the others have the rights to the name. Now that they'd actually decided to use it, he was enraged, and he immediately instigated proceedings to have the rights to the name withdrawn, claiming that he was Pink Floyd. It was Waters's megalomania versus Gilmour's abject frustration at his former colleague's arrogance and despotism over the years.

On 10 November, 1986, manager Steve O'Rourke issued a terse, almost humorous statement: "Pink Floyd is alive and well and recording in England." It was the opening salvo in a bitter personal battle that would eventually end up in the High Court in London.

In fact, when the statement was issued, recording had been underway for some five months on Gilmour's houseboat studio, *Astoria*, moored on

Live Aid ***at Wembley, 13 July, 1985.***

the Thames at Hampton. Dave recorded some demos and jammed with people like Bob Ezrin and Jon Carin to come up with ideas, although they were having trouble coming up with a satisfactory concept for the album.

A record company executive from the American label CBS flew over to hear the work in progress, and he was not impressed. "It doesn't sound like the Floyd," he complained. Ezrin and Gilmour agreed that it just didn't have the necessary edge, and recording started again from scratch. "We never sat down and said, 'God, this doesn't sound Pink Floyd enough - let's do this to make it sound more Pink Floyd'," said a defensive Gilmour, in the notes to the *Shine On* box set. "We just worked on the songs until they sounded right . . . that's when it became Pink Floyd. I don't take any notice of record companies anyway, they just manufacture the records . . . . . until such a day comes as they make a loss on one of our records, which they've never done, it'll stay that way."

Roger Waters's reaction to news that tracks were progressing was to state that an attempt was being made to fake the Pink Floyd sound, in order to ensure the financial success of the album.

Phase two of the work began with another attempt to manufacture a concept for the record. Gilmour brought in Liverpudlian poet Roger McGough and Canadian songwriter Carole Pope, who listened to some of the material and tried to make it coalesce. After several weeks of unsatisfactory brainstorming, Ezrin and Gilmour gave up on the idea of a unifying theme, preferring to believe that the album had a pervasive atmosphere instead, dictated by the fact that most of the tracks had been recorded on Gilmour's turn of the century houseboat. The river would become the album's theme.

Things began to run more smoothly. With creative collaborators on lyrics, and session players who could help him interpret his ideas, Gilmour's ideas began to fall into place, and by the early months of 1987 most of the tracks were complete. Finally, it came time to retrieve Rick Wright from obscurity in Greece. Wright had approached Gilmour in mid-1986, when news that work had begun on a new album had filtered through to him, and he had sent word through his lawyer that he wanted to work with Gilmour again, was prepared to forget the past and, with Waters out of the way, forge something new.

And so it was, in February 1987, that Rick Wright boarded the Astoria for his first serious encounter with Gilmour since the *The Wall* tour had ended in 1981. In the interim, Wright, disillusioned and crippled by feelings of rejection, was content to live out his time sailing his yacht *Gala* round the world. Gilmour saw a changed man, one eager to get work again now that Waters, who had been particularly dismissive of Wright, was out of the picture. More calculating, however, Gilmour saw Wright as providing a greater credibility for the fans and strength for his position in the legal hassles with Waters over the use of the name. It was agreed that Wright would join as a salaried member of the band on $11,000 a week. He would not become a full member of the band again until 1994, and had no real creative input on *A Momentary Lapse Of Reason*, save for a few Fender Rhodes overdubs and the odd Hammond part added during the final mixdown sessions, at A&M studios in Los Angeles during the summer of 1987. The credits on the album belie the fact that Gilmour played most of the parts himself and gave Wright the credit out of kindness, and because it again strengthened his legal position. The same happened with Nick Mason, who is credited with drums and programming, but in an advanced state of creative torpor himself, only contributed only a few tom-tom parts to the album.

With the album completed and mixed, it came time for that all-important cover, and a title. After considering *Signs Of Life* (rejected because it was thought to be ammunition for the kind of journalists who like to take pot shots at middle-aged rock stars), *Of Promises Broken*, and finally *Delusions Of Maturity*, Gilmour decided that the line "a momentary lapse of reason", from the song 'One Slip', was the most Floydian-sounding. "It's a superb title for a so-called Pink Floyd record," commented Roger Waters drily.

For the cover, Gilmour called in Storm Thorgerson, whose last Floyd work had been for *Animals* in 1976, with the idea for an abandoned room that would contain images and references to the past, to failed relationships, the symbol of which was an empty bed. This gave Thorgerson the idea for a river of hospital beds - an image that incorporated the fluvial theme and the slight sense of dislocated madness that the title suggests.

After flying to America to shoot the scene in Los Angeles, Thorgerson discovered there were no suitable beds to be had, so the team returned to the UK and rented 800 NHS hospital beds. Because Thorgerson insisted the photo should be real, and not a computerised manipulation, the group had to employ 30 handlers to shift the beds on and off the sandy headlands of Saunton Sands in North Devon on the morning of 15 June, 1987.

Signs Of Life

(GILMOUR, EZRIN)

The album's opening track has its origins in a guitar demo that Dave Gilmour recorded as a potential track for his first solo album, *David Gilmour*, back in 1978. In the search for material for the new record, each band member had trawled through oddments from their past to scrape together enough material to at least begin working. The fact that the band hadn't really played together for so long meant that the process was slow and difficult at first, despite the enthusiasm of all concerned to rekindle the Floyd sound. Gilmour revised the lead guitar but the backing chords are taken directly from the original demo. Co-written by Dave Gilmour and Bob Ezrin, who was also serving as co-producer on the album, 'Signs Of Life' is one of the Floyd's impressionistic synth and guitar pieces and was briefly considered as the album's title track until someone remarked to Gilmour that it was a gift to sarcastic reviewers.

If there's a theme running through this album, it's the rather cliched notion of the river as a metaphor for life. To establish this, the first sound on the album is that of a boat on the river. Mason, despite not playing many of the drums, did take charge of the sound effects and montages, as he had done on *Dark Side Of The Moon*. "The boat was one of the earliest things we started with as a sound effect because it's such a romantic sound; so clear when we recorded it."

SIGNS OF LIFE

GILMOUR *programming, electric guitars, keyboards*
BOB EZRIN *programming, additional keyboards*
MASON *location ambient sound effects*

Learning To Fly

(GILMOUR, MOORE, EZRIN, CARIN)

The first song to be recorded for the album, in 1986, the original ideas for 'Learning To Fly' came from keyboardist Jon Carin in a jam session with Dave Gilmour, following the latter's appearance in *Live Aid* playing with Bryan Ferry, when the two went off to Gilmour's home studio. "I had to go down to the station to pick someone up," recalled Gilmour in an interview with Floyd fanzine *The Amazing Pudding*. "When I got back, he'd done this, and so we pinched a bit of it. Simple."

As well as Jon, Bob Ezrin helped to write this song, and Anthony Moore lent a hand with the lyrics. Moore had been asked to help out on the album because Dave didn't feel that words were his strong point (although songs like 'Sorrow' would, to some extent, prove him wrong).

On the surface, the song is simply about Gilmour's experiences learning to fly aircraft (he now owns six historic aeroplanes). Anthony Moore was always hard at work, but Gilmour had a habit of showing up late at the studio, and his excuse was all too predictable. Dave would ring in and apologise, "I'm not coming in today, because I'm learning to fly."

In a wider sense, the song was a metaphor for the fact that Gilmour himself was learning to pilot the Floyd. Now in control, he was experiencing a trepidation which he likened to the experience of going up solo in an aircraft. In the middle of the track you can hear Nick Mason, another flyer, going through his pre-flight checks with the control tower.

LEARNING TO FLY

GILMOUR *electric and acoustic guitar, vocals, sequencing, drum programming*
BOB EZRIN *drum programming*
MASON *additional percussion programs, sound effects*
JIM KELTNER *acoustic drum samples*
JON CARIN *keyboards*
TONY LEVIN *bass*
DARLENE KOLDENHAVEN, CARMEN TWILLIE, PHYLLIS ST. JAMES, DONNIE GERARD *backing vocals*

ONE SLIP

GILMOUR *guitars, vocals, programming* **BOB EZRIN** *additional drum programming*
BILL PAYNE *organ*
TONY LEVIN *bass, Chapman Stick*
UNKNOWN *acoustic drums* (APPICE, MASON OR KELTNER)
BACKING VOCALS: SEE 'LEARNING TO FLY'.

THE DOGS OF WAR

GILMOUR, BOB EZRIN.
BILL PAYNE *organ*
TOM SCOTT *alto and soprano sax*

DRUMS, BACKING VOCALS: SEE 'ONE SLIP'.

ON THE TURNING AWAY

GILMOUR, BOB EZRIN.
RICK WRIGHT *organ*
STEVE FORMAN *percussion*
TOM SCOTT *alto and soprano sax*

DRUMS, BACKING VOCALS: SEE 'ONE SLIP'

Right: Phil Manzanera, co-writer, One Slip.

Thriller writer Frederick Forsyth.

According to Mason, the song was intended to be an optimistic way of saying that the band were taking off once more, after a period of being grounded by events beyond their control. "The first demo that Dave gave me had the 'Learning To Fly' idea, it had the 'Dogs Of War' idea; everything was potentially a good track and that's what the album launched from. 'Learning To Fly' actually started out more spiritually uplifting than it sounded when it was finished. I like it because every time I hear it, I hear my own voice doing this take-off."

The Dogs Of War

(GILMOUR, MOORE)

Taking its title from Shakespeare's *Julius Caesar* ('Cry havoc and let slip the dogs of war'), this song took its theme from Frederick Forsyth's novel about mercenaries, both spiritual and physical, who sell themselves to whichever side offers the highest price, and it benefitted from Anthony Moore's help on the words.

Dave Gilmour: "I had the idea, and explained it to Anthony, and he came up with the first draft of words - we chopped and changed it over quite a long time until it wound up as it is. The music was done, fairly much, when we had a computer accident that took a sample of someone laughing and accidentally played it. In the background, this laughter actually sounded like dogs yapping, and the way I'd sung the demo also had elements of that long before we had that lyric."

One Slip

(GILMOUR, MANZANERA)

This song, considered one of the more important on the album, is a regretful and speculative song of hindsight concerning an illicit sexual encounter, possibly one resulting in an unwanted pregnancy. The uncharacteristically candid Gilmour lyric also provided the album with its title. Phil Manzanera, former guitarist with Roxy Music, was a key contributor.

Dave Gilmour: "Most of the music for 'One Slip' came from him. We spent a couple of days throwing ideas around, and this was the one that fitted the album best."

Jon Carin: "When Dave gets involved with different people it brings out different aspects of his personality. Working with Phil Manzanera on 'One Slip', he wrote lyrics that he might not have ordinarily written."

Gilmour: "I personally get uncomfortable going out on choruses . . . so much a pop formula that I try to avoid it. We didn't quite do it on 'One Slip', which was going that way. In the end we did a chorus, then went out with an instrumental."

On The Turning Away

(GILMOUR, MOORE)

While Roger Waters was always one for nailing his red flag to the mast for all to see, Gilmour had always shied away from making his political thinking overt. Though the clearly humanitarian lyric to this song came mostly from Anthony Moore, it met with Gilmour's wholehearted approval. "It's a social commentary I suppose - one can't say much more than that. We did argue at length about whether in the last verse one should get preachy, but in the end we said 'Let's preach!'. Anthony Moore came up with the basic idea and wrote the first set of lyrics, so I can't claim to have been the instigator, but as soon as I saw them, I said, 'That's perfect, that's exactly what we want'."

Unfortunately, Rick Wright's one keyboard solo on the album, which was in this song, ended up on the cutting-room floor. Rick Wright: ". . . not because they didn't like it, they just thought it didn't fit." Additionally, this song was originally supposed to have an orchestral accompaniment, composed by Bob Ezrin and Jon Carin, but this idea, also, was dropped.

Humphrey Bogart, in **Casablanca.**

Yet Another Movie

(GILMOUR, LEONARD)

Certainly one of the stand-out tracks from the album, 'Yet Another Movie', co-written with one-time Madonna collaborator Patrick Leonard, features two soundbites, one from Marlon Brando in *On The Waterfront*, the other from the film *Casablanca* at the end, and the lyric 'a vision of an empty bed,' which was the inspiration for the cover.

The most surreal lyric that Gilmour had attempted thus far, the images of 'Yet Another Movie' are simple, yet evocative. There are clear echoes of the 'One Slip' scenario - a wronged woman, a contrite man - but it is much less specific. "It's hard to explain 'Yet Another Movie'," admits Gilmour. "I've tended to stick within personal experience and reality very much; but I have a desire, without getting into fiction and little stories about other people (which I generally don't care for), to find a broader base to write things about - and that's an attempt to do that. I'm very fond of it, but I don't even know what all of it means myself!"

Nick Mason: "It's one of my favourites on the album, I think just because of the way it was recorded. It was an unforgettable occasion: this enormous studio with more drums than I've ever seen in my whole life. We had Jim Keltner's kit, my kit, Steve Forman the percussion player with all his stuff, and two of these people known as 'drum doctors' who are ultra-specialist drum people. They set the drums up, tune them and so on - bring you seven snare drums and say 'Which one do you think you would like to use for this?' Just the power and the sound of all that air being moved by these drums . . . real 'drum city' in there that day! In the past, we've used musicians other than the group, even if they haven't always been credited: it doesn't mean that I'm not playing on all the tracks. On 'Yet Another Movie', all three of us played together - the percussionist, Jim Keltner and me. We drummed in unison but, at other times, I kept the rhythm whilst the others played fills. It's a different approach which benefits the music."

YET ANOTHER MOVIE

GILMOUR, BOB EZRIN. PAT LEONARD *synths,* **TONY LEVIN** *bass,* **BILL PAYNE** *organ*
MASON *drums*
BACKING VOCALS:
SEE 'LEARNING TO FLY'.

Round And Around

(GILMOUR)

Labelled as track '6a' on the album, 'Round And Around' was the instrumental coda to 'Yet Another Movie' and segues into 'A New Machine Part 1'. It was a snatched instrumental segment that Gilmour rescued from earlier demos. On the live album, *A Delicate Sound Of Thunder*, the track lasts for just 30 seconds and is the shortest ever released by Pink Floyd.

ROUND AND AROUND

GILMOUR *guitars vocals keyboard programing*
BOB EZRIN *additional programming*

Live, '6a' featured firework bursts.

Gilmour, the reluctant frontman.

A New Machine Part 1

(GILMOUR)

A NEW MACHINE PARTS 1 & 2
GILMOUR *vocals, Vocoder vocals, keyboard programming*
BOB EZRIN *additional programming, keyboards, treatments*

The Vocoder was not a new instrument to Pink Floyd, although, in the age of MIDI digital keyboards and processing, the strange electronic vocals provided by the device are considered somewhat passé. In 1977, on *Animals*, it had been used to treat the barking of the dogs, and also for a parody of the 23rd Psalm. On this album, using it in conjunction with noise gates, the band achieved effects no one had before.

Gilmour had always believed that the problem with latter Pink Floyd albums had been Roger Waters's tendency to be too specific in his lyrics, jeopardising the subtle balance between the music and the concept. Not a natural poet, many of Gilmour's self-penned lyrics are very oblique and, as the author himself admits, they often have no discernible meaning at all. This is one such song, although it ostensibly deals with seeing yourself and wanting to change. The song has nothing to do with 'Welcome To The Machine' from *Wish You Were Here*, and many fans mark 'A New Machine Part 1' as one of the worst recordings the band ever made.

Terminal Frost

(GILMOUR)

TERMINAL FROST

GILMOUR *guitars, vocals, keyboard programming*
BOB EZRIN *additional drum programming*
TONY LEVIN *bass*
BILL PAYNE *organ*
RICK WRIGHT *organ, piano*
TOM SCOTT *alto and soprano sax*
MICHAEL LANDAU *Spanish guitar*

Both 'Terminal Frost' and 'A New Machine' were tracks that Gilmour had recorded as demo ideas some two years before *A Momentary Lapse Of Reason*, when he was planning a third solo album. At that point Gilmour had not entertained the idea that he would end up fronting Pink Floyd himself, and was resigned to a low level solo career. Of the two songs, 'Terminal Frost' bears the greatest resemblance to the original demo. "There was a long period where I thought I might get words for it and turn it into a song. In the end it decided for itself that it would remain the way it was." Cryptic as ever, the only lyric is "Never again, never again", echoed again and again. The title is thought to refer to Gilmour's relationship with Waters.

Some who worked on the album suggest that 'Terminal Frost' was originally designed to segue into a track called 'Peace Be With You', a gentler farewell to Roger that was recorded for the album, but left off. Those who heard it claim it was by far the best thing on the record. It is thought that the band felt it to be too personal and downbeat for the album. When the track was released as a single it included a 'Do Your Own Lead' version, in which some of Gilmour's guitar track was mixed out, allowing the bedroom guitar fantasist to play along.

A New Machine Part 2

(GILMOUR)

A reprise of 'A New Machine' dating from demos Gilmour had recorded two years earlier.

Sorrow

(GILMOUR)

Sorrow', the album's finale and longest song, was originally inspired by a poem Dave recalled, from which it actually draws its first line. "I've not actually managed to find the poem that the first line comes from. I probably should have put a credit on there to the person who inspired that line, but I just can't find the poem."

'Sorrow' was a rarity in that Dave went on to write the words in a more or less complete form before any of the music was written. "Most of 'Sorrow' got put down the day after I wrote it: the vocal of the verses, the background guitars, the drum parts and the lead guitar. The solo was done first take . . . I never got around to doing it again. (It was) done on the boat, my guitar going through a little Gallien-Krueger amp."

The solo features one of the most elaborate effects ever devised. The tapes of the track were flown to Los Angeles, where a 24 track mobile studio truck was waiting to be driven to the empty Los Angeles Sports Arena, so that Gilmour's solo could be played though a huge 30,000 watt PA. Special Q-Sound microphones were used to re-record the sounds in ambient 'stadium sound' 3D. According to Ezrin, it made Gilmour's solo through the tiny amp sound "like the Guitar From Hell".

SORROW

GILMOUR *guitars, vocals, keyboard programming*
BOB EZRIN *drum programming, additional keyboard textures*
RICK WRIGHT *Kurzweil*
TONY LEVIN *bass*
MASON *sampled percussion*
DARLENE KOLDENHAVEN, CARMEN TWILLIE, PHYLLIS ST JAMES, DONNIE GERARD *backing vocals*

Far left, middle: Roger Waters was changing his image after years of Floyd obscurity.* Terminal Frost *was Gilmour's first attempt to deal with his relationship with the estranged bassist.

Far left, below: Mason had invested wisely in vintage automobiles and was now the owner of one of the most valuable collections in the world.

Gilmour, bathed in chrysanthemum of light playng his Fender lap steel guitar during the Madision Square garden show on* Momentary Lapse of Reason *Tour.

The Division Bell

1994

Following *A Momentary Lapse Of Reason*, the Floyd leviathan hit the road for the first time in a decade, and successfully exorcised the ghost of Roger Waters. It was clear to the remaining members of the band that their fears at being seen as incomplete without Waters were unfounded. Pink Floyd had once more transcended the dominance of one individual member and reinvented itself.

Dave Gilmour, always a reluctant figurehead, took on the mantle of leader and succeeded in giving the Floyd a new impetus for the 90s. With their enthusiasm for music renewed, Pink Floyd began production meetings for a new album, at Dave Gilmour's houseboat studio, newly moored on the Thames at Richmond, in early 1993. The band felt it was the right time to go back to their roots and approach the album the way they had approached their 70s classics, *Wish You Were Here* and *Meddle*.

Wright, now reinstated as a full member of the band, observed that Pink Floyd hadn't felt like a proper band for a very long time, and that they should strive to make music that was, for better or for worse, played by the three musicians themselves, instead of nameless session players. Nick Mason, who had contributed very little in the way of drums on any Floyd album since *The Wall*, agreed, adding that he was sick of having session drummers do his job for him: "At least the basic ideas are all designed, and therefore playable, by the principals."

With Bob Ezrin again acting as the Floyd's co-producer, the band spent a fortnight at Britannia Row Studios, improvizing musical ideas, 50 in all, saved onto DAT tapes. Numbered 1 to 50 - the occasional idea given a title such as Rick's Moody One or Dave's Echo Riff - the ideas were then collated just as they had been for *Meddle* two decades earlier. "It's the first time we've done this bouncing-around-in-a-rehearsal-room type operation since 1974, and it feels wonderful," beamed an enthusiastic Gilmour. Even Rick Wright, whose input on albums since *Wish You Were Here* had been minimal, was enjoying renewed creative confidence. "I was involved right from the beginning with both the writing and the singing. It was a completely different situation . . . a partnership with the others. It was the three of us making a genuine Pink Floyd album. We were kind of thinking of *Wish You Were Here*, which happens to be my favourite album."

RECORDED *February-December, 1993, on Astoria (Gilmour's houseboat studio on the Thames at Richmond), and at Britannia Row, Abbey Road Studio 1 and 2, Metropolis, The Creek.*
MIXED BY *CHRIS THOMAS AND DAVID GILMOUR*
PRODUCED BY *BOB EZRIN AND DAVID GILMOUR*
RELEASED *5 April, 1994*
CHART PLACING *Number 2 in the UK; Number 1 in the US*
COVER DESIGN BY *STORM THORGERSON*

The spectacular **Division Bell** *tour.*

MPs rushing to a division, c. 1840.

CLUSTER ONE

WRIGHT *piano, sample loops, programming, Hammond organ*
GILMOUR *tremoloed Stratocaster guitar, keyboards, programming*
MASON *live drums*
BOB EZRIN *keyboards, percussion*

WHAT DO YOU WANT FROM ME?

MASON *sampled and live drums*
WRIGHT *digital Rhodes piano, keyboards*
GILMOUR *lead vocal, electric guitars, bass*
BOB EZRIN *keyboards, percussion*
SAM BROWN, DURGA MCBROOM, CAROL KENYON, JACKIE SHERIDAN, REBECCA LEIGH-WHITE *backing vocals*

The resulting record is, despite Waters's attestations that it was a very credible fake, the first true Pink Floyd album in over a decade, bearing all the unique trademarks that have made the band internationally known. Many of the songs deal with the fallout from the preceding decade in the tempestuous life of Pink Floyd. The theme for the album was another Floydian classic, non-communication, something all three band members knew all too much about, having wasted years in courts fighting each other, and going through messy divorces.

Once again the only potential stumbling block was the lyric writing. "I'm not a natural lyric writer," Gilmour reiterated, "and it has never been easy for me to write anything, certainly not of the standard of Roger, who was very focused and in my opinion an inspired writer." In an attempt to get around these problems, Gilmour farmed out various songs to different writers. The notion of a communications breakdown in a relationship was fresh in Gilmour's mind, as he was just surfacing from a broken marriage and had formed a new attachment to journalist and publishing executive Polly Samson, who is credited with breaking his writer's block and encouraging him to explore some of the feelings he harboured towards his ex-partners, particularly Waters. Samson contributed lyrics for seven of the album's eleven tracks.

Sonically, *The Division Bell* mixes digital and analogue recording technology, and is laden with the Floyd's characteristic impressionistic soundscapes. While it might lack the focus and flow of *Wish You Were Here*, and may not aspire to the conceptual daring of *The Wall*, it achieves a universal humanism and lyricism that usually eluded Waters, whose work was often harsh and solipsistic, and could sometimes be exclusive.

Cluster One

(WRIGHT, GILMOUR)

Just as *Wish You Were Here* opens with over four minutes of atmospherics before the first voice is heard, so *The Division Bell* begins with a mysterious, ominous feel, a classic Floyd sound collage of synths and a full six minutes of Gilmour laying down tasteful guitar over Wright's Satie-like piano lines. It is said that just as the introduction to 'Shine On You Crazy Diamond' was a musical paean to Syd Barrett, so 'Cluster One' was the new line-up's attempt to salute the departed Roger Waters. That said, the track was perfect as an atmospheric intro piece for when the band would arrive on stage.

What Do You Want From Me?

(GILMOUR, WRIGHT, SAMSON)

Gilmour's girlfriend Polly Samson lent a hand on lyrics for this song. Working on the principle that it takes two to make an argument, she provided at least half the inspiration. "A lot of the lyrics were the result of a collaboration between myself and Polly . . . and some, unfortunately, came after moments of lack of communication between us. The title came out of exactly one of those moments." In fact this was Gilmour's stock phrase whenever arguments between him and his new girlfriend got too much; he would simply turn and shout, "What do you want from me?". The song also refers, in true Waters-like fashion, to the experience of playing live and wondering what the crowd really want from a performer playing on the stage. Gilmour had long protested that Floyd fans elevated him to the status of a minor deity, with answers to problems of which he had no conception or understanding. "I'm just the guitar player in a rock 'n' roll band" was his stock answer when faced with questions that were beyond his scope. It is also thought that the middle section of the song refers to Waters "selling his soul for complete control". Again Gilmour has never been specific about this, but in the context of the court case it makes sense.

The bassline to the song, one of the first elements

Gilmour laid down on tape at the Astoria sessions, was inspired by 'Have A Cigar', which Gilmour had always felt could have been developed further.

Poles Apart

(GILMOUR, SAMSON, LAIRD-CLOWES)

It was a mark of how far the band had come, in the ten years since the break with Waters, that they were now able to deal with their embattled past and turn it into a paean for lost friendship. Roger Waters had been using his relationship with Syd Barrett for everything from single songs to full-blown concept albums. Gilmour's precise thoughts on what occurred back in the late 60s in the unhappy life of his old Cambridge friend remained largely unknown, save for the mournful four note refrain of 'Shine On You Crazy Diamond'. It was Polly Samson and Nick Laird-Clowes of The Dream Academy (who, like Kate Bush, had benefitted in the past from Gilmour's patronage), who helped Dave explore his own turbulent relationships with both Barrett and Waters.

The first verse concerns Syd, in particular his sad mental decline. Gilmour is very frank when he asks whether Syd knew that it was all going to go so wrong for him, while things would run smoothly for Gilmour himself. He also reprimands those sycophants who told Syd he was a genius, adding to the pressure Syd could never live up to. These words were apparently triggered by recollections of a particular event, when Gilmour first realised that his old friend was mentally fragmenting in front of him: Gilmour, in 1967, returned from a gig in France with his band Jokers Wild, and decided to drop in on Syd and the Floyd, who were recording 'See Emily Play' at Sound Techniques in Chelsea. Syd was acting very oddly, even for Syd, to the extent that he failed even to acknowledge Gilmour. The other period when Gilmour felt profoundly sad was during the recording of Syd's last solo album in 1970. The incapacitated Syd, confused and semi-incoherent, had to have his hand held during the sessions, and also had to be accompanied to the toilet. It was a profoundly disturbing time for Gilmour, who was producing the album, and felt awkward that he was entering the Floyd just as Syd was being ousted. "That had a very deep effect on David," says engineer Peter Bown. "He knew that this was the end for Syd, that he would never ever make it back to reality." On the other hand, Gilmour has always stated that the influence of Barrett on latterday Floyd is overestimated and that Syd is deified by those who do not understand what really went on back in 1968.

The second verse, with its references to the "steel in your eyes", is aimed at Roger Waters and deals, in particular, with Gilmour's belief that Waters was running from his own problems by alienating himself from the band, and just about everyone else; becoming 'Pink' from *The Wall*. By the final line, Gilmour has come to the conclusion that both Syd and Roger had lost the "light in their eyes". The protagonist is determined not to let it happen to him, seeking to express that Waters and Syd are poles apart from him in temperament.

Marooned

(WRIGHT, GILMOUR)

Based around a Rick Wright chord sequence that arose from the initial sessions on *Astoria*, Gilmour wanted to include the track as an epic and emotive jam "of the kind we used to do all the time in the old days". Reminiscent of 'Comfortably Numb', the track builds from an atmospheric synth and piano intro, with the sound of seagulls wheeling overhead, into a full blown Floydian epic. "For me music is very lyric-dominated these days and I love lyrics and I love songs," commented Gilmour of his own work. "But I also like listening to a good instrumental, and a good piece of playing on any instrument. A beautiful chord sequence can be very provocative and emotional."

A Great Day For Freedom

(GILMOUR, SAMSON)

This must rank among the most personal things Gilmour has ever committed to tape. The inspiration for the song came from a newspaper headline that Gilmour had seen concerning the fall of the Berlin Wall, and the first verse is about the fall of communism. The lyric also examines the fallout from the German unification process and whether it has worked in the best interest of all concerned. However, Gilmour uses the wall as a metaphor for his own failing relationship with Ginger, his American wife since 1976, who he was in the process of divorcing, and for his love reborn in Polly Samson. It was she who had metaphorically brought Gilmour out from behind his own emotional wall (shades of Roger Waters shock). The song is a reflective song for love that faded, hope reborn and a powerful optimism. "There was a wonderful moment of optimism when the

Syd in Amsterdam, 1967.

POLES APART

MASON *live drums*
WRIGHT *digital Rhodes piano, Hammond organ*
GILMOUR *lead vocal, electric guitars, lap steel guitar*
GUY PRATT *bass*
BOB EZRIN *keyboards, percussion*
SAM BROWN, DURGA MCBROOM, CAROL KENYON, JACKIE SHERIDAN, REBECCA LEIGH-WHITE *backing vocals*

MAROONED

(INSTRUMENTAL)

MASON *live drums, sound effects*
WRIGHT *sampled keyboards, piano, Hammond organ*
GILMOUR *keyboards, electric guitars*
BOB EZRIN *keyboards, additional percussion*
SAM BROWN, DURGA MCBROOM, CAROL KENYON, JACKIE SHERIDAN *backing vocals*

A GREAT DAY FOR FREEDOM

(INSTRUMENTAL)

MASON *live drums*
WRIGHT *digital Rhodes piano, Hammond organ*
GILMOUR *lead vocal, electric guitars, lap steel guitar*
GUY PRATT *bass*
BOB EZRIN *keyboards, percussion*
DICK PARRY *tenor saxophone*
TIM RENWICK *guitars*
JON CARIN *programming, additional keyboards*
GARY WALLIS *played and programmed percussion*
SAM BROWN, DURGA MCBROOM, CAROL KENYON, JACKIE SHERIDAN, REBECCA LEIGH-WHITE *backing vocals*
ORCHESTRA ARRANGED BY MICHAEL KAMEN

The fall of the Berlin Wall, on 10 November, 1989: inspired 'A Great Day For Freedom'.

wall came down - the release of eastern Europe from the non-democratic side of the socialist system. But what they have now doesn't seem to be much better."

It is possible that Gilmour also took inspiration from Roy Harper's 1990 track 'Berliners', in which the collapse of the wall was explored, and on which Gilmour played guitar. What is certain is that the track is not about Roger Waters, or his 1990 staging of *The Wall* in the Potsdamer Platz. Gilmour has denied that it has anything at all to do with his former bandmate.

WEARING THE INSIDE OUT

MASON *live and programmed drums*
WRIGHT *lead vocal, piano synthesizers, Hammond organ*
GILMOUR *electric guitars*
GUY PRATT *bass*
BOB EZRIN *keyboards, percussion*
GARY WALLIS *played and programmed percussion*
DICK PARRY *tenor saxophone*
SAM BROWN, DURGA MCBROOM, CAROL KENYON, JACKIE SHERIDAN, REBECCA LEIGH-WHITE *backing vocals*
ORCHESTRA ARRANGED BY MICHAEL KAMEN

Wearing The Inside Out

(WRIGHT, MOORE)

Rick Wright had always felt that his contributions to the Floyd were undervalued by Roger Waters. "Roger and I never got on, not even at the beginning. We never saw eye to eye on anything and I don't think were ever what you'd call friends. Nothing I ever did was quite good enough." Wright suffered a huge crisis of confidence in the late 70s as his role became ever smaller, often limited to a few piano and Hammond organ parts. Rather than confront Waters, whom he felt was an emotional bully, Wright would spend as much time as he could away from the band, holidaying in Greece, sailing his yacht around the Med, living the life of a playboy millionaire and, increasingly, seeking refuge in cocaine. When Wright opted to stay in Greece during the final sessions for *The Wall*, Waters reacted by delivering a cruel ultimatum. Accusing him of having been an unproductive freeloader for years, he demanded that Wright leave the band and partnership, and be placed on a session player's wage, or else he would scrap the entire album. "I wasn't about to call his bluff. That's just the kind of thing he is capable of going through with," said Wright. As with Syd nearly a decade earlier, Waters had effectively thrown Wright out of Pink Floyd, albeit for reasons - it was partly to shock Wright into pulling himself together - with which, at the time, Gilmour agreed. However, it only served to plunge him further into a trough of depression and drug abuse from which it would take him nearly a decade to climb out.

'Wearing The Inside Out' is a poignant moment of public confession for Wright. His nervous quavering vocals describe a man barely alive, cowering from responsibility and emotion, adrift and lost, emotionally crippled. It was Wright's first lead vocal since 1973. "It was very fulfilling . . . I have to say, I've never, ever, had any confidence in my voice. But I wrote this song and so I had to sing it . . . basically I hadn't really sung for

Rick Wright returned to the Floyd fold for **The Division Bell.**

Mason: eager return to the essence of the classic Floyd sound.

TAKE IT BACK

MASON *live and programmed drums*
WRIGHT *piano, synthesizers, Hammond organ*
GILMOUR *lead vocal, electric guitars*
GUY PRATT *bass*
BOB EZRIN *keyboards, percussion*
GARY WALLIS *played and programmed percussion*
DICK PARRY *tenor saxophone*
SAM BROWN, DURGA MCBROOM, CAROL KENYON, JACKIE SHERIDAN, REBECCA LEIGH-WHITE *backing vocals*
ORCHESTRA ARRANGED BY MICHAEL KAMEN

twenty years."

Gilmour was overjoyed at Wright's return to song writing, which represented a major milestone in his return to the creative fold. "Everyone who listens to it goes, 'God, it's that voice, it's that voice,' that used to be a part of the Pink Floyd sound." The track includes old Cambridge friend Dick Parry on saxophone, who had also played on *Dark Side* and *Wish You Were Here*.

Take It Back

(GILMOUR, EZRIN, SAMSON, LAIRD-CLOWES)

The song appears to refer to a vengeful girl, but the female in question is in fact Mother Nature. Gilmour proclaims that she will one day become so angered by the abuse meted out to her by humankind that she will "take back" what is hers, wreaking a terrible revenge. The inspiration came from a TV news programme concerning the emergence of a breed of super-viruses resistant to all drugs. The programme concluded that we would reach a point in our 'development' where the misuse of drugs and chemicals would be so out of balance with nature that she would react to re-establish an equilibrium. This idea is reinforced by the use of the nursery rhyme 'Ring-a-Ring-a-Roses' in the instrumental middle section, a song thought to refer to the symptoms and consequences of bubonic plague, which raged through Europe in the seventeenth century.

Coming Back To Life

(GILMOUR)

'Coming Back To Life' chronicles David Gilmour's emotional rescue. During the High Court battles, the guitarist split with his wife of years, Ginger. Though the split seemed inevitable, it upset Gilmour deeply and he descended into a whirl of transient relationships and a late spurt of reckless behaviour.

COMING BACK TO LIFE

MASON *live and sampled drums*
WRIGHT *synths, Hammond organ*
GILMOUR *lead vocal, electric guitars*
TIM RENWICK *guitars*
GUY PRATT *bass*
BOB EZRIN *additional programming*
SAM BROWN, DURGA MCBROOM, CAROL KENYON, JACKIE SHERIDAN, REBECCA LEIGH-WHITE *backing vocals*

Gilmour: enjoying his new role.

Worried that he was getting overweight, having indulged in the Epicurean delights to excess, and that he was losing his drive to perform on stage, Gilmour felt "burned out, shell-shocked and unhappy". It was this concern, only observable in retrospect, that formed itself into this powerful and emotive song, addressing how Gilmour felt revitalised by his love for Polly Samson, which had brought about the return of his lust for life, and of enthusiasm for his work. According to the writer, the song is about that "dangerous but irresistible pastime . . . sex, obviously. Sex and procreation".

Keep Talking

(GILMOUR, WRIGHT, SAMSON)

KEEP TALKING

MASON *programmed drums*
WRIGHT *piano, synths, Hammond organ*
GILMOUR *lead vocal, electric guitars*
GUY PRATT *bass*
BOB EZRIN *keyboards, percussion*
GARY WALLIS *played and programmed percussion*
SAM BROWN, DURGA MCBROOM, CAROL KENYON, JACKIE SHERIDAN, REBECCA LEIGH-WHITE *backing vocals*
STEPHEN HAWKING *electronic vocal*

Like many of the Floyd's latter songs, the music for 'Keep Talking' was written some months before the lyrics. A reluctant lyricist at the best of times, Gilmour had a few vague ideas in mind, when inspiration finally hit. He was sitting with Polly one night, watching TV, when the pair saw an advert for British Telecom in which Stephen Hawking - the gifted cosmologist and author of the groundbreaking bestseller *A Brief History Of Time* - provided the voice-over using his computerised voice synthesiser. Hawking suffers from motor-neurone disease, and is confined to a wheelchair, unable to speak without the aid of this device. It was Hawking's struggle to express himself that provided Gilmour with an overview for the song. "It nearly made me weep," recalls Gilmour. "This was the most powerful piece of television advertising that I've ever seen in my life." Gilmour decided to use Hawking's electronic voice on the track, to symbolise the need for communication in all people, if humanity is to advance. Once again, the sentiments were manifested in Gilmour's feelings over the breakdown of his first marriage to Ginger, and to the communication difficulties inherent in developing a new relationship with Polly Samson.

Another obvious parallel is with the breakdown in his relationship with Waters. Despite the fact that they never considered themselves close friends, it was still a source of some distress to Gilmour that he and Waters could no longer even speak to each other, because they had spent so much productive time together over the years.

The advertising company Saatchi & Saatchi were called, and permission sought from BT and Hawking himself, before the symbolic voice could be used. Hawking, a Pink Floyd fan, later turned up to see the band perform at Earl's Court.

Lost For Words

(GILMOUR, SAMSON)

LOST FOR WORDS

MASON *live drums*
WRIGHT *piano, synths, Hammond organ*
GILMOUR *lead vocal, acoustic and electric guitars*
GUY PRATT *bass*
BOB EZRIN *keyboards, percussion*
TIM RENWICK *guitars*
SAM BROWN, DURGA MCBROOM, CAROL KENYON, JACKIE SHERIDAN, REBECCA LEIGH-WHITE *backing vocals*

Gilmour v Waters again. In the post-Barrett Floyd, Waters would construct the lyrics and the conceptual foundations, while Gilmour provided much of the musical framework and the commercial gloss. This song is Gilmour's examination of the apparently irreconcilable breakdown of this successful and influential partnership. Encouraged by Polly Samson, who acted as a surrogate therapist, Gilmour was able to begin exploring the deep feelings of sadness and anger that his former partner had provoked in him over the years. The track, illustrated in the CD booklet by a pair of boxing gloves, and featuring the recordings of a boxing match, is a thinly disguised reference to the court room pugilism that had taken place, and comes almost in the form of a rhetorical open letter to Waters, asking him whether he sees what a disagreeable and unhappy individual he has become.

Central to the song is Gilmour's upset at Waters's rejection of the olive branch that was extended half-way through the battle over the rights to the use of the Pink Floyd name. Gilmour, fearing that his ex-colleague was teetering on the brink of a breakdown, suggested to Waters's lawyers that they should call off the expensive and emotionally damaging court case, and attempt to come to some amicable out-of-court settlement. The memorable line "And I ask if we could wipe the slate clean/But they tell me to please go fuck myself" is a reference to a note that Gilmour received from Waters (through his lawyers) in response to his overtures. The song also includes a reference to the "right one walking out of the door", possibly referring to Rick Wright's departure in 1979.

The melody may well have been influenced by Bruce Springsteen's 'Independence Day'.

High Hopes

(GILMOUR, SAMSON)

The album's high point was a last minute addition. In July 1993, during a break from the recording, Gilmour and Samson decamped to a *gite* in France to work on lyrics. By chance, Gilmour took with him a cassette of various chord progressions, reminiscent of Roger Waters's mournful 'Cymbaline'. Listening to the tape, Samson began to hum the phrase "before time wears you down", triggering a feverish bout of lyric

Pink Floyd launching their first sponsored tour since the early 70s.

writing that resulted, several hours later, in this autobiographical observation on the present, wrapped inside recollections of Gilmour's childhood past.

Returning from the retreat, Gilmour went straight to the studio and laid down a rough demo. "I did everything myself on it, and it was virtually complete in a day, but the best ideas always take the least time," recalls the guitarist.

Like The Beatles' 'Strawberry Fields Forever', the track uses people and places from adolescence (from the River Cam, where Gilmour would swim as a youth, to The Cut, the path that leads from the road to Grantchester Meadows - a meeting point where the young dope smokers of Cambridge would gather to score) to evoke a sense of mourning for the loss of idealism and childhood innocence. Gilmour, like Lennon, was plagued by the sense that the optimism of youth was so often sacrificed to the brutal reality of life as an adult. The song tells of how ambition and desire can cloud your enjoyment of life, friendship and happiness. But the song also displays the revitalised middle-aged Gilmour, and climaxes with one of his finest languid solos.

The Division Bell, the bell that summons members of parliament to The House Of Commons to vote, gave the album its title, and it is used here as a symbol of the separation from innocence, beginning at birth. The image was seized upon by writer Douglas Adams (author of *The Hitchhiker's Guide To The Galaxy*), a friend of Gilmour's, who was brought in to work on the lyrics. Although none of his work actually found its way on to the record, he nevertheless receives a credit. "I had given a talk at The Royal Geographical Society, in aid of the Environmental Investigation Agency's work on rhino conservation. Both Dave and Nick came along, and we all went out to dinner afterwards. Dave was a bit preoccupied about the title problem - they had to have the title by the following morning, and no one could decide what it should be. I said, 'Okay, I'll give you a title, but it'll cost you a £5,000 contribution to the EIA.' Dave said, 'Well, tell me what your title is and we'll see.' So I suggested *The Division Bell*. And Dave said, 'Hmmm, well, seems to work. Sort of fits the cover art as well. Yeah, okay'." Gilmour wrote the cheque there and then.

In an additional allusion to the album's theme of non-communication, at the very end of this track, a coda to the entire album, there's a brief confused telephone conversation between Floyd manager Steve O'Rourke and Polly Samson's four year old son (by writer Heathcote Williams), Charlie. It ends when Charlie simply hangs up on the hapless O'Rourke, who had always begged the band to let him appear on a Floyd album.

HIGH HOPES

MASON *programmed and sampled drums*
WRIGHT *piano, synthesizers, Hammond organ*
GILMOUR *lead vocal, piano acoustic and electric guitars, bass*
GUY PRATT *bass*
BOB EZRIN *keyboards, percussion*
TIM RENWICK *guitars*
SAM BROWN, DURGA MCBROOM
CAROL KENYON
JACKIE SHERIDAN
REBECCA LEIGH-WHITE
backing vocals
ORCHESTRA ARRANGED BY MICHAEL KAMEN

Chronology

1943 **September 9:** Roger Waters born in Great Bookham, Surrey, as George Roger Waters.

1944 Roger Waters's father killed in Anzio during World War Two.

1945 **January 27:** Nicholas Berkeley Mason born in Birmingham.

July 28: Richard William Wright born in London.

1946 **January 6:** Syd Barrett born in Cambridge as Roger Keith Barrett.

1947 **March 4:** David Gilmour born in Cambridge.

1961 **December 11:** Syd Barrett's father dies of sudden inoperable cancer,

1962 **September:** Roger Waters moves to London to attend Regent Street Polytechnic after leaving architecture practice where he was an apprentice.

1963 **March:** Bob Dylan tours Britain for the first time. Syd is among the first to get tickets to the London show at the Albert Hall.

1964 **August:** Syd Barrett moves to London to attend Camberwell Art College. Barrett and Waters move in together at the house of Mike Leonard. They meet Nick Mason and form an embryonic band who play two short gigs at pubs, under the name Leonard's Lodgers. They soon rename themselves The Pink Floyd after two grizzled Georgia bluesmen, Pink Anderson and Floyd Council.

1965 **August:** Barrett and school friend David Gilmour go busking in the south of France, where they get arrested.

September: Syd Barrett takes first LSD trip in garden of Dave Gale's parents home in Cambridge. Is rejected as 'unsuitable' for Sant Mat, an eastern religion.

1966 **January:** Pink Floyd make their debut at The Marquee Club in Wardour Street, at the *Spontaneous Underground*. 20 people present at their first afternoon show.

September 30: 'Pink Theme', 'Snowing', 'Flapdoodle Dealing' and 'Let's Roll Another One' performed live for the first time at All Saints Hall, Powis Gardens, London.

October 11: Floyd play The Roundhouse.

October 14: Band ditch all R&B influenced material at Peter Jenner's request, and play their first full 'underground' set at All Saints Hall, Powis Gardens, London.

October 15: Band play *International Times 'All Night Rave'* party at London's Roundhouse.

October 21: London Free School established. Band play to their first capacity audience. They are paid £15.

October 31: Band sign six-way management contract with Jenner and King, forming Blackhill Enterprises.

November 18: 'Philadelic' music for *Simian Hominids* event staged at Hornsey College of Art, with full light show.

November: Studio demos of 'Interstellar Overdrive', 'I Get Stoned', 'Silas Lane' and 'Let's Roll Another One' recorded at Thompson Private Recorders, Hemel Hempstead.

December 12: Band plays Royal Albert Hall.

December 18: Pink Floyd play the *Night Tripper* at The Blarney Club in Tottenham Court Road. The following week it is renamed the UFO Club. The Floyd become regulars.

1967 **January 11 & 12:** Band records 'Interstellar Overdrive', 'Nick's Boogie', 'Arnold Layne' and 'Let's Roll Another One' at Sound Techniques, Chelsea, with Joe Boyd. This version of 'Interstellar Overdrive' was edited and released on the soundtrack to the Peter Whitehead film *Tonite Let's All Make Love in London*, early in 1968.

January 20: Granada TV film the band at the UFO for documentary. Pink Floyd are named 'house band'.

February 1: Pink Floyd turn professional.

February 7: Granada TV documentary on the UFO and underground scene, featuring Pink Floyd, is televised.

February 27: Re-record 'Arnold Layne' and a retitled 'Candy And A Currant Bun' at Sound Techniques, Chelsea. Joe Boyd Produces.

March: Pink Floyd sign to EMI records for a £ 5,000 advance.

April: Work begins on *The Piper At The Gates Of Dawn* at Abbey Road, Studio 3.

April 6: Syd achieves lifelong ambition when he plays with the band on TV, on *Top Of The Pops*.

April 22: 'Arnold Layne' b/w 'Candy And A Currant Bun' charts at number 20.

April 24: Roger Waters is injured by a coin thrown at a gig.

April 29: 14 hour *Technicolour Dream* event at Alexandra Palace. Pink Floyd play to 10,000

people as dawn breaks.

May 12: *Games For May* at the Queen Elizabeth Hall. Syd writes the event's theme song. It later becomes 'See Emily Play'.

May 23: 'See Emily Play' is recorded at Sound Techniques.

June 16: 'See Emily Play' released. Climbs to number 6.

July 6: Band promote 'Emily' on *Top Of The Pops*. Syd wears a collection of dirty rags.

August 5: *The Piper At The Gates Of Dawn* released.

August 7: Tour of Denmark.

August 21: Tour of Germany is cancelled midway through. Syd goes AWOL.

October 24: First US tour begins.

October 26: First of three nights at San Francisco's legendary Fillmore West.

October 30: Pat Boone Show is taped. Barrett fails to answer any questions and doesn't lip-synch.

November 2: Abbey Road recording sessions for next single, 'Paintbox'.

December: Floyd tour with package of bands including Jimi Hendrix. Davy O'List of the Nice stands in for Syd at some shows when he either fails to show or cannot play.

December 22: *Christmas On Earth Revisited*. Syd stands on stage and stares blankly at crowd during the set. The band and managers are worried. Waters decides that the band cannot go on with Syd in this condition and tells the others of his concerns.

1968

January: Dave Gilmour deputises on guitar when Syd is incapable of playing at a show in Brighton

February 11: Sessions for BBC *Top Gear* compered by John Peel. Band play Syd's new tunes 'Vegetable Man' and 'Scream Thy Last Scream'.

March 2: Band meet at Ladbroke Road offices and Syd is asked to stop touring and contribute as a songwriter.

April 6: Syd Barrett's departure from the band is officially announced.

May: Peter Sykes asks Pink Floyd to record soundtrack for his film *The Commitee*.

May 26: *Oz* benefit gig at Middle Earth.

June 29: *A Saucerful Of Secrets* released in UK. Floyd play first free concert in Hyde Park, organised by Blackhill Enterprises.

July 4: Floyd arrive in US to promote *A Saucerful of Secrets*.

July 27: *A Saucerful of Secrets* released in US.

1969

March: Sessions for *More* film soundtrack begin.

April 14: *More Furious Madness From The Massed Gadgets Of Auximenes* (*The Man* and *The Journey*) performed live at the Royal Festival Hall.

June: Band play Mothers Club Birmingham and Manchester College of Commerce, recorded for inclusion on *Ummagumma*.

July: *More* released.

July 10: Pink Floyd music 'Moonhead' is used to accompany Apollo 11 landings on BBC TV.

July 26: Royal Albert Hall, London, final show of the British tour.

December 2: Rome, Italy, for recording of soundtrack to *Zabriskie Point*.
Syd Barrett's first solo single, 'Octopus' is released.

1970

January: *The Madcap Laughs*, Syd Barrett's first solo album is released on Harvest. 'It's quite nice but I'd be surprised if it did anything.' was the verdict from its creator.

January 18: 'The Amazing Pudding' performed live.

March: *Zabriskie Point* released. Work on *Atom Heart Mother* begins.

June 27: *Atom Heart Mother* premiered at Bath Festival.

July 18: Free concert in Hyde Park attended by 20,000 people.

September 12: World tour begins. Band's equipment is stolen in New Orleans.

November: *Barrett*, Syd's second and last solo album is released.

December: 40 ft posters of Lullubelle III, the cow from the cover of *Atom Heart Mother*, adorn Sunset strip billboard.

1971

January 4: Floyd block-book Abbey Road and begin sessions for their follow-up album to *Atom Heart Mother*. Pink Floyd turn down Stanley Kubrick's request to use music from *Atom Heart Mother* in *A Clockwork Orange*.

April 22: 'Return Of The Son Of Nothing' - the piece that would become 'Echoes' - is played live for the first time.

July 31: Band depart for their first tour of the Far East.

August: Band play *The Garden Party* at Crystal Palace. A giant inflatable octopus rises out of the lake in front of the stage.

August 23: Work continues on *Meddle*.

November: *Meddle* released.

1972

January 2: Syd Barrett makes unannounced guest appearance at the King's College Cellar in Cambridge with Twink and Eddie Guitar Burns. This band evolves into Stars.

February 17: *Eclipse* performed live at The Rainbow. The show is praised by critics who proclaim it as rock's first conceptual masterpiece.

February: Syd Barrett plays ill-fated gig at the Cambridge Corn Exchange under the band name

Stars. He leaves the stage with his hand badly cut.

February 23: Studio recording for *Obscured by Clouds* begins.

March 3: Band tour Japan.

May 23-31: Live filming and recording of *Pink Floyd Live at Pompeii* in a Roman amphitheatre.

June 1: Pre-production sessions at Abbey Road.

June 3 *Obscured By Clouds* released. Pink Floyd rehearse 'Echoes' for premiere of Roland Petite ballet.

June 4: Sessions begin for *Eclipse*, which later became *Dark Side Of The Moon*, at Abbey Road Studio 2.

September: Film *Pink Floyd Live At Pompeii* premiered in Edinburgh. Band tour US with *Eclipse*.

1973

March 13: *Dark Side Of The Moon* released.

May 18: *Dark Side Of The Moon* played at Earl's Court.

March 28: *Dark Side Of The Moon* hits Billboard number 1.

June: US tour.

November: Studio recording sessions begin for *Household Objects* album, but are soon abandoned.

December: *A Nice Pair* released. Later pressings have photo of W.R. Phang, dentist, removed at Mr Phang's request.

1974

July: 'Raving and Drooling' performed live during brief French tour.

November: Barrett makes his final attempt to record, prompted by the success of *The Madcap Laughs* in the US. It is described by those who hear it as desperately sad.

1975

January 6: Sessions for *Wish You Were Here* begin at Abbey Road.

May: Syd Barrett is spied at Harrods of Knightsbridge, carrying a huge carrier bag of confectionery, which he then drops in his attempts to flee.

June 5: Barrett turns up at Abbey Road unrecognisable, bald and fat, during the final mix of the album. Dave Gilmour marries first wife, Ginger.

June 6: Band depart on US tour.

June 28: Roger Waters spits at audience member and, shocked, starts thinking about the idea of a polythene wall between himself and the audience.

July 5: Knebworth Festival. Two World War Two Spitfires perform a flyby, starting the Floyd's most spectacular show of the year.

September: *Wish You Were Here* released.

1976

April: Gilmour produces Unicorn's album *Too Many Cooks*.

April 1: Thieves break into Gilmour's London home and make off with £7000 of guitars.

May: Band establish Britannia Row - recording studio is fitted out to record the band.

August 2: Peter 'Puddy' Watts, Floyd road manager and one of the voices heard on *Dark Side Of The Moon*, dies of heroin overdose.

December 2: Hipgnosis stage photo shoot at Battersea Power Station, South London. Inflatable pig slips its moorings and takes off across London. It eventually comes to earth in a Kent field.

1977

January 19: *Animals* is premiered to the press at Battersea Power Station.

January 20: John Peel premieres *Animals* on his BBC Radio One show.

January 23: *Animals* released. World tour begins.

1978

January: Nick Mason produces The Damned, a British punk band. They wanted Syd Barrett, but made do with Nick Mason instead. Dave Gilmour works on his first solo album in France. Rick Wright starts work on his first solo album.

February 14: Rick Wright completes work on his solo album at Superbear Studios in France.

May 25: Dave Gilmour's first, eponymous, solo album is released.

1979

January: Work continues on untitled follow up to *Animals* in France, Los Angeles and London, to avoid looming tax bill.

March: Gilmour plays solo shows.

June 1: Band deliver tapes of their new album to EMI. No one can decide whether to make it a double or single album, so work continues until November.

November 16: 'Another Brick in The Wall Part II' released. Goes straight to number one - it's the band's first and only number one single.

November 30: *The Wall* is released.

1980

January 24: Floyd erect huge vanity billboard on Sunset Strip. Each day workmen add another brick to the wall until it is completely filled in.

February 7: *The Wall* is premiered at The Los Angeles Sports Arena. Fireworks set fire to a drape and the concert is held up early on.

March 22: *Dark Side Of The Moon* finally eclipses Carole King's *Tapestry* as the longest chart run on the Billboard top 100.

March: New York DJ breaks the story that if you play *The Wall* backwards, the hidden message,

"Congratulations. You have just discovered the secret message. Please send your answers to Old Pink, care of The Funny Farm, Chalfont," can be heard just before the track empty spaces. It was claimed to be a reference to Syd.

1981

March: Pink Floyd sue Norton Warburg for £1 million, alleging fraud. Chairman Andrew Warburg flees to Spain.

May: Nick Mason releases solo album.

June 13: Band play *The Wall* at Earl's Court for inclusion in the film. It is the last occasion Pink Floyd play together with Roger Waters.

August 4: *The Wall* performed at Earl's Court in London. The Floyd use a surrogate band to open the show.

1982

July: Sessions begin at Britannia Row on *The Final Cut*.

July 14: World premiere of the film *The Wall* at The Empire, Leicester Square.

1983

March 20: Waters receives BAFTA award for 'Another Brick In The Wall Part 2'.

March 21: *The Final Cut* is released.

1984

March 5: Dave Gilmour releases second solo album *About Face*. Pete Townshend of the Who is Gilmour's co-writer.

April 9: Rick Wright releases his *Zee* album. Roger Waters releases track '5.01 a.m.' from his fist solo album - *The Pros and cons of Hitch-Hiking*.

July 16: Waters begins tour of the world. Eric Clapton plays guitar in his touring band. Gilmour tours North America.

1985

July 13: Live Aid, Gilmour plays as part of Bryan Ferry's band.

August 19: Nick Mason and Rick Fenn's *Profiles* album released.

1986

October 11: Gilmour plays on *The Tube* TV show advertising Pete Townshend's Double O charity.

October: Waters appears on the soundtrack to the TV film *When the Wind Blows*, the story of two elderly people caught in the aftermath of nuclear war.

November 11: Pink Floyd issue a statement to the effect that they intend to continue and are working on a new album.

1987

April 6: Waters's lawyers issue a statement to the effect that he considers himself the main creative force behind Pink Floyd, and that he will be contesting the use of the name Pink Floyd by Gilmour, Wright and Mason.

May 28: *Beyond The Wildwood*, a tribute to Syd Barrett, is released.

June 15: Waters releases *Radio Chaos*.

August 14: *Radio Chaos* world tour begins.

September 7: *A Momentary Lapse Of Reason* is released under the name of Pink Floyd.

September 9: Pink Floyd embark on their first tour for a decade. It is scheduled to last for 11 weeks and ends up running for 22 months.

November 21: Vocalist Clare Torry guests on 'Great Gig In The Sky' as part of Roger Waters tour.

December 23: Waters and Gilmour sign a binding legal document effectively ending their feud. Waters would receive a royalty payment for the use of the Pink Floyd 'trademarks' like the flying pigs and the visuals to accompany *The Dark Side Of The Moon*.

1988

January 28: Giant inflatable bed is sailed down the Thames past Parliament to announce the new Floyd tour.

June 16: The Floyd play West Berlin, next to the wall. 2,000 East German fans congregate on their side of the wall to listen.

June 21: Pink Floyd play next to The Palace of Versailles in France. The show ended with a spectacular firework display and was filmed for the *Delicate Sound Of Thunder* video.

August: Shows filmed for the *Delicate Sound Of Thunder* video on the east coast leg of the US tour. Band stop off to start recording the new album of the same name.
Band play sell out Wembley date.

October 17: Release of *Opel*, a collection of Barrett out-takes and previously unreleased tracks.
Syd Barrett hits the national press when reporter Mick Hamilton tracks the reclusive former Floyd frontman down to his Cambridge home. The *News Of The World* runs pictures and quotes anonymous neighbours as saying that Syd was a lunatic who barked like a dog and shrieked late at night.

November 21: *Delicate Sound Of Thunder* released.

November 26: The Floyd finally fulfil their space-rock legacy by becoming the first band to have their music taken into space. A *Delicate Sound Of Thunder* cassette is taken by Russian cosmonauts onto Soyuz 7.

1989

April: It is reported that Gerald Scarfe has designed a sleeve to Roger Waters's new album *Amused To Death* that features

Waters's former bandmates floating inside a cocktail glass.

June 3: Band play in Moscow.

July 15: Band play in Venice to 200,000, from a floating barge on one of the canals. It is alleged that the band's sound equipment caused hundreds of thousands of pounds worth of damage to the ancient buildings, in places sending chunks of marble falling to the ground.

September: Waters issues a writ claiming Pink Floyd have not paid him the requisite $800 per performance for the use of the inflatable pig. The band claim they have added testicles to the pig, so it is substantially different.

October 11: Pink Floyd play as 'Leave Those Kids Alone' at The Barbican in London to raise funds for National Society For The Prevention Of Cruelty To Children.

November 5: Nick Mason completes his fourth London to Brighton rally for vintage cars, in his 1901 Panhard-Levassor.

1990

April 10: Dave Gilmour and his wife Ginger, who married on the eve of the band's 1975 US tour, split.

May 23: Nick Mason marries second wife, Annette Lynton, at Chelsea Registry Office.

June 30: Knebworth festival is attended by over 125,000 people. Pink Floyd play a set that begins with a 20 minute film by Storm Thorgerson, which includes promos from the band's early days.

July 21: Roger Waters performs *The Wall* in its entirety at the Potsdamerplatz in Berlin. The show is now recognised as one of the most spectacular in rock history and was witnessed by an estimated 400,000 people. Those who helped out included Van Morrison and Sinead O'Connor.

August 5: The Knebworth album is released. It includes three Floyd tracks 'Comfortably Numb', 'Shine On....' and 'Run Like Hell'.

September 17: *The Wall - Live in Berlin*, released.

1991

Pink Floyd take time off to "race cars and fly planes".

October 18: Roger Waters performs at the *Guitar Legends* festival in Seville Spain and includes 'Comfortably Numb' and 'Brain Damage' in his set.

1992

April: Atlantic Records offer Syd Barrett's family £75,000 for any new Syd recordings - regardless of quality or format. It is suggested that Peter Buck and Mike Mills from REM would collaborate. The family decline.

April 30: Roger Waters announces his engagement to Priscilla Phillips, longtime friend of the Duchess of York.

June 22: Dave Gilmour plays guitar with veteran pop singer Tom Jones at London's Town & Country Club.

Pink Floyd return to the studio to start work on a new and as yet untitled album.

July 28: Dave Gilmour plays Roger Waters's original acoustic demo of 'Money' on Nicky Horne's Radio One Saturday afternoon Show.

September 7: The long awaited Waters solo album *Amused To Death* is released. Despite lukewarm reviews, it is widely perceived by Floyd fans to be one of his finest albums ever.

November 9: *Shine On* box set is released.

1993

Gareth Cousins remasters Syd's recordings for *Crazy Diamond*, at Abbey Road.

February: Dave Gilmour officially reveals that Pink Floyd have begun work on a new album.

February 23: TV documentary program *Without Walls* traces the history of psychoactive drugs in *The Art Of Tripping*. Storm Thorgerson conceives and directs the programs. Gilmour provides the low-key soundtrack.

March 24: The twentieth anniversary of *Dark Side Of The Moon* is marked with a specially remastered and repackaged reissue.

April 26: EMI release the Syd Barrett box set *Crazy Diamond-the Complete Syd Barrett*. It includes all of Syd's solo albums including *Opel* plus bonus tracks and alternate versions

Vexfilms releases a 12 minute Standard 8 film shot by Nigel Gordon (Syd's flatmate from 101 Cromwell Road) that purports to show Syd, tripping on mushrooms for the first time in the Gog Magog Hills near Cambridge. Gordon admits this is probably not Syd's first trip but "it was marketed that way". Most of the footage "appears to have been shot through a jar of marmalade". Also includes footage of The Pink Floyd outside Abbey Road just after signing with EMI.

May 6: Newbury by-election candidate Colin Palmer announces that his 21st Century Party derives its political beliefs from Pink Floyd albums.

July 28: Roger Waters marries Priscilla Phillips at Romsey Registry Office.

December 1: Press conference announces Pink Floyd dates for 1994 tour.

1994

February: Rehearsals begin for world tour in a disused aircraft hangar near Palm

Springs, California.

March 21: Pink Floyd fly a huge painted airship over Battersea Power Station, site of the *Animals* cover shoot.

March 30: *The Division Bell* is released. No promotional interviews or press conferences are given, reinforcing the album's theme - lack of communication.

May 16: Band release 'Take It Back' from *The Division Bell* and back it with a live version of 'Astronomy Domine', in tribute to Syd. "I've really enjoyed playing 'Astronomy Domine', which we haven't played live for 20 years. It's a reminder of how Syd wrote and an opportunity to use some updated psychedelic effects," said Gilmour.

June 25: Bootleg dance remix of *Wish You Were Here* is released. Five tracks include 'Shine On You Crazy Diamond (Fluffy Cloud Version)' and 'Have a Cigar (Take A Joint Version)'. The Orb and their managers deny any knowledge, and EMI offer no endorsement on behalf of Floyd. It is the first of many Floyd remix albums.

June: George Harrison appears backstage at their Pasadena gig and chats for 10 minutes to someone he believes to be Steve O'Rourke, only to find to his embarrassment that it is Nick Mason.

July 15: The audience at Detroit, Michigan are treated to the first complete rendition of *Dark Side Of The Moon* in nearly twenty years.

July 22: European tour kicks off in Lisbon, Portugal, sponsored by Volkswagen in a £9m deal. They release an exclusive edition of the Golf Cabriolet - the Pink Floyd Cabriolet - to coincide with the European tour. Only 30 were available to collectors in the UK, at £16,898. Features Pink Floyd graphics, and comes in 'sonic blue' metallic paint. VW had previously done a similar deal with Genesis. The Lisbon date took $750,000 to stage, and the tour crew of 400 tucked into 1000 eggs and 300 loaves of bread a day, washed down by tea made from 1,300 teabags, and 50 pints of milk.

July 25: EMI re-release remastered versions of *A Saucerful of Secrets*, *Dark Side of The Moon*, *Wish You Were Here* and *Animals*.

July 29: Dave Gilmour marries Polly Samson at Marylebone Registry Office. Gilmour invites Roger Waters, but the reclusive star does not attend.

August 7: *The News of the World* reports that Rick Wright's accountant, Martin Stainton, 45, has disappeared with £3m of his money. Stainton also did accounts for Rod Stewart, Tina Turner, Simple Minds and Bon Jovi. Investigators found that he was up to his limit on all his credit cards.

September 7: The band play Prague in the Czech Republic. President Vaclav Havel attends. Dave Gilmour and Havel end up talking well into the night.

Roger Waters announces that he is planning a stage version of *The Wall*, (just as Pete Townshend adapted Tommy into a Broadway musical). He says the film doesn't do his composition justice, lacking humour and humanity.

October 12: The band play the first of 14 nights at Earl's Court, London, a homecoming concert. The opening night's show is stopped after seating collapses resulting in several hospitalisations.

December: It is announced that the *Division Bell* tour took in 68 cities, grossed £150 million and played to an estimated 5.5 million people. This makes the Floyd the biggest grossing rock act in history.

1995

Band take time off. Gilmour flies his planes. Mason drives his cars. Wright sails his yacht.

August: *Pulse*, a double album of the *Division Bell* tour, is released. The first 2 million copies appear with a 'limited edition' LED that blinks to the rhythm of a heart beat. This was Storm Thorgerson's idea.

September: Nick Mason's projected biography of the band is withheld. Gilmour decides he wants to make the history an official one that involves all three remaining members of the Floyd.

November: Pink Floyd make tentative bookings at some of the world's largest arenas and stadiums for the end of 1996 - suggesting another world tour may be imminent.

December: Pink Floyd inducted into the Rock'n'Roll Hall Of Fame at a ceremony at the Waldorf Astoria in New York. Their fellow inductees include Brian Wilson and David Bowie.

Discs/Videos/Books

SINGLES

'Arnold Layne'/'Candy And A Currant Bun', March 11, 1967, EMI Columbia DB 8156.

'See Emily Play'/'The Scarecrow', June 16, 1967, EMI Columbia DB 8214.

'Apples And Oranges'/'Paintbox', November 18, 1967, EMI Columbia DB 8310.

'It Would Be So Nice'/'Julia Dream', April 12, 1968, EMI Columbia DB 8410.

'Point Me At The Sky'/'Careful With That Axe, Eugene', December 17, 1968, EMI Columbia DB 8511.

'Another Brick In The Wall Part II'/'One of My Turns', November 16, 1979, EMI Harvest HAR 5194.

'When The Tigers Broke Free'/'Bring The Boys Back Home', July 26, 1982, EMI Harvest HAR 5222.

'Not Now John'/'The Hero's Return Parts I & II', April, 1983, EMI Harvest HAR 5224.

'Learning To Fly'/'One Slip'/'Terminal Frost' and 'Terminal Frost (DYOL version)', September 7, 1987, EMI EM 26.

'On The Turning Away'/'Run Like Hell (Live)'/'On The Turning Away (Live)', November 24, 1987, EMI EM 34.

'Take It Back'/'Astronomy Domine (Live)' May, 23, 1994, EMI.

ALBUMS, COMPILATIONS AND BOX SETS

The Piper at the Gates of Dawn, August 5, 1967, EMI Columbia SX/SXC 6157; Tower T/ST 5903 (U.S.). Astronomy Domine; *Lucifer Sam; Matilda Mother; Flaming; *Pow R Toc H; Take Up Thy Stethoscope And Walk; Interstellar Overdrive; The Gnome; Chapter 24; The Scarecrow; Bike. US copies omit tracks marked * and include 'See Emily Play'.

Tonite Let's All Make Love In London, 1968, Instant INLP 002
Interstellar Overdrive (Parts 1-3).

A Saucerful Of Secrets, June 29, 1968, EMI Columbia SX/XCS 6258 (U.K.); Tower T/ST 5131 (U.S.) Let There Be More Light; Remember A Day; Set The Controls For The Heart Of The Sun; Corporal Clegg; A Saucerful Of Secrets; See-Saw.

More, July 1969, EMI Columbia SCX 6346 (U.K.); Tower ST 5169 (U.S.).
Cirrus Minor; The Nile Song; Crying Song; Up The Khyber; Green Is The Colour; Cymbaline; Party Sequence; Main Theme; Ibiza Bar; More Blues; Quicksilver; A Spanish Piece; Dramatic Theme.

Ummagumma, October 25, 1969, EMI Harvest SHDW 1/2 (U.K.); STBB 388 (U.S.).
Astronomy Domine; Careful With That Axe Eugene; Set The Controls For The Heart Of The Sun; A Saucerful Of Secrets; Sysyphus (Parts 1-4); Grantchester Meadows; Several Species Of Small Furry Animal Gathered Together And Grooving With A Pict; The Narrow Way; The Grand Vizier's Garden Party.

Zabriskie Point, March 1970, MGM 2315 002 (U.K.); SE-4468ST (U.S.). Soundtrack compilation: Heart Beat, Pig Meat; Crumbling Land; Come In Number 51, Your Time Is Up.

Picnic, June 1970, EMI Harvest
Compilation includes 'Embryo'.

Atom Heart Mother, October 10, 1970, EMI Harvest SHVL 781 (U.K.); SKAO 382 (U.S.). Rise And Shine; Sunny Side Up; Morning Glory; Remergence; Father's Shout; Breast Milky; Mother Fore; Funky Dung; Mind Your Throats Please; If; Summer '68; Fat Old Sun; Alan's Psychedelic Breakfast.

Relics, May 1971, EMI Starline SRS 5071 (U.K.); Harvest SW 759 (U.S.).
Compilation with Arnold Layne; Interstellar Overdrive; See Emily Play; Remember A Day; Paintbox; Julia Dream; Careful With That Axe Eugene; Cirrus Minor; The Nile Song; Biding My Time; Bike.

Meddle, November 1971, EMI Harvest SHVL 795 (U.K.); SMAS 832 (U.S.). One Of These Days; A Pillow Of Winds; Fearless (interpolating You'll Never Walk Alone); San Tropez; Seamus; Echoes.

Obscured by Clouds, June 3, 1972, EMI Harvest SHSP 4020 (U.K.);ST 11078 (U.S.) Obscured By Clouds; When You're In; Burning Bridges; The Gold It's In The; Wot's....Uh The Deal; Mudmen; Childhood's End; Free Four; Stay; Absolutely Curtains.

Dark Side Of the Moon, March, 1973, EMI Harvest SHVL 804 (U.K.); SMAS 11163 (U.S.). Speak To Me; Breathe; On The Run; Time; The Great Gig In The Sky; Money; Us And Them; Any Colour You Like; Brain Damage; Eclipse.

A Nice Pair, 1974, EMI Harvest SHDW 403 (U.K.); SABB 11257 (U.S.)
Including The Piper at the Gates of Dawn and A Saucerful of Secrets.

Pink Floyd: Masters Of Rock Vol. 1, 1974, EMI Harvest. Re-release of The Best of Pink Floyd. Europe only but heavily imported into UK

Wish You Were Here, September 15, 1975, EMI Harvest SHVL 814 (U.K.); Columbia PC 33453 (U.S.). Shine On You Crazy Diamond (Parts 1-9); Welcome To The Machine; Have A Cigar; Wish You Were Here.

Animals, January 23, 1977, EMI Harvest SHVL 815 (U.K.); Columbia JC 34474 (U.S.).
Pigs On The Wing (Part One); Dogs; Pigs (Three Different Ones); Sheep; Pigs On The Wing (Part Two).

The Wall, November 30, 1979, EMI Harvest SHDW 411 (U.K.); Columbia PC2 36183 (U.S.). In The Flesh; Thin Ice; Happiest Days Of Our Lives; Another Brick In The Wall (Part 2); Mother; Goodbye Blue Sky; Empty Spaces; Young Lust; One Of My Turns; Don't Leave Me Now; Another Brick In The Wall (Part 3); Goodbye Cruel World; Hey You; Is There Anybody Out There?; Nobody Home; Comfortably Numb; Show Must Go On; Run Like Hell; Waiting For The Worms; Stop; The Trial; Outside The Wall.

A Collection Of Great Dance Songs, November 23, 1981, EMI Harvest SHVL 822 (U.K.); Columbia TC 37680 (U.S.). One of These Days; Money (remake); Sheep; Shine On You Crazy Diamond (remix); Wish You Were Here; Another Brick In The Wall (Part 2).

The Final Cut, March 21, 1983, EMI Harvest SHPF 1983 (U.K.); Columbia QC 38243 (U.S.). The Post-war Dream; Your Possible Pasts; One Of The Few; The Hero's Return; The Gunner's Dream; Paranoid Eyes; Get Your Filthy Hands Off My Desert; The Fletcher Memorial Home; Southampton Dock; The Final Cut; Not Now John; Two Suns In The Sunset.

A Momentary Lapse Of Reason, September 7, 1987, EMI CDP 7 480682 (U.K.); Columbia CK 40599 (U.S.).
Signs Of Life; Learning To Fly; The Dogs Of War; One Slip; On The Turning Away; Yet Another Movie; Round And Around; New Machine (Part 1); Terminal Frost; New Machine (Part 2); Sorrow.

Delicate Sound Of Thunder, November 26, 1988, EMI CDS 7914 802 (U.K.); Columbia C2K 44484 (U.S.).

Tonite Let's All Make Love in London . . . Plus, 1990, See For Miles SEE CD 258. Full version of 'Interstellar Overdrive' and 'Nick's Boogie'.

Knebworth: The Album, 1990, Polydor 843 921 (U.K.); 847 042-2 (U.S.) 'Comfortably Numb' and 'Run Like Hell'.

Shine On, February 1995, EMI. EMI boxed set with 9 CDs: A Saucerful Of Secrets, Meddle, Dark Side Of The Moon, Wish You Were Here, Animals, The Wall, A Momentary Lapse Of Reason, and the Early Singles CD. This last CD included 100 page booklet on the band.

Pink Floyd London 66-67, September 1995 See For Miles. Interstellar Overdrive (Full length version): Nick's Boogie.

The Division Bell, April 5, 1994, EMI. Cluster One; What Do You Want From Me?; Poles Apart; Marooned; A Great Day For Freedom; Wearing The Inside Out; Take It Back; Coming Back To Life; Keep Talking; Lost For Words; High Hopes

Pulse, August 1995, EMI, CD EMD 1078. Shine On You Crazy Diamond; Astronomy Domine; What Do You Want From Me?; Learning To Fly; Keep Talking; Coming Back To Life; Hey You; A Great Day For Freedom; Sorrow; High Hopes; Another Brick In The Wall (Part Two); Speak To Me; Breathe; On The Run; Time; The Great Gig In The Sky; Money; Us And Them; Any Colour You Like; Brain Damage; Eclipse; Wish You Were Here; Comfortably Numb; Run Like Hel

SYD BARRETT ALBUMS

The Madcap Laughs, January, 1970, Harvest, SHVL 765 (U.K.). Terrapin; It's No Good Trying; Love You; No Man's Land; Dark Globe; Here I Go; Octopus; Golden Hair; Long Gone; She Took A Long Cold Look; Feel; If It's In You; Late Night. Variously produced by Dave Gilmour and Roger Waters, the late Malcolm Jones (the founder of Harvest), Dave Gilmour with Syd Barrett and Peter Jenner. The album includes Syd's one and only solo single 'Octopus/Golden Hair (Harvest HAR 5009), a James Joyce poem that Syd set to music as early as 1965.

Barrett, November, 1970, Harvest, SHSP 4007 (U.K.). Baby Lemonade; Love Song; Dominoes; It Is Obvious; Rats; Maisie; Gigolo Aunt; Waiving My Arms In The Air; Wined And Dined; Wolfpack; Effervescing Elephant.
With the unexpected success of the stripped down and loose *Madcap Laughs*, EMI whisked Syd back into Abbey Road in 1970 to make a follow-up. Syd's condition had deteriorated markedly, and engineer Peter Bown, a Floyd veteran who had also worked on *The Piper At The Gates Of Dawn*, recalls that the sessions were closed at Dave Gilmour's instruction, "David was very upset because Syd didn't know who he was, simply didn't recognise him. Syd was incapable, a cabbage. At one point I had to accompany him to the lavatory, unzip his fly and point his penis at the pan because he was incapable of doing it himself. It was so terribly sad. What surprises me is that when we listened back to the tapes, he actually managed to sound reasonable."

Opel, October 17, 1988, Harvest, CDP 7 91206 2 (U.K.); Capitol C2 91206 (U.S.). Opel; Clowns And Jugglers; Rats; Golden Hair; Dolly Rocker; Word Song; Wined And Dined; Swan Lee (Silas Lang); Birdie Hop; Let's Split; Lanky (Part 1); Wouldn't You Miss Me (Dark Globe); Milky Way; Golden Hair (instrumental) A compilation of lost, overlooked and alternate versions of material from Syd's post-Floyd career.

Syd Barrett-Crazy Diamond, April 26, 1993, Harvest, SYDBOX 1 CDS 7 81412 2. Box set containing original albums *The Madcap Laughs*, *Barrett* and *Opel*. Each album includes bonus tracks of alternate versions from, and represents the very best of what was left in, the Abbey Road archives. There is some material from aborted sessions in 1975 that has not been heard, but this is, in the words of engineer John Leckie, "just a lot of unlistenable noises. There were no vocals recorded apart from the track called Bob Dylan Blues on which Syd sings, 'I got the Bob Dylan blues I got the Bob Dylan blues, my hats in a mess, but I don't care about that,' It was very sad to see him like that."

VIDEOS

Syd Barrett's First Trip
Silent 8mm art-house style footage taken by Cambridge friend, Nigel Gordon, of Syd Barrett under the influence of mushrooms in the Gog Magog hills outside Cambridge. Released by UFO Films, London 1994

Pink Floyd Live In London 66-67
Filmed by Peter Whitehead, England 1966 and 1967 this is amongst the earliest film of the Floyd. 16mm footage of the Pink Floyd at their first session at Sound Techniques studio, Chelsea and live at the 14 Hour Technicolour Dream. Also includes John Lennon. Released by, See For Miles films, 1995.

Tonite Let's All Make Love in London
Directed by Peter Whitehead, England, 1968. Includes Pink Floyd playing short extracted excerpts of *Interstellar Overdrive* . Released by, Kona Films, in Japan only, 1993.

More
Directed by Barbet Schroeder, France, 1969.
Released by ,Columbia video 1987.

Zabriskie Point
Directed by Michelangelo Antonioni, USA, 1970. Starring Mark Frechette and Daria Halprin. Released by, MGM video 1984.

La Vallée
Barbet Schroeder, France, 1972. *The Valley: Obscured by clouds*, Released by, Conniseur Video 1986 US only.

Pink Floyd — Live at Pompeii
Directed by Adrian Maben, France, 1972. Important live document of the Floyd circa 1972, experimenting with their old set without. Also includes footage of band at work on *Dark Side Of The Moon* at Abbey Road. Released by, 4-Front video 1986.

Pink Floyd — The Wall
Directed by Alan Parker, England, 1982. Screenplay by Roger Waters. Starring Bob Geldof. Released by, MGM/UA video1989.

The Final Cut
Compiltion of music videos for the Final Cut album. Screenplay by Roger Waters. Includes 'The Gunner's Dream', 'The Final Cut', 'Not Now John', and 'The Fletcher Memorial Home'. Released by, Picture Music International 1983

Delicate Sound of Thunder
Concert video recorded at Nassau Coliseum, New York, in August of 1988 and at the legendary Versailles concert in France during the *Momentary Lapse of Reason* tour. Includes some songs not on the CD album release: 'Signs of Life', 'On the Run', 'The Great Gig in the Sky', and 'One Slip'. Released by, Picture Music International, 1989

La Carrera Panamericana
Verité documentary of the 2000-mile car race in Mexico which Nick Mason and Dave Gilmour took part in. Also includes, Pink Floyd and Dave Gilmour solo recordings as part of the soundtrack. Released by, Sony Music Video 1991.

Pulse
Live concert footage from the *Division Bell* tour. Includes 'Dark Side Of The Moon', 'Shine On You Crazy Diamond' as

well as some early favourites. Released by, Picture Music International 1995

BOOKS

About Pink Floyd

MacDonald, Bruno (editor). *Pink Floyd-Through The Eyes Of...* Sidgwick & Jackson, London, 1996.

Dallas, Karl. *Bricks In The Wall*. Shapolsky Publishers, New York, 1987.

Miles & Mabbett, Andy. *Pink Floyd-The Visual Documentary*. Omnibus Press, London 1994.

Bertrando, Paolo (editor). *Pink Floyd, Tutti I Testi Dal 1970 AL 1994* Volume secondo Arcana Editrice, 1994.

Welch, Chris. *Pink Floyd - Learning To Fly*. Castle Communications, London 1994

Sanders, Rick. *Pink Floyd*, Futura Books, London 1975.

General

Various contributors. *Hot Wacks Book XV-The Last Wacks*. The Hot Wacks Press, Canada, 1992.

Lewisohn, Mark. *The Complete Beatles Sessions*.

Green, Jonathan. *Days In The Life - Voices from the English Underground 1961-1971*. Minerva Press London, 1988.

Kent, Nick. *The Dark Stuff*.

Roseman, Bernard. *LSD The Age Of The Mind*. Wilshire Books, Hollywood California, 1966.

Caute, David. *Sixty-Eight - The Year Of The Barricades*. Hamish Hamilton, London 1988.

Thorgerson, Storm. *Walk Away Renee*. Paper Tiger Books, London 1978.

Jones, Malcolm. *The Making Of The Madcap Laughs*. Orange Sunshine Press, 1986

Garner, Ken. *In Session Tonight, The Complete Radio 1 Recordings*. BBC Books 1993.

Hogg, Brian. *Syd Barrett - Crazy Diamond*. CD Box set with accompanying booklet, EMI Records, London 1993.

NEWSPAPERS & MAGAZINES

Though numerous magazine and newspaper articles were referred to in the book, the most revealing and oft-quoted were the following:

'The 30 Year Struggle For The Soul Of Pink Floyd' from *Mojo* issue 6, May 1994

'30 Years Backstage At The Greatest Show On Earth' from *Mojo* issue 20, July 1995.

John Walsh's interview with Pink Floyd from *Q 98*.

International Times Number 29.

Melody Maker, January 14 1967.

Connor McNight's interview with Roger Waters and Nick Mason from *ZigZag* magazine, July 1973.

David Fricke's interview with David Gilmour from *Musician*, December 1992.

David Fricke's feature 'Pink Floyd, The Inside Story' from *Rolling Stone*, November, 1987.

Mick Brown And Kurt Loder's feature 'Behind Pink Floyd's Wall' from *Rolling Stone*, September 1982.

Timothy White's feature on Pink Floyd in US *Penthouse Magazine* 1988.

Phil Sutcliffe's feature 'And Pigs Will Fly' *Q Magazine* September 1990.

Notes to accompany *Shine On* box set, designed by Storm Thorgerson and Stylorouge. EMI Records Ltd, 1992.

Notes to accompany the anniversary reissue of *Dark Side Of The Moon*, EMI Records Ltd 1993.

The New Musical Express.

The Melody Maker.

Brain Damage Magazine. Floyd quarterly edited by Jeff Jensen and available at P.O. Box 109 Westmnst Il 60559 U.S.A.

The Amazing Pudding. The now defunct Floyd fanzine whose back issues were invaluable.

Eskimo Chain Fanzine. Edited by Iain Smith and available at 2, White Cottages, Long Garth, Durham City. DH1 4HL UK.

Terrapin, the Syd Barrett fanzine (No longer published due to 'Lack of Syd')

REG The Roger Waters Fanzine. Edited by Michael Simone at 112 Bennett Road, Aptos, CA 95003 U.S.A.

Broadcast & Video Sources

'The Pink Floyd Story': Six part documentary made by and broadcast on Capital radio, London. December 17 1976-January 21 1977.

Roger Scott's unedited interview with Roger Waters. Produced for Capital Radio, London, 1987 (Courtesy of Capital Radio, London).

Alan 'Fluff' Freeman's unedited interview with Roger Waters produced for Capital Radio, London, 1989 (Courtesy of Capital Radio, London).

Tommy Vance interview with Roger Waters, BBC Radio One, November 30. 1979.

David Jenson's unedited interview with David Gilmour. Produced for Capital Radio, London 1988 (Courtesy of Capital Radio, London).

Classic Albums Documentary for BBC Radio 1. Produced by John Pidgeon.

INTERNET NEWSGROUPS & ARCHIVE SITES

alt.music.pink-floyd

Author's Acknowledgments

For interviews carried out specifically for this book I am indebted to Peter Bown, John Leckie, Nigel Gordon, Bob Ezrin, Joe Boyd, Bob Close, Miles, Lyndsey Korner, Peter Jenner, Andrew King, Graham Forbes, Storm Thorgerson, Ron Geesin, Roger Mintov, Wayne Shuman, Richard Wright, Peter Barrett, Alan 'Fluff 'Freeman, Roger Quested, Alan Parsons, Peter Mew, Ian Humphries, Lucienne Watts and John Peel.

The big bouquet goes to Nicholas Crowe, fellow Floyd head, for his endless trawling of press cuttings, books, fanzines, radio interviews and stray scraps of Floyd related debris. 'Yoooooou do it.'

I also drew on radio and TV interviews conducted with all five band members throughout the years, and for letting me raid his collection I thank Mr Sad - David Freymann at Radical Tendency. To Malcolm Jones at Capital Radio I doff my titfer in gratitude for granting access to the excellent and underutilised Capital Radio tape archives for unedited interview material; the same again goes to John Pidgeon Associates whose excellent Radio 1 documentary material on the making of *Dark Side Of The Moon* proved to be indispensable. Thanks also go the BBC sound archives, The National Sound Archives in Kensington and Abbey Road Studios, St John's Wood.

For their help in tracking down rare Floyd pressings and fanzines I thank Bill Forsyth at Minus Zero Records, London- the finest rare, collectable, psych, prog and contemporary pop rock shop on the big blue marble. Hearty handshake goes to Jeff Jensen at Brain Damage, P.O. Box 109, Westmnst Il 60559, USA. Tel. 708 968 4921. To Iain Smith of *Eskimo Chain* Barrett fanzine (cheques and Money Orders for £1 payable to Iain Smith, 2 White Cottages, Long Garth, Durham City, DH1 4HL, UK, please) and to Michael Simone at REG, the English language fanzine for Roger Waters devotees, available at 112 Bennett Road, Aptos, CA 95003 USA.

However, my special and heartfelt thanks go to the many unknown and shifty bootleggers out there who have allowed me to trace the origins of tracks through live performances and studio outtakes. You may have taken the Floyd for a few quid, what you do may be utterly illegal, but as rock becomes social history, you serve an ever more valauable purpose.

For his deft editorial sheering and his incisive and scholarly insights into much of the material in this book, I thank Jim Irvin - the cheque is in the post. For editorial help and breakdown recovery I thank Paul Trynka of *Mojo* Magazine, the greatest Rock magazine in the world, or so it says on this piece of paper he gave me. For helping me with phone numbers and contacts, Richard Allen, of Delirium Records, and Ivor Trueman (watch for his forthcoming book on the Floyd Live shows). Thanks too go to Floyd heads from time, Ashley Heath and Adrian O'Reilly, whose considered opinions have all made it into the book, making me look clever. For help in researching the film soundtracks, I thank Adrian and Juliette Moreton of Kinépix in Wakefield.

Echoes was also compiled using a great deal of archive material from the Internet. In particluar the various Floyd newsgroups and ftp archive sites (alt.music.pink-floyd). I am particularly indebted to the mysterious 'Pink Daddy', who provided me with some crucial information on the making of *Atom Heart Mother* and *Meddle*. Appreciation also goes to San Francisco Public Library, the best microfilm and Rock'n'Roll repository I know of, and to Wandsworth Public library which isn't, but is still very nice. To Wildcat Records of Illinois, the least expensive repository of Floyd-related material in the world. Another valuable source for this book was the unpublished work of Chris Wallis. Where are you? No e-mail, no address and no numbers check out anymore. Thanks to Jeff Jensen, head honcho at *Brain Damage* Magazine for supplying the manuscript.

To Richard Philpott and Charlotte Bush for their photo research, and my ever-patient editor at Carlton, Lorraine Dickey. I would like to thank Paul DuNoyer, who put my name forward for this project in his capacity as advisor to Carlton Books.

Now for the personals: gratitude and eternal friendship goes to Tim Forster for his stoical patience and friendship through strange times. Finally to my parents Lynda and Geoffrey and to lil' sis Julia too, for buying me *The Piper At The Gates of Dawn* for Christmas 1980; I love you.

Index

All numbers in *italics* refer to illustrations.

A

B

C

D

E

F

G

H

I

J

K

L

M

N

O

P

Q

S

T

U

V

W

Y

Z

Picture Credits

The publishers would like to thank the following sources for their kind permission to reproduce the pictures in this book:

AKG London/Erich Lessing; Peter Anderson/Barrett Family Collection, Irene Winsby Collection; Bridgeman Art Library/Christie's, London; British Film Institute; Cambridge Newspapers; Colorsport; Corbis; Corbis-Bettmann/UPI; Ron Geesin/Richard Stanley; Ronald Grant Archive; Yvonne Haines; Hulton Getty/Nick Hale; Images Colour Library; Cliff Jones; Kinema Collection; Roger Kohn; London Features International/Steve Granitz; Mansell Collection; Dr. Strange TM & Copyright © 1996, Marvel Characters, Inc. All Rights Reserved; Mirror Syndication International; News Team; Pictorial Press; Barry Plummer; Redferns/Glenn A Baker, Ian Dickson, Colin Fuller, Mick Gold, Mick Hutson, Michael Ochs Archive, David Redfern, Brian Shuel; Repfoto/Robert Ellis, David Warner Ellis, Barrie Wentzell; Retna Pictures/Adrian Boot, Gary Gershoff, Karl Grant, Jeffrey Newbury, Neal Preston, Michael Putland, Steve Rapport, Brian Rasic, Timothy White; Rex Features/Dezo Hoffman, Andrew Laenen, SIPA, The Times, The Tolkein Society, Jeremy Young; Science Photo Library/Jean-Loup Charmet, Tony Craddock, Petit-Format/Nestlé, L Steinmark/Custom Medical Stock Photo, Ron Sutherland; S.I.N/Frederick.

Thanks are due to Ron Geesin and Peter Anderson.